Controlling
the
Bureaucracy

Bureaucracies, Public Administration, and Public Policy

Kenneth J. Meier
Series Editor

Bureaucracies, Public Administration,
and Public Policy

Controlling
the
Bureaucracy
Institutional Constraints
in Theory and Practice

WILLIAM F. WEST

M.E. Sharpe
Armonk, New York
London, England

Library of Congress Cataloging-in-Publication Data

West, William F.
Controlling the bureaucracy : institutional constraints
in theory and practice / William F. West.
p. cm. — (Bureaucracies, public administration,
and public policy)
Includes bibliographical references and index.
ISBN 1-56324-513-2.　—　ISBN 1-56324-514-0 (pbk.)
1. Bureaucracy—United States.
2. Administrative agencies—United States—Management.
3. United States—Politics and government.
I. Title.　II. Series.
JK421.W44　1995
350′.000973—dc20　　　94-45048
CIP

Printed in the United States of America

The paper used in this publication meets the minimum requirements of
American National Standard for Information Sciences—
Permanence of Paper for Printed Library Materials,
ANSI Z 39.48-1984.

⊗

BM (c)　10　9　8　7　6　5　4　3　2　1
BM (p)　10　9　8　7　6　5　4　3　2　1

Contents

Foreword

The M.E. Sharpe series Bureaucracies, Public Administration, and Public Policy is designed as a forum for the best work on bureaucracy and its role in public policy and governance. Although the series is open with regard to approach, methods, and perspectives, especially sought are three types of research. First, the series hopes to attract empirical studies of bureaucracy. Public administration has long been viewed as a theoretical and methodological backwater of political science. This view persists despite a recent flurry of research. The series seeks to place public administration at the forefront of empirical analysis within political science. Second, the series is interested in conceptual work that attempts to clarify theoretical issues, set an agenda for research, or provide a focus for professional debates. Third, the series seeks manuscripts that challenge the conventional wisdom about how bureaucracies influence public policy or the role of public administration in governance.

Controlling the Bureaucracy: Institutional Constraints in Theory and Practice fits into the second and third categories. Bill West has given us a thoughtful and challenging argument concerning the relationship between bureaucracy and political institutions. Since much has been written about political control, the potential for making an original contribution seemingly is not large, but Professor West has challenged what we thought we knew about the issues. In his discussion of courts, he presents a provocative argument that courts and their decisions have no impact on the policy priorities of bureaucracies. Even in areas where deadlines make courts proactive (EPA), they can only force *some* type of action rather than a specific action. Professor West argues that agencies determine policy long before court-defined procedures kick in. At best such procedures assist only those with the resources and expertise to participate.

In assessing presidential control, the author casts doubt on the validity of the existing arguments in two ways. First, he notes that recent presidents have made appointments that undermine their own leadership and control of bureaucracy, especially in regard to economy and efficiency. Second, he reminds us that the president may actually represent interests far narrower than those represented by the bureaucracy. Presidential efforts at controlling the bureaucracy, as a result, could undermine both its competence and its responsiveness to the people.

Bill West has long been associated with cutting-edge research on congressional control of bureaucracy. He uses this expertise to challenge the notion of "fire-alarm" oversight; we can only hope that this argument will be read by scholars everywhere and result in the elimination of this fuzzy notion from the debate.

But the most exciting and creative part of the book is Professor West's effort to place the debate over controlling the bureaucracy back into its constitutional context. The bureaucracy has been a battlefield where the political branches of government have applied their checks and balances. Political control of the bureaucracy must be understood in the full context of the Constitution and all three branches of government. Anything less leaves us with an incomplete and inaccurate view of bureaucracy and public policy.

Controlling the Bureaucracy is a must read for all students of public administration. The time-honored debate about the relationship between bureaucracy and democracy remains relevant today, and Bill West has given us an informed guide to the issues.

Kenneth J. Meier

Acknowledgments

Several people have been helpful to me in preparing this book. I am grateful to Jim Anderson and Kim Hill for their excellent criticisms of selected chapters. Ken Meier thoroughly reviewed an early draft of the whole manuscript and offered insightful suggestions throughout. Although Joe Cooper did not have a direct role in this, I have benefited a great deal from our past collaborations—especially in dealing with issues of executive and legislative control. Finally, I would like to thank my wife, Pat McDaniel, for all of her support on the domestic front and for her reactions to sections of the book where I was having an especially hard time expressing myself clearly.

1

Ideas and Politics: The Context for Understanding and Evaluating Institutional Controls

Although the growth of bureaucracy has accompanied modernization throughout the world, this development has been especially unsettling for our peculiar, tripartite system of democracy. Thus, American government has adapted to the rise of the administrative state through three often-conflicting means of promoting accountability. It has sought to ensure desired qualities in agency decision making through participatory opportunities and standards of rationality that are enforced through the courts. In addition, both the president and Congress have sought to monitor and shape agencies' implementation of statutes in accordance with their own policy preferences.

Each of these controls has received considerable attention, yet there are few up-to-date discussions of all three that go beyond the brief accounts found in public administration and administrative law texts. The following chapters seek to fill this void by providing a balanced overview of the institutional powers and resources associated with administrative due process and executive and legislative oversight at the federal level. Special attention is given to how each has expanded in recent decades in direct relation to the growth of bureaucracy as a locus of policy-making discretion and as an arena for political conflict.

A more ambitious goal of this book is to evaluate controls over public administration. This entails a consideration of the decision-making qualities that different constraints promote in light of the criteria that we feel should guide statutory implementation. Equally as important, it may also entail a rethinking of the "process values" that we want from controls in light of what we can realistically expect. The reciprocal linkage between normative and empirical concerns, which underlies the allusion to "theory and practice" in the subtitle of this book, provides a partial justification for such a broad undertaking. Much has been written on the topics discussed here, yet the complementary relationship between prescriptive and descriptive analysis has frequently been slighted. Political scientists have often failed to make explicit, much less critically examine, the normative premises that ultimately must give meaning to the empirical questions they ask. Conversely, prescriptive works by legal scholars and others have often reflected faulty assumptions about the nature of administration and about its relationship to the incentives and capabilities that define the effects of institutional controls.

The scope of this book is further justified by a second interrelationship that is also crucial to the evaluation of controls over public administration. Although due process and executive and legislative oversight are often treated separately, one cannot adequately discuss the effects or the desirability of any of them in isolation from the others. This is because controlling the bureaucracy is a "negative-sum game" from a constitutional perspective. The values, political interests, and institutional prerogatives furthered by one type of constraint inevitably undermine the values, political interests, and institutional prerogatives promoted by each of the other two. Indeed, the most critical structural choices facing American government today concern the balance that should be struck among the three "named" branches within the administrative process. At one level or another, this concern underlies almost everything that is written about institutional controls over the bureaucracy.

In turn, the most important and vexing constitutional issues have to do with the control of delegated policy-making authority. Who should oversee bureaucracy and pursuant to what criteria were relatively easy questions to answer under the traditional assumption that administration was a matter of carrying out legislative goals objectively and efficiently. Thus, there was a fairly broad consensus during the early decades of this century that adjudicatory decisions affecting important individual rights should be subject to rigorous procedural constraints and judicial review, and that the remainder of the administrative process should fall under the executive's managerial control. The issues surrounding bureaucracy's role and its relationship to legislative, executive, and judicial power have become much more complex with the realization that implementation is also frequently a political function of balancing competing values.

A coherent and widely accepted doctrine has not emerged concerning the principles and institutional mechanisms that should constrain the quasi-legislative dimensions of public administration. What is striking, though, is the popularity of the belief that agency policy making should reflect qualities of rationality that differ markedly from the kinds of pluralistic processes that our political system is seemingly designed to encourage. These prescriptions can be traced in large measure to institutional analyses that describe Congress's delegation of authority and the structure of bureaucratic politics that has resulted from it in pathological terms. As such, they provide useful reference points for describing and assessing the roles played by due process and presidential and congressional oversight. Much current thinking about administrative accountability derives from simplistic empirical and normative assumptions about the role of administration in American government.

The Context for Limited Controls

The bulk of the discussion in the chapters that follow focuses on the determinants and the effects of expanded controls. Given this, and given the interrelationship between prescriptive and descriptive concerns in institutional analysis, it is useful to begin with a broad overview of the ideals and the realities that were associated with less-demanding constraints in the past. Lax controls over public administration were often justified by normative theories of administration that viewed agency discretion in sanguine terms. They could also be attributed in part to the low levels of conflict that accompanied policy implementation in many policy areas, and to correspondingly low incentives for affected groups to seek controls over the bureaucracy that would protect their interests.

Limited Constraints

Administrative due process and presidential and congressional oversight were not very extensive or rigorous at midcentury. This is a subjective and relative judgment that must be defended in the context of more recent developments. Deferring a discussion of these changes to later chapters, it is possible to characterize in broad terms the most important features of the old system of limited controls over administrative discretion.

Attempts to confine bureaucratic discretion through administrative due process were haphazard and generally undemanding through the 1950s. This owed in part to judicial modesty. Courts were initially reluctant to review administrative decisions at all unless authorized to do so by the enabling statutes under which agencies operated. Although a general "presumption of reviewability" evolved during the twenties and thirties, and was eventually codified in the Administrative Procedure Act,[1] judicial precedent and professional norms continued to call for restraint in questioning agencies' factual and policy determinations. This was especially true when decisions were based on administrators' judgment in weighing evidence and assessing likely outcomes within their areas of expertise. The role of the courts was thus usually limited to questions of procedure and statutory interpretation.

The courts' reluctance to interfere with administration was both a cause and an effect of undemanding or nonexistent procedural requirements and terms of judicial review in many statutes. Enabling legislation in the early part of the century occasionally stipulated the procedures that agencies were to use in carrying out their mandates, but bureaucrats were usually left to their own devices. Sentiment to impose some order on the administrative process began to mount in the early 1930s and eventually culminated in the passage of the Administrative Procedure Act in 1946. If the avowed purpose of the APA was to standardize the administrative process and render bureaucracy more accountable, however, its requirements evinced a continued reluctance to question the exercise of agency discretion. One limitation was its unwillingness to interfere in a substantial way with bureaucratic policy decisions. Another was that the applicability of its requirements for both rulemaking and adjudication was confined to regulatory administration and little else. Although the APA was never the sole source of administrative procedures and judicial review, its limited provisions remained the primary constraints on administrative output during the two decades following its passage.

The laxness of administrative due process until the 1960s coincided with a limited interest in policy implementation by the two political branches of government. It was only after the Second World War that presidents began to view the appointment of political executives as a management tool rather than as a source of patronage.[2] In addition, the White House and Executive Office lacked the institutional capacity for systematic review and influence over agency policies before the 1970s. Centralized control over the bureaucracy only emerged as a significant strategy for promoting presidential objectives during the Nixon administration.[3]

Congress displayed a similar lack of interest in oversight. The conventional wisdom that had emerged among scholars by 1970 was that the mundane aspects of day-to-day administration were neither personally interesting nor politically salient to most legislators. Studies concluded that oversight sometimes did occur, but that it tended to be a sporadic response to constituent pressures or to widely publicized failings in the administrative process that provided opportunities for legislators to generate name recognition and to claim credit as protectors of the public trust. It was seldom informed by programmatic concerns, and its overall effects were often characterized as being negligible.[4]

Normative Foundations of Limited Control

The system of limited controls over administration that existed during the first half of the twentieth century initially found legitimacy in the normative theory of public administration that dominated thinking about bureaucracy and its role in government from the late 1800s into the 1930s. The premise of the so-called traditional model was that politics and administration were conceptually distinct functions and practically separable activities. Politics, which involved value judgments, was the process of accommodating and responding to society's demands through the articulation of policy objectives. In contrast, administration was the task of accomplishing those objectives. As Luther Gulick stated, "Administration has to do with getting things done."[5] Although sophisticated scholars such as Gulick did not believe in this distinction as something that actually existed or that even could exist in an absolute sense (notwithstanding the misinformed ridicule they have received), they did embrace the politics/administration dichotomy as an approximation of reality that could serve as a unifying premise for normative theory and institutional design.

The traditional model is well known to those familiar with the intellectual history of public administration. Woodrow Wilson advocated as early as 1887 that bureaucracy and the processes by which it carried out legislative mandates should be studied systematically. In so doing, he argued that, given the instrumental function performed by agencies, we could borrow many of the principles of sound administration that had already been discovered by Europeans, irrespective of the differences in our political institutions.[6] The common assertion that Wilson's essay was a seminal influence on the field of public administration is debatable.[7] In any case, optimism that administration could be an efficient, instrumental process had become widespread among scholars by the early part of the century. As with Wilson, the foundation for this belief was the Progressive faith, born of positivist philosophy and an awareness of the wonders wrought by technology in the private sector, that government and law, as informed by science, could be successfully applied to the problems facing society. The thrust of their work was to prescribe techniques of organization and management that would enhance the effectiveness and efficiency of administration. Many of these techniques were felt to be equally applicable to public agencies and private firms based on the assumption that both types of organizations pursued hierarchically ordered goals.

As the traditional model gained widespread adherence, its prescription of neutral competence naturally instilled confidence that agencies not only could be but would be effective "transmission belts" for attaining policy objectives articulated in the legislative process. This, in turn, translated into a wariness of excessive outside interference that would undermine effective implementation. Rigorous administrative procedures and judicial review were to be confined to areas where agency decisions impinged on important individual rights, and oversight by politically driven legislative amateurs was to be limited to a passive, supervisory function. The emphasis on executive power that evolved within the traditional school ultimately proved difficult to reconcile with the premise that administration was an instrumental process. In an attempt at consistency, however, the president's role as chief executive was vaguely defined in objective terms as that of a general manager.[8] At any rate, disappointment over presidents' limited interest in administrative management was mitigated by a generally positive view of bureaucracy.

It is important to add that broad legislative mandates conferring substantial discretion upon the bureaucracy were difficult for many to ignore. This condition had always obtained to some extent, but the delegation of policy-making authority became especially apparent during the 1930s. The violence this did to separation of powers and to the principle of representative democracy was a source of much concern to constitutional purists, and it moved the Supreme Court in 1935 to invalidate two statutes as abdications of legislative responsibility.[9] Yet as Elihu Root observed as early as 1916, the cession of discretionary authority to the administrative state was bound to continue, "whether we approved theoretically or not."[10] His prescience was confirmed by the quick abandonment of the nondelegation doctrine as a concession to the need for modern government to respond effectively to society's policy demands. As the Court noted in 1940, delegation was necessary in order that the "expression of legislative power [did] not become a futility."[11]

New Deal intellectuals subtly recast the traditional model's conception of neutral competence in an initial effort to justify delegated authority. Administrative policy making pursuant to general directives was still viewed (very ambiguously) in instrumental terms, and was often perceived to be salutary under the assumption that bureaucracy would identify and implement effective means of carrying out objectives that Congress wanted to achieve but lacked the time and the knowledge to confront in an intelligent way. Theorists thus began to emphasize the virtues of substantive as well as managerial expertise.[12] As James Landis noted in defending the broad powers often given to regulatory agencies:

. . . with the rise of regulation the need for expertness became dominant: for the art of regulating an industry requires knowledge of the details of its operation, ability to shift requirements as the conditions of the industry may dictate, the pursuit of energetic measures upon the appearance of an emergency, and the power through enforcement to realize conclusions as to policy.[13]

Yet this effort to reconcile bureaucratic discretion with the principle that political authority should be confined to electorally accountable institutions was a stopgap at best. Notwithstanding its strong appeal, the portrayal of administrative policy making as solely a technical enterprise became an increasingly tenuous article of faith. Scholars began to come to grips with the fact that agencies were called upon to balance competing social objectives just when the defense of delegation in terms of bureaucratic expertise was reaching its fullest expression. For example, Pendleton Herring observed in 1936 that the "task of interpretation is a continuation of the legislative process," and that administrators are thus "subject to the same pressures that assailed the legislators."[14] By the end of the 1940s, scholars such as John Gaus and Paul Appleby had issued convincing general attacks on the politics/administration dichotomy as a realistic basis for either descriptive or prescriptive theory.[15]

At the same time, the realization that administration frequently involved political decisions was not initially a cause for alarm among many theorists. Indeed, early pluralists often viewed the delegation of authority to agencies in positive terms as something that facilitated the accommodation of interests. As such, the existence of bureaucratic power was in keeping with the spirit if not the letter of the Constitution. Norton Long developed this thesis brilliantly in his 1949 essay "Power and Administration." Long argued that the dispersion of policy-making authority among agencies was a logical extension of the American constitutional system of separated and shared powers, and that it both reflected and reinforced the accompanying political system in which interest groups rather than parties and elections played the dominant role in shaping policy. The absence of centralized accountability to elected officials through hierarchically structured government institutions and disciplined parties forced American bureaucrats—much more so than their counterparts in parliamentary regimes—to seek support from clientele groups as a means of establishing their own political viability.[16]

In this latter respect, Long and some other theorists drew an analogy between agencies and business firms seeking customers. Just as the decentralization of economic power led to an efficient allocation of resources through the invisible hand of competition, the political marketplace worked best, not through hierarchical planning and direction, but through "mutual partisan adjustment" among the various interests affected by government action. This was made possible or was at least facilitated by the availability of multiple points of access for group influence created by the dispersion of institutional power. It was both inevitable and desirable under the pluralist model that politics should find its expression everywhere. Viewed in such a context, even the redundancy and conflict in the structure of bureaucracy that had become increasingly troublesome to those with a managerial bent was functional from the standpoint of "political efficiency."[17] It resulted from but further enriched the medium for interest-group politics created by the dispersion of authority through other institutional features such as separation of powers, federalism, bicameralism, and the congressional committee system.

The Political Foundations of Limited Control

If constraints on public administration are justified and evaluated in terms of appealing process values, such as neutral competence or democratic responsiveness, they can also frequently be explained in terms of politics. Procedural constraints and terms of judicial review are seldom neutral in their implications for those who stand to be affected by agency decisions. Presidential and congressional interest in what the bureaucracy does are also obviously tied to constituent demands and perhaps to broader institutional concerns as well. In these regards, the system of limited constraints on bureaucracy that existed into the 1960s was consistent, not only with optimistic normative assessments of unconstrained bureaucratic discretion, but with the political climate surrounding the implementation of many programs. Ironically, this was because the realities of administrative politics often did not conform with the pluralist description.

Incentives to control agency discretion were especially low in "distributive" areas involving such things as public works, grants, and subsidies, where the costs of individual programs were so widely dispersed that "losers" (taxpayers for the most part) did not perceive themselves as such (or at least were not sufficiently upset by the fact to mobilize for effective opposition).[18] Regulatory administration also frequently involved low conflict before the 1960s. Much of the traditional "economic" regulation sought to nurture new industries or to protect established ones from the destabilizing effects of competition or from crises in public confidence that might result from the disreputable behavior of a few firms. Many regulatory programs were, in fact, analogous to distributive policy in their effects and their political dynamics. Activities such as ratemaking and licensing could impose artificial limits on competition, in effect subsidizing industry at the expense of diffuse consumer interests.

To the extent that agencies were already committed to homogeneous clientele who perceived themselves as being affected in a positive way by implementation, and to the extent that these clientele dominated the political environment of public administration, there was little reason for groups to attempt to secure procedural constraints on bureaucratic discretion that would promote their interests. This same feature of administrative politics accounted for a lack of emphasis on executive and legislative oversight. Notwithstanding their rhetoric to the contrary, neither the president nor Congress has ever shown a strong interest in administrative efficiency as an end in itself. Even compliance with statutory goals, insofar as they can be discerned, has been of limited concern on its own merits (especially for the president). Given the incentives that dominate presidential and congressional behavior, oversight was a relatively low priority because the administrative process was relatively low in conflict and thus lacking in political salience.

This is not to say that all administration took place within harmonious environments. Of particular note is that the politics of regulation was always sufficiently diverse and complex as to defy neat generalization. If many programs ultimately worked to their benefit, the orientation of business groups toward regulatory policy was still often one of caution or ambivalence at best and hostility at worst. This owed to the fact that even friendly agencies were generally given the power to apply potentially damaging sanctions that they might use under different political circumstances.

As a matter of degree, however, conflict was constrained in regulatory politics. Even to the extent that the thrust of policy was to impose costs on industry, agencies were often less than aggressive in carrying out their mandates. The relatively low point of equilibrium at which procedural constraints on agency discretion were consistent with the political environment of regulation was reflected in the Administrative Procedure Act, which was the dominant source of structural controls on agency discretion in the two decades following its passage in 1946. Business interests were never ignorant of the value of formal due process as a means of slowing down or blocking unwanted agency action. Indeed, they lobbied Congress to impose such requirements across a broad range of administrative activities in the decade before the APA was enacted. As it turned out, however, the act's much less demanding requirements for rulemaking were generally satisfactory to regulated interests given administrators' preference for adjudication (which was constrained by trial-like procedures). As a less forceful regulatory strategy that stepped on fewer toes, the practice of implementing mandates incrementally on the merits of individual cases also limited the incentives for intervention by the president and Congress in regulatory administration. Even where the political branches might have wanted to inter-vene, the quasi-judicial character of agency action rendered their interfer-ence difficult to defend on ethical and legal grounds.[19]

The New Environment of Public Administration

This brief description of the old normative and political environments of administration provides a context for appreciating developments that have occurred over roughly the past three decades. Administrative procedures and judicial review have become more rigorous and extensive during this period. In addition, both the president and Congress have expanded their efforts to influence administrative policy. If limited constraints were sus-tained by optimism concerning the effects of bureaucratic discretion and by the low conflict that attended policy implementation in many areas, the new regime of more extensive controls has resulted from the opposite condi-tions. Delegated authority has become more troubling from the standpoint of democratic theory, and administrative action has become salient to a broader range of interests. These observations are critical to the task of evaluation as well.

Growing Normative Concerns

Whether public administration currently suffers from a "crisis of legiti-macy" is a complex question.[20] The public's level of resentment no doubt varies among areas of administration. Whereas one would hardly expect to find that many small businesspeople have warm feelings toward OSHA, for example, several studies suggest that people have quite favorable views of the bureaucrats who provide them with social services.[21] Resentment is also higher in the abstract than in the particular. While there is little doubt that the term *bureaucracy* has negative connotations for many of us, opinion polls show high levels of support for most of the functions that agencies perform. Even many regulatory programs enjoy the approval of a substan-tial majority of the American public.[22]

These qualifications miss the point to some extent, however, for if the legitimacy of administration is not a pressing concern for most people, it has become increasingly important to those who write about and make institutional policy. It is discussed frequently in academic literature and newspaper editorials, and it has become almost a common denominator in the rhetoric of presidential candidates. Although intellectual and political elites may misperceive the issue as a matter of widespread disaffection, and although they, themselves, are largely reconciled to delegated authority, their reservations about bureaucracy have provided compelling rationales for subjecting agencies to more stringent controls in recent decades. These have often been expressed in constitutional terms, but have also been grounded to a large extent in policy analyses that equate administrative discretion with program failure.

As with the traditional model of public administration, the justification for bureaucracy as a healthy medium for group politics began to encounter challenges just as it was reaching its zenith. This was largely due to the tension between the empirical assumptions of pluralist theory and the realities of bureaucratic politics alluded to above. A growing body of research in the 1950s and 1960s attested to the fact that much policy making was characterized by logrolling rather than by conflict. In many accounts, the fragmentation of power among numerous agencies, congressional committees and subcommittees, and groups did not create a maelstrom in which all relevant interests were somehow accommodated. Rather, it led to "subsystem politics" in which well-organized and often well-heeled interests dominated the allocation of scarce resources at the general public's expense. Agency discretion thus came to be viewed by many as both a symptom and a cause of inequity and irrationality in program implementation and within American government generally. Writing in the mid-1970s, James Wilson noted:

> . . . the Madisonian system makes it relatively easy for the delegation of public power to private groups to go unchallenged and, therefore, for factional interests that have acquired a supportive public bureaucracy to rule without submitting their interests to the effective scrutiny and modification of other interests.[23]

Although his analysis had many precursors, Theodore Lowi expressed this theme most persuasively in his 1969 book, *The End of Liberalism.*[24] Drawing on evidence from a broad range of policy areas, Lowi argued that bureaucratic discretion was closely associated with "interest group liberalism," a corrupt system of governance in which public authority had been appropriated for private ends. Broad delegations of power, which might be justified to the public in terms of noble or otherwise widely appealing goals, were frequently administered in such a way as to serve the special interests of agency clientele. Urban renewal ended up helping developers rather than inner-city residents. Grants for underprivileged children in public schools were diverted to the needs of the middle class and professional educators. A host of subsidies and public works programs involved a similar dynamic. According to Lowi and others, such administrative distortions of policy goals often involved the complicity of the legislators initially responsible for broad delegations. They, like the bureaucrats who carried out their mandates, could benefit or suffer in accordance with the reactions of intense, well-organized interests to policy implementation. This tendency was arguably reinforced by the way Congress organized its legislative and oversight responsibilities. Thus, the functional fragmentation and constituency ties of the committee system frequently coincided with the functional fragmentation and constituency ties of the bureaucracy itself.

The problems associated with bureaucratic discretion were deemed to be especially acute in areas of regulation, where influential studies identified vague statutory mandates as a root cause of "agency capture." Open-ended congressional instructions to regulate business in the "public interest, convenience, or necessity," which had been justified in terms of administrators' technical expertise, ironically meant that bureaucracy would have to make the hard choices resolving competing interests and social values. Given this, industry groups naturally enjoyed a substantial advantage over the ostensible beneficiaries of regulation in the administrative process. The disparity in financial, organizational, and informational resources became especially telling over time under the "life-cycle" version of this thesis.[25] Partially successful in persuading Congress to confront a problem with vague legislation, diffused interests typically found it impossible to maintain a level of monitoring and political support for aggressive action that could compete with the sustained efforts of industry to influence policy implementation.

The institutional developments discussed in this book can be partly understood as a reaction and a counterreaction precipitated by indictments such as these. The so-called public-interest movement, which was energized by allegations of agency clientelism, sought to redress the deficiencies of the existing system of administration by creating more programs and by delegating more authority. At the same time, greater care was taken to ensure through administrative procedures and political oversight that programs would be carried out faithfully and aggressively, and that relevant interests would have viable opportunities to participate in policy decisions. In new areas of "social regulation," for example, agencies could not proceed slowly and incrementally as their older siblings had done, but were typically required to issue rules in dealing with problems—sometimes within prescribed time periods.[26] Program beneficiaries were also frequently given substantial opportunities to secure injunctions from the courts that would force agencies to act.[27]

These developments are reflected in the growth of the *Federal Register*, the *Code of Federal Regulations*, and other commonly cited indexes of policy activism by federal agencies that began in the 1960s and that intensified in the 1970s. Yet this trend had normative ramifications of its own. If the accommodation of the administrative state with representative democracy had always been difficult, it became more so with the tremendous expansion of bureaucratic output. It was not only the increased number of administrative programs that was important in this regard. Equally as significant was the manner in which programs were carried out. Agencies' emphasis on rulemaking as a means of accomplishing regulatory and other objectives rendered the legislative content of administration more precipitous and more difficult to ignore. The need to hold administrators accountable as they exercised broad political discretion thus provided the justification for further efforts to control the bureaucracy through oversight and administrative procedures.

The Increased Political Saliency of Administration

If it has reflected popular ideas about the proper role of administration in American government, the expansion of procedural constraints and legislative and executive oversight has also both resulted from and contributed to fundamental changes in bureaucratic politics. According to Hugh Heclo and others, subgovernments have been superseded by larger, more diverse, more fluid, and more conflictual configurations of actors in many areas.[28] In truth, the cozy-triangle metaphor was always a considerable exaggeration. Notwithstanding its frequent use as an abstract characterization, classic works on administrative politics during the 1960s by scholars such as Emmette Redford noted that subgovernments could overlap with one another, that they could be internally conflictual, and that their stability could be upset when policy issues escalated to the arena of "macropolitics."[29] As a matter of degree, however, the popularity of Heclo's amorphous concept of an issue network bespeaks fundamental developments that have occurred in the general environment of program implementation.

One such change has been the increased scarcity of fiscal resources. Growing budget deficits and a growing tax burden have resulted in a more widespread and acute awareness of the fact that distributive programs create losers as well as winners.[30] The politics of mutual non-interference has also been eroded by the rise of new, competing interests to play a role in areas of policy making once dominated by homogeneous clientele groups. Although there are no definitive data describing what has occurred, scholars agree that the number of groups involved in national politics has increased dramatically.[31] Many of the new concerns that have complicated agency (and congressional) decision making are driven, not by immediate economic motives, but by ideological commitments (environmentalists and consumer advocates, for example) and by intellectual and professional interests (economic analysts and experts in water policy, for example).

The growth in complexity and contentiousness of bureaucratic politics has been intermeshed with government action. Some new or newly powerful interest groups have secured their own programs, their own legally protected rights, and their own agencies to administer such entitlements.[32] Other groups have formed to take advantage of new subsidies, grants, contracts, benefits, and the like rather than vice versa. Moreover, existing public institutions, such as other agencies and state and local governments, have become increasingly active in administrative policy making.[33] In important respects, one might conceive of the change that has taken place as a proliferation of subgovernments whose defining functional or policy concerns have come to overlap.[34] As one prominent illustration, environmental interests, agencies, and programs are often affected by and affect policy making in areas, such as public works and natural resource management, that were once dominated by narrow "producer" interests.

Key changes in the political environment of public administration have been closely associated with increased incentives to control bureaucracy. The growth of competition, instability, and uncertainty in the implementation of programs has led groups affected by administration to seek participatory opportunities and standards of justification for agency actions that they can use strategically to further their own interests in policy making. As administration has become more conflictual, it has also drawn more attention from the two political branches of government. Notwithstanding the normative justification of promoting accountability for its own sake, efforts by the president and Congress to extend their control over the bureaucracy can be explained largely in terms of the growing relevance of administration to their institutional roles of accommodating interests and producing policy. In this regard, presidential and congressional incentives to perform oversight have each been amplified by the fact that one branch's gains necessarily limit the other's success in achieving its objectives through the administrative and legislative processes.

Evaluating Institutional Controls

The normative and political contexts for expanded controls over the bureaucracy cannot be delineated as clearly as the preceding discussion may imply. Although some scholars go too far in discounting the independent role of ideas as institutional determinants,[35] there is little denying that normative arguments are frequently intertwined with and are sometimes used to rationalize institutional preferences grounded in self-interest. At the same time, the distinction between political and normative forces is often tenuous or nonexistent. As with the rise of the public-interest movement to compete with economic concerns, the conflicting pressures that come to bear on agencies today often derive as much from ideology as from the prospect of material gain or loss.

An equally important point is that the relationship between formal controls, on the one hand, and the political and normative environments of administration on the other is interactive rather than unidirectional. Institutions shape politics and ideas just as politics and ideas shape institutions. As mentioned, for instance, the emphasis placed on rulemaking has been a response to demands for more aggressive action by regulatory agencies, but in turn it has added to the problem of legitimacy surrounding administration as well as to the complexity and contentiousness of agency decision making. The increased number of pressure groups so widely noted in the literature has also been an effect as well as a cause of institutional change. The creation of new agencies and programs, the expansion of standing by Congress and the courts, the direct subsidization of participants in agency proceedings, and other developments have thus nurtured and sustained various kinds of interests. In some cases, these structural features of administration have provided the necessary incentives for groups to organize. The expanded administrative roles of the president and Congress have similarly contributed to as well as resulted from the multiplication of interests and viewpoints surrounding policy implementation.

If the causal linkages among ideas, politics, and institutions are complex and reciprocal, the preceding overview nevertheless provides a useful foundation for understanding the systemic role played by due process and executive and legislative oversight. Descriptive analysis is, in turn, a necessary component of institutional evaluation. As mentioned at the outset, the assessment of controls over the bureaucracy must be based on a consideration of the values that we want them to promote in light of the values that we can realistically expect them to promote. Sound normative doctrine thus cannot be divorced from an understanding of the character of administration and its relationship to the motives and capabilities that define judicial, executive, and legislative behavior. Beyond this, evaluation must consider the compatibility of institutional controls and their associated effects with underlying constitutional norms.

Organization of the Book

The material in this book might be organized in a number of ways, but the most straightforward approach is to begin by examining the three types of institutional constraints on bureaucracy individually.[36] Chapters 2 and 3 focus on administrative due process, chapters 4 and 5 focus on the administrative presidency, and chapters 6 and 7 focus on legislative oversight. The organizational framework is not consistent across the three areas. Roughly speaking, however, the first chapter in each pairing describes the most important legal prerogatives, techniques, and resources that define institutional controls, giving special attention to developments that have occurred in recent decades. It also outlines the limitations of institutional constraints and broadly addresses the issue of effectiveness.

The second chapter in each pairing turns to the task of evaluation. In so doing, the roles that constraints on public administration are commonly expected to play serve as reference points for describing the roles that they actually play. The former assessments necessarily entail broad interpretations of themes in the accounts of scholars and other observers, and because of this the analysis must be sensitive to the danger of relying on straw men. In fact, there is not a consensus regarding the policy implications of any of the three types of control discussed here. At the same time, the literature in each area suffers from widely held if not universal misconceptions about the nature of agency decision making, about institutional motives and effects, and about the process values that are and should be served by different constraints.

The questions addressed in these chapters obviously relate, either directly or indirectly, to "metapolicy" issues of how government decisions ought to be made. Constitutional analysis in this generic sense must just as obviously be integrated with constitutional analysis in a formal, legal sense. If the federal Constitution contains little explicit guidance concerning the role of bureaucracy in American government, its general precepts still provide the basis for judging the legitimacy of any institutional arrangements. The Constitution is also the source of authority for ordering interbranch conflict within the administrative process.

To place the values that should inform institutional analysis in clearer perspective, the final chapter deals more directly with administrative due process and presidential and congressional control of the bureaucracy from the standpoint of separation of powers and checks and balances. The concerns about institutional behavior and effects discussed in the earlier chapters are relevant to this end, as are broader questions having to do with the relationship between the growth of administrative discretion and the balance of power among the three formal branches of government. In this latter respect, as well, the core values applied in evaluating controls over the bureaucracy are frequently based on simplistic and conflicting premises.

Administrative Values, Political Values, and Institutional Effects

The criteria that should be used to assess bureaucracy and its role in American government once seemed to be relatively straightforward. Again, the traditional model of public administration conceived of bureaucracy as an instrument for carrying out rather than establishing the will of the state. This perspective allayed misgivings about the role of administrative discretion in a representative democracy. It also yielded prescriptions for judicial, executive, and legislative oversight that were roughly compatible with a simple conception of separation of powers.

The traditional model did not furnish perfectly neat prescriptions for institutional control. Agencies apply policy to individuals, and this has always deviated from an unambiguous equation of all administration with execution. The inevitable fusion of executive and judicial functions is especially salient in regulatory administration, but its significance is by no means confined to those areas. The conflict that exists between the need for effective management and the assurance of fairness afforded by administrative due process and rigorous judicial review (and the delay and resource costs that accompany such guarantees) has been an enduring source of tension. At the same time, this problem is mitigated by the fact that, while they incorporate different means and stress somewhat different outcomes, both adjudication and execution are properly grounded in the norm of objectivity.

The fact that administration has important legislative components has posed more troublesome issues than has the commingling of executive and judicial power. Ambivalence and confusion concerning the proper basis for bureaucratic accountability have accompanied the realization that agencies make as well as carry out policy. Three distinct doctrines stand out in this regard. The goals of objectivity and technical competence have remained popular as bases for statutory implemention, notwithstanding the demise of the politics/administration dichotomy as a foundation for serious academic discussion of bureaucracy's systemic role. In addition, centralized management pursuant to broad national objectives and interest representation have emerged as alternative, politically based models for administrative policy making.[37] The evaluation of due process and executive and legislative oversight is largely a matter of assessing the desirability and the feasibility of these competing objectives. This involves a consideration of the relationship between the administrative process and the constitutional structure and political dynamics of American government.

Theorists have been schizophrenic concerning the goals of due process. Scholars and policy makers have frequently described and justified the extension of rigorous procedural requirements and judicial review from administrative adjudication to agency policy making as means of ensuring balanced interest representation under open-ended mandates. Due process has been endorsed in this capacity as an antidote to agency clientelism and to the narrow policy orientations often associated with bureaucrats' specialized knowledge and organizational responsibilities. Yet while such constraints do guarantee viable participation in some ways, the ultimate goal of adversary hearings and review based on a record is to guarantee that agency decisions are justified in terms of sound factual assertions and accurate interpretations of legislative intent. In this regard, due process has sought to ensure that administrative policy will be informed by dispassionate, objective considerations. Its ultimate goal is to institutionalize the qualities that New Dealers imputed to bureaucratic expertise in their original efforts to reconcile broad delegations of legislative authority with the traditional model's transmission-belt metaphor. Other procedural constraints such as economic analysis have sought to promote traditional values as well.

The appropriateness of due process is therefore contingent upon the degree to which administration is or can be objective, as well as upon the degree to which adversary procedures and judicial review are capable of promoting technically sound policy. All agency decisions have important empirical components, and due process has undoubtedly produced more rigor and objectivity in bureaucratic policy decisions. At the same time, the extension of demanding procedures and judicial review from their original use as assurances of accuracy and consistency in adjudication to the control of bureaucratic policy making has been problematic for two reasons. To the extent that such actions are based on technical premises, effective decision making has often been hindered by judges' lack of expertise and by a procedural framework that inhibits appropriate dialogue on empirical issues. A second and perhaps more important limitation stems from the fact that legislative intent is frequently unclear. Administrative delay has often been acute in areas where formal procedures have required agencies to provide tight, means–ends justifications for their actions but where open-ended mandates necessitate the balancing of competing interests.

An even more profound source of tension has to do with the balance that should be struck, not between objectivity and politics, but between different political institutions and representative principles within the administrative process. Here as well, however, evaluation is often conditioned by a traditional administrative norm. Control over bureaucratic policy making by the president is frequently envisioned as a means of reconciling attractive representative principles with a broader standard of rationality. Few modern scholars labor under the illusion that presidents will be content merely to ensure that the laws are carried out faithfully. Indeed, the traditional model's goal of objective statutory implementation was always logically if not explicitly at war with its other instrumental goal of coordinative management across agencies and programs. Unified executive control is (and probably always has been) advocated under the latter criterion as a force that naturally integrates political and administrative values by rationalizing the performance of bureaucracy (and public policy generally) on the basis of broad national interests. The administrative presidency has become increasingly appealing in this regard given the frequently alleged role of delegated authority as a vehicle for promoting narrow clientele interests.

Notwithstanding its plausibility, this characterization exaggerates the institutional dynamics of presidential oversight. The argument for centralized executive control does not suffer from the same internal inconsistency and misconceptions about the character of agency policy making as the justification for due process, but neither does it accurately portray the president's motives as they relate to the bureaucracy. There is little evidence to suggest that the sound internal management and coordination of agency programs are important executive priorities in and of themselves. A fact that is perhaps less widely appreciated is that the influence of the institutionalized presidency on public administration does not always reflect general as opposed to special interests. Nor does it always involve the application of pre-established, hierarchically ordered goals to administrative issues. Although the presidency can serve as a centralizing and rationalizing force, executive oversight is just as often characterized by the case-by-case resolution of conflict precipitated by specific agency proposals. The expansion of the administrative presidency has been as much a reflection of the need to accommodate competing interests within the departments, the Executive Office, and society generally as of the need to promote coherent policy agendas across agencies and programs.

Congressional oversight has received less enthusiastic support than presidential management (and probably even less than due process) as a means of controlling delegated legislative authority. This is partly attributable to the perception that legislators are unconcerned with statutory intent and ignorant of the details of program implementation. Increasingly, however, congressional intervention in agency affairs has been attacked, not because it reflects political rather than technical and managerial concerns, but because of its specific political content. In particular, legislative influence is alleged to subvert the same desirable goals of coordination and accountability to a national constituency that inhere in the administrative presidency. It is also sometimes alleged to subvert the kind of balanced interest representation promoted by administrative procedures. These assessments are typically linked to the organizational characteristics of Congress that define oversight. The facts that much review is reactive and that it is grounded in the committee system are thus portrayed as sources of parochialism and irrationality that reinforce the policy fragmentation inherent in the bureaucracy itself.

In reality, legislative oversight is not as ill-informed as is often claimed. Congress brings substantial expertise to bear in reviewing administrative programs. Just as presidential oversight is more pluralistic and less hierarchical than commonly recognized, moreover, congressional oversight is more pluralistic and less fragmented. In fact, congressional influence in the administrative process has come to represent a more diverse and conflictual array of interests in recent years as oversight has become a higher legislative priority. This development, which has coincided with the rise of "subcommittee government," has been both an effect and a cause of the fundamental changes in bureaucratic politics alluded to above. While review by multiple committees and subcommittees with differing policy orientations is often a source of delay and confusion in administration, it is hardly synonymous with the kind of policy fragmentation often associated with Congress's decentralized structure and parochial constituency ties. The oversight process has become a primary means of accommodating conflicting interests in controversial areas of administration.

In brief, the need to accommodate the competing interests surrounding specific administrative policy issues has not been given its due as a defining characteristic of American government that has both precipitated and conditioned the effects of expanded controls over bureaucracy. This has obvious implications for institutional policy. The courts have shown some appreciation of the tension between rigorous procedural constraints and the political realities of bureaucratic policy making in recent years. Although precedent has been far from consistent on the subject, there has been at least a modest retrenchment on the extension of rigorous due process to agency decisions that are legislative (rather than judicial) in a functional sense. This has resulted in part from the realization that formal procedures and judicial review are poor mechanisms for resolving the kinds of conflicting forces associated with policy implementation pursuant to broad mandates.

Anomalously, however, judges have generally sought to discourage direct congressional involvement in agency policy making in favor of a unified executive. They have usually done so through a "formalistic" (rather than a functional) analysis that simply equates all administration with execution. This preference for hierarchy over shared control is most probably rooted in the popular indictments of fragmented bureaucratic and congressional power alluded to above. In this regard, hegemonic presidential control over the administrative process would undoubtedly produce more coherency in government—notwithstanding the exaggerated claims that are often made for it. Yet a more important point is that, although it might be desirable in important respects, such an arrangement fundamentally ignores the relationship between the growth of delegated authority and our constitutional system of decentralized power. Legislative processes and outcomes would undoubtedly be more efficient under a parliamentary system as well. The question that remains is why efficiency should be preeminent in administrative policy making but not in other areas.

Nor, as a practical matter, are the parochial tendencies associated with decentralized power in the administrative process as pronounced as they might have been in the past. As noted earlier, the vindication of delegated authority as something that facilitated the expression of diverse preferences was frequently belied by the realities of logrolling and privileged access to the administrative process by narrow group interests. Institutional evaluation today is often characterized by a disjuncture between theory and reality that is, in some respects, the inverse of the one that existed at midcentury. Thus, although the pluralist system will never operate in a perfectly equitable manner, the political environment of public administration has become more pluralistic in the "healthy" sense envisioned by scholars such as Norton Long. Both presidential and congressional oversight have resulted from and contributed to this trend.

Notes

1. *Administrative Procedure Act,* U.S. Statutes at Large 60 (1946): 237.
2. G. Calvin McKenzie, *The Politics of Presidential Appointments* (New York: Free Press, 1981).
3. Richard Waterman, *Presidential Influence and the Administrative State* (Knoxville: University of Tennessee Press, 1989).
4. Morris S. Ogul, *Congress Oversees the Bureaucracy* (Pittsburgh: University of Pittsburgh Press, 1976); Randall B. Ripley and Grace A. Franklin, *Congress, the Bureaucracy, and Public Policy* (Pacific Grove, Calif.: Brooks/Cole, 1991).
5. Luther Gulick, "Science, Values, and Administration," in *Papers in the Science of Administration,* ed. Luther Gulick and L. Urwick (New York: Institute of Public Administration, 1937), p. 192; see also Frank J. Goodnow, *Politics and Administration* (New York: Macmillan, 1900).
6. Woodrow Wilson, "The Study of Administration," *Political Science Quarterly* 2 (June 1887): 197–222.
7. Paul Van Riper has argued convincingly that the leading public administration theorists in the early part of the twentieth century were unaware of Wilson's article, and that both it and subsequent efforts that seemed to follow its prescriptions were independent reflections of ideas that were gaining currency among intellectuals. "The Politics–Administration Dichotomy: Concept or Reality?" in *Politics and Administration: Woodrow Wilson and American Public Administration,* ed. Jack Rabin and James S. Bowman (New York: Marcel Dekker, 1984), pp. 203–17.
8. The classic articulation of this view is contained in The President's Committee on Administrative Management, *Report with Special Studies* (Washington, D.C.: U.S. Government Printing Office, 1937).
9. *Panama Refining Co. v. Ryan,* 293 U.S. 388 (1935); *A.L.A. Schecter Poultry Corp. v. United States,* 295 U.S. 495 (1935). Prior to these two cases, the Court had paid lip

service to the "non-delegation doctrine," but had always found that the statutes under consideration contained sufficiently clear policy standards that they were not abdications of legislative responsibility.

10. Elihu Root, in an address as president of the American Bar Association, 41 *American Bar Association Review* 355 (1916); pp. 368–69. Quoted in Kenneth Culp Davis, *Administrative Law and Government* (St. Paul, Minn.: West Publishing, 1975), p. 11.

11. *Sunshine Anthracite Coal Co. v. Adkins* 310 U.S. 381, 389; 60 Sup. Ct. 907 (1940).

12. See Frederick C. Mosher, *Democracy and the Public Service* (New York: Oxford University Press, 1968), especially chap. 3.

13. James Landis, *The Administrative Process* (New Haven: Yale University Press, 1938) pp. 23–24.

14. Pendleton Herring, *Public Administration and the Public Interest* (New York: McGraw-Hill, 1936), p. 218.

15. Paul H. Appleby, *Policy and Administration* (University, Ala.: University of Alabama Press, 1949).

16. Norton Long, "Power and Administration," *Public Administration Review* 9 (Autumn 1949): 257–264; idem, "Bureaucracy and Constitutionalism," *American Political Science Review* 46 (September 1952): 808–18.

17. See also Martin Laudau, "Redundancy, Rationality, and the Problem of Duplication and Overlap," *Public Administration Review* 29 (July/August 1969): 346–58.

18. Theodore Lowi, "Four Systems of Policy, Politics, and Choice," *Public Administration Review* 32 (July/August 1972): 298–310.

19. As discussed in chapters 2 and 8, the APA and judicial precedent proscribe direct, substantive influence by the president and Congress in such areas.

20. James O. Freedman, *Crisis and Legitimacy: The Administrative Process and American Government* (Cambridge, Mass.: Cambridge University Press, 1978).

21. See, for example, Charles Goodsell, "Looking Once Again at Human Services Bureaucracy," *Journal of Politics* 43 (August 1981): 763–78.

22. For a recent critical discussion of the issue of legitimacy, see Kenneth F. Warren, "We Have Debated Ad Nauseam the Legitimacy of the Administrative State—But Why?" *Public Administration Review* 53 (May/June 1993): 249–54.

23. James Q. Wilson, "The Rise of the Bureaucratic State," *The Public Interest* 41 (Fall 1975): 77–103; quotation p. 94.

24. Theodore Lowi, *The End of Liberalism* (New York: Norton, 1969).

25. Marver Bernstein, *Regulating Business Through Independent Commission* (Princeton, N.J.: Princeton University Press, 1955). A colleague has pointed out to me that the word *capture* never appears in Bernstein's text, but his arguments are certainly consistent with that notion as it is generally understood. An equally popular alternative to the life-cycle theory was the thesis that regulatory agencies were originally created to serve regulated interests. This interpretation was espoused by such different bedfellows as Marxist historians and neoconservative economists.

26. Bruce Ackerman and William Hassler, "Beyond the New Deal: Coal and the Clean Air Act," *Yale Law Journal* 89 (1980): 1466–1571.

27. Teresa M. Schwartz, "The Consumer Product Safety Commission: A Flawed Product of the Consumer Decade," *George Washington Law Review* 51 (1982): 32–95.

28. Hugh Heclo, "Issue Networks and the Executive Establishment," in *The New American Political System,* ed. Anthony King (Washington, D.C.: American Enterprise Institute, 1978).

29. Emmette S. Redford, *Democracy in the Administrative State* (New York: Oxford University Press, 1969). See also J. Leiper Freeman, *The Political Process* (New York:

Random House, 1965); E.E. Schattschneider, *The Semisovereign People* (New York: Holt, Reinhart and Winston, 1960).

30. Indeed, although there is a good deal of conceptual confusion on the subject, distributive policy is often defined by the absence of *perceived* losers.

31. Jack L. Walker, "The Origins and Maintenance of Interest Groups in America," *American Political Science Review* 77 (June 1983): 390–406.

32. Walker, "The Origins and Maintenance of Interest Groups."

33. Walker, "The Origins and Maintenance of Interest Groups"; Robert H. Salisbury, "Interest Representation: The Dominance of Institutions," *American Political Science Review* 78 (March 1984): 64–76; Samuel H. Beer, "The Adaptation of General Revenue Sharing: A Case Study in Public Sector Politics," *Public Policy* 24 (Spring 1976): 127–96.

34. For the argument that a subgovernment (although not a cozy triangle) is still a useful analytical concept, see Daniel McCool, "Subgovernments as Determinants of Political Viability," *Political Science Quarterly* 105 (Summer 1990): 269–94; and idem, "Subgovernments and the Impact of Policy Fragmentation and Accommodation," *Policy Studies Review* 8 (Winter 1989): 264–87.

35. As discussed in chapter 2, this is especially true of recent efforts by rational choice theorists to explain administrative procedures.

36. An alternative organizational scheme would be to focus on desired qualities in administration, such as technical accuracy and efficiency, political accountability, and so on. Another would be to focus on different kinds of administration, such as adjudication and rulemaking.

37. For a discussion of these models, see Herbert Kaufman, "Emerging Conflict in the Doctrines of Public Administration," *American Political Science Review* 50 (December 1956): 1057–73.

2

Administrative Due Process

The term *administrative due process* is used very broadly here to refer to the formal structure of agency decision making. It includes the types of actions agencies use in carrying out their mandates, as well as the procedures that constrain those actions. Given Congress's inability to provide detailed substantive guidance in many instances, together with bureaucracy's occasional tendency to deviate from statutory goals that have been articulated, structural constraints seek to ensure abstract qualities in agency decision making. Although administrative due process can be viewed as a system of "internal" controls in this sense, it cannot be disassociated from judicial review. Thus, the courts play a central role in enforcing the structural constraints that they and Congress have imposed. By the same token, judicial review of agency action is heavily dependent on the procedures agencies are required to use.

Bureaucratic discretion has become more tightly constrained in a number of ways since the 1960s. An important development has been the courts' extension of the protections afforded by the Fifth and Fourteenth amendments beyond regulatory adjudication to individual interests not covered by the Administrative Procedure Act and other statutory requirements. In addition, both Congress and the courts have sought to shape the character of agency policy making through various stipulations. Among the most important have been the encouragement of rulemaking, the expansion of opportunities to participate in and challenge agency decisions, the extension of formal due process to rulemaking, and the requirement that agencies justify their actions on the basis of economic analysis. This chapter briefly describes these developments, together with their limitations and effects as means of control. Although it is necessarily general, it provides a useful overview of structural constraints—especially for those with little background in the area.

Introduction

Numerous types of actions shape administrative policy. Among the most significant are agenda-setting decisions, such as when the Federal Trade Commission allocates limited prosecutorial resources in antitrust enforcement or when the Consumer Products Safety Commission assigns priorities for the investigation of potentially dangerous products. As Kenneth Davis notes, "Often the most important discretionary decisions are the negative ones, such as not to initiate, not to investigate, not to prosecute, not to deal, and the negative decisions usually mean a final disposition."[1] In an immediate and legally binding sense, however, administration comes to bear on society primarily through application decisions and rulemaking. These two types of action provide the foci for most internal constraints on bureaucratic discretion.

Application is the implementation of policy in individual cases. The Department of Transportation, the Veterans Administration, and the Department of Education make application decisions when they bestow or withhold highway grants, disability claims, and student loans. Similarly, the Federal Trade Commission makes application decisions when it orders particular firms to cease and desist from deceptive advertising practices, and the Federal Communications Commission makes application decisions when it allocates broadcast licenses. A contested application decision may be referred to as *adjudication.* This term is used imprecisely and inconsistently, and some scholars implicitly or explicitly equate it with a decision that is reached through courtlike procedures and that results in formal findings. Yet there is ample precedent for defining adjudication in substantive terms as the settlement of any controversy between an agency and someone subject to an application decision.[2]

In contrast to application decisions, rules are standards that pertain to classes of individuals and activities. The Veterans Administration, the Department of Education, and the Federal Communications Commission engage in rulemaking when they establish general criteria to guide the allocation of disability claims, student loans, and broadcast licenses. The Federal Trade Commission engages in rulemaking when it defines commercial activities within and across industries that fall within the meaning of "deceptive practices."

Unless otherwise noted, the term *rule* here refers to general statements that have the force of law and that therefore preclude the need for an agency to demonstrate the correctness of its construction of statutory directives in subsequent application decisions. Unlike such *substantive* or *legislative* rules, *interpretive* rules are mere statements of how agencies plan to construe their enabling legislation in the future. As such, they cannot be used as unchallenged premises for future decisions. Agencies also issue many rules of *internal practice and procedure* that guide the behavior of their members in carrying out organizational tasks. These include organizational SOPs for substantive and interpretive rulemaking, and for the application of policy in individual cases.

The equation of rulemaking and adjudication with policy making and policy application, respectively, should not be taken too far. Application decisions can create what we normally think of as policy, either by establishing general standards through precedent or by individual actions that have broad effects (a decision by the Department of Transportation to build a bridge across the Potomac River, for example). Conversely, abstract standards in the form of rules may affect one or a few individuals. If it is imperfect in these ways, however, the distinction between rulemaking and adjudication has traditionally been a key basis for prescribing procedural constraints on agency discretion.

A brief historical overview provides a foundation for describing and evaluating constraints on application decisions, rulemaking, and other elements of the administrative process. Although enabling statutes sometimes stipulated the procedures that agencies were to use in carrying out their mandates, bureaucrats were often left to their own devices in the early decades of the twentieth century. Practices varied tremendously as a result, and indeed many agencies chose what procedures they would use on an ad hoc basis. As one scholar noted:

> Just what the procedure is in any particular department or special agency at one time is difficult to get at; departmental practices are not for the outsider. A governmental employee . . . sometimes gives a glimpse of what actually happens. Usually such glimpses, since they are given with an initial cautiousness and finger-on-the-lip sign, are of little documentary value. Few departments give freely.[3]

The role of the courts in the administrative process was similarly limited. Judges typically assumed that they lacked the authority to review agency actions unless they were explicitly granted the power to do so by enabling legislation. Where review did occur, it tended to be limited by a procedural focus and by judicial deference to agency expertise on factual issues.[4]

The first attempt to impose uniform standards on the exercise of bureaucratic discretion was the Administrative Procedure Act of 1946.[5] Among its provisions, the APA specifies when and how certain types of administrative decisions and internal operating procedures must be made available to the public. The act's central features are its definitions of adjudication and rulemaking, together with its prescription of participatory opportunities and standards of rationality for each. In the first instance, it requires agencies to hold formal, trial-like hearings to resolve disputed issues, and it stipulates that decisions must be based exclusively on evidence contained in a record subject to judicial review. In the second, it requires agencies to give public notice and to solicit written or oral comments concerning the merits of proposed rules.

The APA is a notable effort to standardize the administrative process and to render agency decisions more accountable, and it remains the single most important source of federal administrative law. At the same time, the constraints it imposes are limited. Its procedural requirements and standards of judicial review for rulemaking establish only very loose controls on agencies' policy-making discretion, and its formats for both rulemaking and adjudication are circumscribed by broad exemptions and by other provisos that limit their coverage primarily to regulatory administration. Individual enabling statutes usually did not go beyond the APA's requirements during the first two decades following its passage, moreover, and the courts were reluctant to impose procedural constraints on their own initiative.

This brief description of the administrative process as it existed before the 1960s, together with the conditions that sustained it, provides a basis for understanding the more demanding system of procedural requirements and judicial review that exists today. Constraints on agency discretion have expanded along several dimensions. Although one should take care not to exaggerate the reach or the impact of these developments, their direct and indirect effects on public administration have been substantial.

The Growth of Structural Constraints

Much of what has happened in the administrative process over the past three decades can be described in term of two broad trends, the components of which overlap. One trend has been a redefinition of individual rights affected by bureaucracy and an accompanying extension of the protections afforded by due process to new types of adjudicatory actions. Another, which is perhaps more important from the standpoint of political science, has been an abandonment of the deference to agencies' policy-making expertise that underlay the APA and that otherwise characterized judicial and legislative attitudes before 1960. The latter trend has, in turn, resulted from several important institutional developments, each designed to ensure different qualities in bureaucratic decision making.

Protecting Individual Rights

The task of fashioning appropriate procedural constraints on agency adjudication is normally conceived of as one of balancing immediately affected individual interests against the public's interest in efficient administration. Congress and the courts have weighed these competing needs in dealing with a variety of issues, including such things as the circumstances under which administrators must obtain warrants in conducting physical inspections and the kinds of testimonial and documentary evidence that may be subpoenaed by agencies. The most important constraint on agency discretion in individual cases is adjudicatory due process. Although it was originally intended as a safeguard against the abuse of discretion in regulatory areas, the courts have transformed its practical definition in recent decades by extending procedural rights to a broader range of interests affected by a broader range of agency actions.

As mentioned, the APA's adjudicatory procedures set forth most of the same elements of formal due process associated with judicial proceedings. The act and its legislative history encourage agencies and those affected by their decisions to resolve disputed issues of fact and law informally. To the extent that this fails, however, Section 556 of the statute requires agencies to hold hearings at which presiding officials (often called administrative law judges) are given the responsibility to "administer oaths and affirmations, issue subpoenas . . . , rule on offers of proof and receive relevant evidence, take depositions or have depositions taken where the ends of justice would be served, . . . hold conferences for the settlement or simplification of the issues of the issues by the consent of the parties, and dispose of procedural requests or similar matters."[6] Parties to adjudication are entitled to submit "oral or documentary evidence, to submit rebuttal evidence, and to conduct such cross examination as may be required for a full and true disclosure of the facts." Section 557 of the APA stipulates that a presiding official must base his or her recommendations explicitly and exclusively upon findings contained in a record. Courts are empowered to review these conclusions and the decisions of agency heads (who often bear final responsibility for acting on the recommendations of presiding officers) to ensure that decisions are supported by "substantial evidence."[7]

The APA protects the integrity of its formal adjudicatory procedures and of pursuant judicial review by limiting ex parte (or off-the-record) communications between administrative decision makers and "interested persons outside the agency." The latter category includes lobbyists, as well as members of the legislative and executive branches. Even communications within agencies between officials performing prosecutorial and judicial functions have been limited through judges' interpretations of the APA's intent. Given the needs of congressional oversight and executive management, however, the proscription of ex parte contacts is restricted to "matters relevant to the merits of the proceeding," as opposed to such things as inquiries about the status of pending actions or the procedures being employed.[8]

Despite their rigor, the APA's procedures do not pertain to most types of adjudication. Excluded from its requirements are application decisions dealing with: "matters subject to a subsequent trial of the law and the facts de novo in a court; the selection or tenure of an employee . . . ; proceedings in which decisions rest solely on inspections, tests, or elections; the conduct of military or foreign affairs functions; cases in which an agency is acting as an agent of a court; and the certification of worker representatives." Further, the act's adjudicatory procedures apply only to decisions "required by statute to be determined on the record after an opportunity for an agency hearing" (or words to that effect). Now, as in 1946, triggering language of this sort is confined largely to regulatory mandates.[9]

Although it is not discussed in the legislative history of the APA, what is commonly referred to as the "privilege doctrine" undoubtedly provided the justification for this last limitation in its coverage. Nonregulatory actions, such as the allocation of benefits, subsidies, and contracts, as well as the bestowal or termination of government jobs, were thought to involve the distribution of public largess rather than property or liberty interests. It followed that the need for procedural safeguards against improper decisions was not as compelling a reason to inhibit agency efficiency in these areas as it was in cases where administrative proscriptions or prescriptions directly affected individuals' economic and social freedoms.

Against this background, a significant development in administrative law since the passage of the APA has been the courts' extension of due process to some nonregulatory adjudication. A seminal case in this area was *Goldberg v. Kelly* (1970), in which the Supreme Court held that Aid to Families with Dependent Children should not be viewed as a public gratuity.[10] Instead, recipients had what amounted to property and liberty interests in continued benefits pending a showing by administrators that they no longer met eligibility criteria. In protecting these interests, the Court required a pre-termination hearing at which affected parties must be apprised of the bases for administrative decisions and be allowed to challenge the agency's factual assertions and legal interpretations. Other cases have found due process to be relevant to the termination of public employment, the suspension of students from public schools, and other administrative actions previously thought to fall outside the protection of the Fifth and Fourteenth amendments. These procedural developments resulting from the courts' redefinition of constitutionally protected rights in the administrative process have been accompanied by heightened substantive review of decisions affecting individual interests.[11]

One should take care not to exaggerate the expansion of due process in agency adjudication. It has not been extended to all types of individual-level discretion, and agencies have not been required to conduct formal hearings in most nonregulatory areas where it has been found to apply. Rather, the courts have prescribed a contextual analysis in determining whether due process is required and, if so, what its nature is to be. First, one must ask whether a liberty or a property interest is at stake. In termination from public jobs, for example, such an interest is often equated with tenure—a legitimate, bilateral expectation of continued employment under satisfactory performance.[12]

Assuming that a constitutionally protected interest exists, a balancing test must then be conducted to determine both the formality and the timing of the hearing that is required. One side of the equation contains the importance of the individual right involved, together with the probability that the right will be infringed upon by a wrongful agency decision. The other contains the state's interest in efficient administration. Whereas *Goldberg* stipulated that welfare recipients must be allowed to confront agency officials with their attorneys, for instance, *Goss v. Lopez* (1975) implied that only an informal meeting was required before suspending a student for alleged misconduct.[13] In *Mathews v. Eldridge* (1976), the Court ruled that, because recipients of disability payments were not apt to be wholly dependent upon their benefits and because the medical determinations involved were typically objective and mechanical (and therefore less subject to error), a post-termination hearing satisfied the requirements for administrative due process.[14]

The most frequent explanation for post-*Goldberg* retrenchments is the obvious one—that an undiluted application of formal due process would impose an unacceptable burden on administration. In light of these qualifications, some have minimized the extent to which the expansion of due process has actually changed administrative adjudication.[15] At the same time, however, scholars' assessments of the changes that have occurred are necessarily dependent upon their expectations. Ardent supporters of individual rights have been more conservative in describing the extent of recent changes than have champions of administrative efficiency. Notwithstanding important limitations as to the character and effects of due process, the erosion of the privilege doctrine has had a significant impact on agency adjudication.[16]

Interest Representation

In addition to the extension of guarantees designed to ensure accuracy, consistency, and reasonableness in the application of statutory provisions, a number of other developments over the past thirty years reflect an abandonment of the premise that administrative policy making should be left to bureaucratic discretion. One general trend has been heightened interest representation. Just as the expansion of adjudicatory due process has entailed a redefinition of individuals' constitutional rights as they relate to government, the extension of new participatory opportunities in administration by the courts and by Congress has sought to ensure that agencies give adequate weight to all statutorily protected interests in making rules and arriving at application decisions that have broad policy effects.

One of the most important developments in administrative law during the middle of the twentieth century was the courts' relaxation of the threshold criteria required for citizens to participate in and seek judicial review of agency decisions. Standing to sue an agency and to participate in some types of administrative proceedings was traditionally based on one's ability to demonstrate that he or she had suffered or would suffer substantial economic or physical harm as the result of a bureaucratic action. Since the 1960s, however, judges have afforded the intended beneficiaries of programs (such as consumers and environmentalists) opportunities to challenge agency decisions even though their individual stakes have been small materially, or aesthetic or ideological in nature. In *United States v. Students Challenging Regulatory Agency Procedures (SCRAP)* (1973), for example, the Supreme Court upheld the standing of individuals to challenge increased railway freight rates because the policy would have impinged indirectly on their enjoyment of the environment by increasing the cost of recyclable goods. (It was argued that the corresponding use of nonrecyclable commodities would consume more natural resources and would also produce more refuse in national parks.)[17] The liberalization of standing has applied to challenges of rules and of adjudicatory actions with policy effects that go beyond the parties immediately involved in the decisions. In the latter regard, the courts have become especially receptive to representatives of diffuse and nonmaterial interests in areas such as ratemaking and the issuance of some types of licenses and permits, where the allocation of government-controlled resources in individual cases has important social or economic implications.

Judicial precedent has not moved ineluctably toward broader standing. The courts have had second thoughts about decisions extending opportunities for surrogate parties to act on behalf of individuals who might not have the wherewithal to challenge agencies in the courts.[18] Other cases have required individuals to demonstrate a high probability rather than a mere possibility that they will be adversely affected by an agency policy in a substantial way. In *City of Los Angeles v. Lyons* (1983), for example, a citizen who had been stopped for a missing tail light was rendered uncon-scious by policemen applying a chokehold. In denying standing to sue the city to proscribe that procedure, the Court stressed the low "'odds' . . . that Lyons would not only again be stopped for a traffic violation but would also be subjected to a chokehold without any provocation. . . ."[19] Access to the courts may also be impeded by a variety of other "threshold determina-tions" that are similar to standing, such as "ripeness," "primary jurisdic-tion," and the "exhaustion of available administrative remedies."[20]

As a general trend, however, a significant liberalization of standing has enhanced the ability of a broader range of individuals and groups to challenge agency decision making. The expansion of standing before the courts has, in turn, forced agencies to accommodate a broader range of affected interests in their proceedings. In its *Office of Communications of the United Church of Christ v. FCC* decision,[21] for example, the D.C. Circuit Court ruled in favor of a citizens' group that had not been allowed to participate in a Federal Communications Commission proceeding to renew a broadcast license. The FCC had denied the group's request for an eviden-tiary hearing at which it could intervene because its members were not competing for the license and had not otherwise asserted an economic interest in the decision. Treating the question of administrative intervention and judicial standing as one, the Court held that it was enough that the group—as listeners in the area and members of the public that the FCC was charged to serve—objected to the types of entertainment and political mes-sages broadcast by the current licensee. In general, an important effect of the expansion of standing has been to force agencies to open up application decisions that have broad policy implications. Some agencies already solic-ited public comment in such areas, either voluntarily or as the result of requirements in their enabling legislation, but many did not.

Although the APA allows for any interested parties to participate in rulemaking, the expansion of potential litigants has forced agencies to take seriously a broader range of interests there as well. It has also likely con-tributed to the voluntary adoption of notice-and-comment procedures in many areas exempted from the APA's requirements, such as military and foreign affairs, matters of internal practice and procedure, and the adminis-tration of "public property, loans, grants, benefits, subsidies, and con-tracts."[22] Although the legislative history of the APA suggested that notice-and-comment would often be desirable in such instances, nonregula-tory agencies generally avoided these procedures in the first two decades following the act's passage.[23] In contrast, today most domestic rulemaking probably involves public notice and comment (although no one has exam-ined the subject in a systematic way).

Requirements imposed by enabling legislation have reinforced the expansion of standing by the courts. Statutes have imposed notice-and-comment in some areas of nonregulatory rulemaking, as well as in some areas of nonregulatory adjudication where agency decisions have broad policy effects (such as in the approval of public works projects). In addition, Congress has demonstrated an increased tendency to create legally enforceable rights of participation that supplement the APA's requirements. This trend has been especially pronounced in areas of social regulation. Some legislation provides early access to the development of policies that will later be subject to notice and comment. For instance, many statutes require agencies to consult with advisory committees as they are formulating decisions, and in some cases provide a formal decision-making role for such bodies. As one illustration, the Occupational Safety and Health Administration is encouraged to appoint an ad hoc committee to formulate and recommend safety standards. Such committees must represent the viewpoints of workers, employers, and state health and safety organizations.[24]

Other legislative requirements go beyond the APA's essentially hortative opportunities for outside parties to petition agencies to investigate alleged violations of the law or to undertake rulemaking proceedings.[25] In its original form, for example, the Consumer Products Safety Act provided that the Consumer Products Safety Commission must offer a compelling justification for denying a request to initiate rulemaking or for terminating a proceeding once begun, and it explicitly authorized interested parties to challenge the reasonableness of such explanations before the courts.[26] As another illustration, the Occupational Safety and Health Act stipulates that a preliminary rulemaking proceeding may be initiated on the basis of information provided by the secretary of labor, the secretary of health and human services, the National Institute for Occupational Safety and Health, a state or political subdivision thereof, or any "interested person." Perhaps the most notable action-forcing provisions are those that have enabled environmentalists to obtain injunctions requiring the EPA to issue regulations dealing with problems outlined in its enabling legislation.

The Rulemaking Revolution

Fundamental changes in the form of agency action have both contributed to and helped to justify expanded participation. Although the use of devices such as advisory committees has a long history, dating back well into the nineteenth century, they were formerly much more common in distributive administration than in regulatory areas. In this regard, the increased use of rulemaking in lieu of case-by-case adjudication to carry out regulatory statutes has provided both a normative rationale and a political impetus for greater interest representation. If regulatory administration could once be conceived of primarily as a quasi-judicial function that should be insulated from outside pressures, its legislative dimensions have become much more difficult to ignore.

In addition to being the foci for most procedural constraints, rulemaking and adjudication often represent alternative strategies for carrying out statutory mandates. The essential function of the former is to guide or constrain the latter, and as such rulemaking may preclude the need to settle individual controversies by establishing policy in terms clear enough to elicit voluntary compliance from regulates or to dispel uncertainty concerning eligibility for government services and benefits. Greater reliance on rulemaking thus represents a fundamental transformation in the institutional form of program implementation in many regulatory areas. Whereas agencies were typically free to choose between general standards and case-by-case discretion in carrying out their mandates before 1970, they have since been required or encouraged to rely on rulemaking as a means of implementing and developing policy in many contexts.

Although most agencies combine rulemaking and case-by-case discretion in varying proportions, the respective merits of decisions to emphasize one or the other have received considerable attention.[27] This has been especially true in regulatory administration, where reliance on rulemaking and adjudication have corresponding advantages and disadvantages along two dimensions. In terms of fairness to affected interests, rulemaking can inhibit the retroactivity and capriciousness that may accompany the ad hoc development of policy. At the same time, an adjudicatory approach can promote fairness by allowing administrators to tailor their decisions to individual circumstances where the diversity of issues faced in implementation prohibits meaningful generalization from one case to the next.

In terms of sound policy development, rulemaking is an expedient way for administrators to achieve desired results, and it is also conducive to planning and to the creation of comprehensive and integrated standards. Unlike adjudication, which is a reactive approach that tends to focus on the facts of individual cases, rulemaking allows administrators to anticipate problems and to consider all relevant interests and policy effects. Rulemaking may also be desirable because it produces policy that is clearer, more accessible, and thus presumably more accountable than standards that must be distilled from a series of individual cases. On the other hand, focusing on relatively small issues as they ripen in the context of individual cases can be attractive where an understanding of problems and the probable effects of alternative solutions is limited. An incremental approach can also limit the effects of bad decisions and allow policy makers more flexibility in reversing their direction.

An important feature of the administrative process before 1970 was that bureaucrats themselves were usually permitted to weigh the pros and cons of issuing general standards to guide the application of policy. Enabling statutes generally authorized agencies to issue rules as deemed appropriate for carrying out their mandates, and the courts were reluctant to interject their own judgments as to what form administration should take. A frequently cited precedent that addressed this issue was *SEC v. Chenery* (1947), in which a company argued that the Securities and Exchange Commission's case-by-case disapproval of stock transactions was improper because it resulted in the retroactive application of policy. Although the Supreme Court encouraged the use of rulemaking whenever practical in the interest of fairness, it held that "the choice between proceeding by general rule or by individual, ad hoc litigation lies primarily in the informed discretion of the administrative agency."[28]

The *Chenery* decision was based on the premise that administrators were best able to judge whether they knew enough about the problems at hand or whether the issues under consideration were sufficiently uniform as to allow the development of general standards. Although this seemed reasonable as an abstract proposition, by the 1960s many had come to feel that agencies were inclined to abuse their discretion by failing to issue general standards when they should in the interest of fair and effective administration. This thesis was expressed in the writings of many authorities on the administrative process. As Kenneth Davis argued in his influential book *Discretionary Justice,* "The typical failure in our system ... is not legislative delegation of broad discretionary power with vague standards; it is the procrastination of administrators in resorting to the rulemaking power to replace vagueness with clarity."[29] The assertion that agencies often failed to use rulemaking when they should spread well beyond academia, and indeed had become common fare in government commission studies, judicial writings, and congressional hearings and reports by the late 1960s.

Partly as a result of assessments such as these, the deference traditionally accorded agencies in choosing the form of administration eroded during the 1970s. Although administrators retained substantial discretion in most areas, exhortations and constraints to articulate new policy and codify old precedents through rules became increasingly common. Describing the role of the courts in this regard, Colin Diver observes that:

> Instances of judicial insistence on rulemaking, though rare, accumulated rapidly enough to provide rulemaking enthusiasts ... the basis for discerning a general tendency. Courts invoked a variety of legal grounds ... for divining

an obligation to proceed by rulemaking. Some cases merely vacated specific agency orders as inadequately justified, while others directly commanded the agency to initiate rulemaking proceedings.[30]

The legislature played yet a more significant part in shaping the form of administration. Congress sometimes pressured agencies to emphasize rulemaking, as it did with the Federal Trade Commission. Beyond this, it required rulemaking as a prerequisite for enforcing policy in most of the regulatory statutes enacted in the 1960s and 1970s. This is most notably true with regard to "social regulation" dealing with health, safety, consumer rights, and the environment. Thus, for example, the Consumer Products Safety Commission and the National Highway Safety Administration lack the discretion enjoyed by older regulatory bodies to develop policy incrementally through administrative adjudication. Enabling statutes have gone even further in some cases by requiring agencies to issue rules dealing with certain problems within specified periods of time.

Judicial and legislative encouragement and constraints have contributed to a profound change in the institutional character of administrative regulation. Today, much more than twenty-five years ago, agencies rely on rulemaking as a means of implementing policy—especially in areas of regulation. As Antonin Scalia notes:

> The 1970s have been aptly described by expert observers of the federal administrative process as the "era of rulemaking." To an astounding degree, a system which previously had established law and policy through case-by-case adjudication ... began setting forth its general prescriptions in rules, leaving little to be decided in subsequent adjudications beyond the factual issues of compliance or non-compliance.[31]

Hybrid Rulemaking Procedures

Although rulemaking can be defended in terms of fairness and effectiveness, its legislative character also renders the political content of administration more visible and direct. Because it creates policy in a more precipitous way than adjudication, often requiring agencies to balance competing interests in the process, the issuance of general standards is more politically salient and more difficult to reconcile with the tenets of representative democracy. In light of this, it is hardly surprising that rulemaking has been subjected to more stringent constraints as it has become more prevalent. In addition to the broadening of participatory rights, the most significant institutional reaction to the rulemaking revolution has been the replacement of the APA's relatively lax procedures with requirements that subject agencies' quasi-legislative actions to a higher burden of justification.

The APA contains two sets of requirements for rulemaking, sometimes referred to as "formal" and "informal" procedures (although the act, itself, does not use these terms). In the first instance, it provides that trial-like adjudicatory procedures also apply to rulemaking where enabling statutes specify that decisions be based "on a record after an opportunity for an agency hearing." This was not contemplated to be a standard or frequently used format, however, and it was probably included in the APA as a sop to conservatives and business groups who had wanted all rulemaking to be constrained by formal due process. As a practical matter, Congress imposed such requirements in only a handful of statutes.[32] The procedures generally prescribed for rulemaking were much less demanding. Section 553 of the APA requires agencies to publish a notice in the *Federal Register* and to solicit written comments concerning the merits and demerits of their proposed rules. Oral hearings are optional. Final rules issued after comments have been received must be accompanied by "a concise general statement of their basis and purpose," and courts are authorized to review decisions in order to ensure that they are not "arbitrary or capricious."

If Section 556 and Section 557 of the APA were designed primarily to control agencies' quasi-judicial activities, Section 553 reflects the premise that rulemaking is a quasi-legislative function that often involves questions of probable policy effect rather than "adjudicative facts" that are subject to proof or disproof. The framers of the act extended this analogy in reasoning that, just as members of a congressional committee would normally collect evidence and opinions through hearings and other means, administrators should take care to ensure that their decisions were informed by relevant views and information. Agencies were only required to solicit written comment, however, and it was assumed that any hearings they might choose to conduct would be of an informal nature. The input obtained in these ways was intended as a decisional aid that administrators could use as they saw fit. Thus, although the meaning of arbitrary or capricious was the subject of scholarly debate and judicial inconsistency from the start, the term clearly implied less stringent scrutiny than the substantial-evidence standard governing regulatory adjudication. At least originally, it was construed to mean that rules would be valid so long as they were supported by some evidence and a plausible argument.

Viewed in this historical context, more recent developments reflect a breakdown of the dichotomy between quasi-judicial and quasi-legislative functions that lay at the core of the APA. Many statutes enacted since the mid 1960s have required agencies to compile records outlining the legal and factual bases for their rules and defending those premises against any challenges. Either explicitly or implicitly, Congress has frequently required such justifications to meet the "substantial evidence" standard of judicial review prescribed for adjudication. These requirements go well beyond the APA's Section 553, which says nothing about a record and, again, which defines judicial scrutiny in more relaxed terms. Statutes have also frequently required agencies to hold hearings, either as a matter of course or when requested by affected interests. In some cases, they have further stipulated that such hearings incorporate elements of formal due process, such as full or limited opportunities for affected interests to engage in cross-examination and submit rebuttal evidence.[33]

Legislatively imposed constraints such as these are prevalent in social regulation, and have crept into other areas as well. Although they are often referred to as "hybrid" rulemaking procedures because they represent a supposed middle ground between the APA's simple notice-and-comment requirements and the much more judicialized constraints prescribed in sections 556 and 557, they frequently contain the most salient aspects of the latter format. By itself, the base requirement that agencies justify their actions on a record subject to rigorous judicial scrutiny may induce administrators to hold adversary proceedings as an assurance to the courts that the premises of their rules have been thoroughly tested.

Judicial precedent has paralleled statutory trends in rulemaking procedure. In *Citizens to Preserve Overton Park v. Volpe* (1971), the Supreme Court remanded a case to a district court because the justices had not been presented with an adequate version of the record upon which the secretary of transportation had based a decision to route an interstate highway through Memphis, Tennessee. The Court reasoned that, in the absence of such a record, it had no way of judging whether the agency had complied with its enabling legislation by accurately determining that there were no "feasible and prudent" alternative routes circumventing a city park and residential area.[34] An implicit premise of *Overton Park* was that judges should subject administrative policy decisions to close scrutiny rather than defer to bureaucratic expertise. This applied to issues of fact and probable policy effect as well as to the questions of statutory interpretation that had been the traditional concern of judicial review.

Although *Overton Park* technically involved informal adjudication (a contested application decision that was not constrained by trial-like adjudicatory procedures), the D.C. Circuit Court of Appeals quickly extended its record-keeping requirement to rulemaking governed by the APA. By the late 1970s, most legal scholars (and agency lawyers) had come to the conclusion that, as informal rulemaking had been redefined by judges, the difference between the arbitrary-and-capricious standard and substantial-evidence review had become "largely semantic." Both implied that judges were willing to take a "hard look" at the rationale for agency decisions as expressed in a record. From that position, it was a logical step to the requirement that agencies ensure the integrity of such records by subjecting their factual evidence and legal reasoning to the crucible of cross-examination, rebuttal, and other adversarial procedures. To many, *Home Box Office* (1977) represented the culmination of the Circuit Court's initiatives in substantive and procedural review of agency rulemaking.[35] This decision placed severe restrictions on off-the-record communications between agency officials and outside parties on the premise that such influences would undermine the integrity of administrative due process and would similarly inhibit meaningful judicial review.[36]

Judicially imposed hybrid rulemaking has been tempered since the late 1970s. Indeed, the Supreme Court's decision in *Vermont Yankee* (1978) seemed to be an outright repudiation of lower courts' efforts to formalize informal rule making. Justice Rehnquist's opinion was especially critical of the imposition of procedures, such as cross-examination and rebuttal, that are nowhere mentioned in the APA. As it stated, "Nothing in the APA . . . permitted the [D.C. Circuit] Court to review and overturn the rule making proceeding on the basis of procedural devices employed (or not employed) by the [Nuclear Regulatory] Commission so long as the Commission employed the statutory *minima*. . . ."[37] The Court's *Baltimore Gas & Electric* (1983) and *Chevron* (1984) decisions have reinforced this precedent, arguing against judicial usurpation of agencies' substantive discretion in areas where decisions rest on political and scientific issues, respectively.[38] Most authorities view *Chevron*'s injunction that courts should not impose their judgment in the absence of discernable statutory intent as being especially important. By the same token, the Court has conceded that ex parte communications are necessary to some extent in the interest of sound executive management, effective administration, and political responsiveness.

It is nevertheless a mistake to conclude that the judiciary's position on rulemaking has returned to anything approaching its lax posture before *Overton Park*. Although the court has given inconsistent signals regarding its willingness to defer to agencies' expertise and political judgments, the potential for rigorous substantive review remains much greater than it was. In 1983 it chided the Department of Transportation for attempting to use *Vermont Yankee* "as though it were a talisman under which any agency decision is unimpeachable."[39] *Chevron* itself leaves ample latitude for courts to determine if agencies have behaved pursuant to "reasonable" or "permissible constructions" of legislative intent. If they have been sanctioned as the "lifeblood of the administrative process," restrictions on informal contacts with affected groups and other government officials also remain more severe than they were in the 1960s. A key observation in these regards is that recent Supreme Court opinions have continued to assume that agencies will justify their decisions on the basis of a record. (Again, the APA does not mention a record, and as a practical matter agencies typically did not compile rulemaking records, as such, before the mid 1960s.)

Whatever its position on rulemaking procedures and the stringency of review, moreover, the Supreme Court has only limited resources for changing judicial behavior. Several authorities have noted in this regard that lower courts have continued to insist that agencies provide meaningful opportunities to challenge the evidence in rulemaking records. Peter Schuck and Donald Elliott find that, whereas *Chevron* immediately led to a modest increase in the willingness of judges to affirm agency decisions of all types (rulemaking, adjudication, and ratemaking), about half of this growth in deference had eroded by 1988. An even more significant point is that the D.C. Circuit, which has original jurisdiction for reviewing most agency rules, has shown a marked resistance to recent precedent. In fact, its affirmation rate actually decreased in the wake of *Chevron*.[40]

Policy Analysis

The rigor demanded by hybrid rulemaking procedures is reinforced in important respects by the popularity of requirements that administrators objectively identify and weigh the probable effects of their actions. Although a variety of specific techniques are used to this end, the most common is cost-benefit analysis. Under this format, some or all policy effects are measured and compared in terms of real or imputed market values to determine whether their total benefits to society will outweigh their total costs. Benefit-to-cost ratios may be used to select the best policy from among several alternatives under the related technique of cost-effectiveness analysis.

The use of "policy" or "economic" analysis has grown tremendously since the mid-1960s, when it came to prominence as a means of evaluating Great Society programs. It has become especially popular in the area of regulation since the mid-1970s. Several presidential directives have required executive agencies to weigh all or some of the positive and negative effects of their regulatory proposals. The most ambitious of these to date is Reagan's Executive Order 12291, a program extended under the Bush Administration. Among other things, the Reagan order required a formal cost–benefit analysis for "major" regulations (defined as those having a projected economic impact of $100 million per year), and what was presumably a less rigorous analysis for other rules.[41] President Clinton has also required cost–benefit analyses of regulations that exceed the $100-million threshold or that are otherwise "significant."

Cost–benefit analysis has also been required by some enabling statutes, and has been implied or encouraged by balancing mandates that require agencies to weigh competing social objectives in issuing general rules or in making individual application decisions that have broad effects. Although judicial decisions have been inconsistent in their willingness to specify the methodology agencies must use in the latter cases, the general tendency for courts to require more rigorous justifications has encouraged the adoption of economic analysis. In addition, the use of this technique has been widely advocated by economists, engineers, and scientists serving as agency consultants and as members of advisory committees.[42]

Generally applicable laws have required rigorous evaluation of policy effects as well. The most important of these is the National Environmental Policy Act (NEPA) of 1969, which requires environmental-impact statements (EISs) for "all major federal actions affecting the quality of the human environment." An EIS must analyze the positive and negative effects of a proposed action on the environment, and must also evaluate possible alternative policies. NEPA does not mandate the quantification of policy effects (although it does encourage a "systematic, interdisciplinary approach which will ensure the integrated use of the natural and social sciences"), but many agencies have seen fit to conduct fully or partially quantified analyses pursuant to its requirements.[43]

Administrative Procedures in Perspective

The preceding discussion is by no means a complete inventory of formal constraints on agency discretion. Other topics that fall under the ambit of administrative law include the scope and limits of agency investigative powers, freedom of information requirements, and tort liability of government officials. It is also important not to leave the impression that internal controls over bureaucratic discretion can be neatly categorized. Despite the homogenizing effects of the APA and more recent institutional trends that cut across agencies, administrative procedures are usually tailored to particular administrative tasks by Congress, the courts, and agencies themselves. This is true of the contextual balancing used to give operational meaning to due process and of the statutory requirements that accompany many programs. Important aspects of the procedures governing the approval of new drugs, nuclear power plants, and mineral leases on public lands are all unique to those activities, for example.[44]

Just as the institutional structure of implementation differs among agencies and among programs within agencies, the effects of particular types of requirements can vary in accordance with numerous factors. These have received little systematic attention, and a thorough assessment of the impact of administrative procedures is beyond the scope of this chapter. It is possible, however, to outline some of the limitations and effects of administrative procedures in a general way. While one should take care not to exaggerate either their reach or their impact where they do apply, administrative procedures nonetheless affect the implementation of policy in important respects.

Limitations of Procedural Constraints

Despite the growth of internal constraints, a large residual of agency discretion remains beyond the reach of such controls. Most agencies retain substantial freedom in choosing between rulemaking and case-by-case implementation. Notwithstanding the erosion of the privilege doctrine and other developments, moreover, administrative procedures and judicial review tend to be more demanding in regulatory administration than elsewhere. Again, the balancing analysis employed by the courts to define administrative due process has not required trial-like proceedings or even pre-termination hearings of any kind in many areas of nonregulatory adjudication. Although notice-and-comment procedures have been adopted in most areas of substantive rulemaking exempted from the APA, the constraints of hybrid procedures have been confined largely to regulatory administration by Congress and the courts.

Another qualification of the theme developed in the preceding section is that the trend toward more rigorous controls reached its zenith in the mid-to-late 1970s. Although the subsequent retrenchment has been relatively modest, more recent Supreme Court decisions dealing with standing, rulemaking procedures, and other dimensions of the administrative process have evinced a greater sensitivity to the adverse effects of excessive procedural demands on flexible and efficient program implementation as well as on bureaucratic accountability to the political branches of government. Congress has also slowed its efforts to structure the exercise of agency discretion. Legislative requirements that particular agencies use hybrid rulemaking procedures are confined primarily to statutes passed in the late 1960s and 1970s, for example. Similarly, there has been little sentiment to revive broad amendments to the APA, endorsed by the Republican Party in 1980 and the Senate in 1982, that would have imposed economic analysis, substantial-evidence review, and other constraints on all agency rulemaking (although there appears to be renewed interest in such provisions among the new Republican majority). Congress has even rescinded some of its procedural constraints in favor of greater administrative discretion.

Perhaps a more important set of caveats pertains to limitations on the effects of administrative procedures that do exist. Numerous informal decisions take place both before and within the interstices of formal procedures, and these often have a crucial bearing on what agencies do. Notwithstanding the existence of extremely detailed procedures that guide policy development by the Nuclear Regulatory Commission, for instance, a veteran staffer from that agency observed that, because of the uniqueness of each proceeding, rulemaking is ultimately an "art rather than a science."[45] Every contemplated action involves different factual and political issues that determine who will be involved at what stage of decision making.

An especially important fact that is frequently overlooked in the literature is that due process, economic analysis, and most other procedural constraints on agency discretion tend to focus on what Herbert Simon refers to as the "alternative-testing" stage of administration, but often have little bearing on prior decisions in agenda setting and policy formulation that are frequently crucial in establishing the direction of program implementation.[46] Interested parties may petition agencies to initiate adjudicatory and rulemaking proceedings in many areas of administration, but the terms of the APA and most enabling statutes generally afford little guarantee that such requests will be given serious consideration. The usual justification for refusal to impose more stringent constraints on agenda setting has been that, unlike final decisions in rulemaking and adjudication, investigatory actions, the selection of cases to prosecute, and the identification of problems that merit rules impinge only indirectly on affected interests. The allocation of scarce resources in such areas must also typically involve subtle balancing considerations, many of which require a thorough familiarity with an agency's capabilities and ongoing activities. Given these facts, agenda setting is often considered to be an "executive function" best left to administrators.

Some statutes have incorporated mechanisms allowing outside interests to force agencies to act, as discussed above, but such provisions are limited to a relatively small percentage of programs. They have also been rescinded in some of the areas where they once applied. In 1981, for instance, Congress amended the Consumer Products Safety Act, deleting the enhanced petitioning rights it had created. The legislature's action came in response to agency complaints that the need to accommodate outside requests prevented it from planning and from pursuing a coherent regulatory strategy.

This same concern is explicit in refusals by judges to entertain challenges to agencies' agenda-setting discretion. Aside from its black humor, *Heckler v. Chaney* is an illustration of the Supreme Court's deference to executive judgment in establishing administrative priorities. Denying a petition by which death-row inmates sought to force the Food and Drug Administration to review the "safety and effectiveness" of lethal injections, it noted that:

> The agency is far better equipped than the courts to deal with the many variables involved in the proper ordering of its priorities. . . . In addition to these administrative concerns, we note that when an agency refuses to act it generally does not exercise its *coercive* power over an individual's liberty or property rights, and thus does not infringe upon areas that courts often are called upon to protect.[47]

Once an issue has been placed on an agency's agenda in the form of a proposed adjudicatory action or rule, much of the decision-making process often occurs well before procedural constraints prescribed by Congress and the courts directly come to bear. In adjudication, administrators may apply a variety of techniques that preclude recourse to formal due process (again, which is only required in the event that the parties involved cannot resolve their differences informally). For example, the FTC may coerce a firm to alter its behavior merely by initiating an investigation of unfair competitive practices, or it may later use the evidence it has collected to persuade the accused to sign a "consent decree" agreeing to "cease and desist" from certain activities without admitting guilt. Similarly, SEC or FCC staff may persuade an applicant for a securities or broadcast license that he or she is not qualified well before the initiation of a formal hearing. Where adversary processes are initiated, moreover, agencies and affected interests frequently use devices such as prehearing conferences to reach agreements on disputed issues and otherwise to simplify and shorten proceedings.[48]

The timing of participation can impose especially significant limits on the impact of public input in the formulation of rules and other agency policies. The informal process of administrative policy development has received only scant attention from scholars,[49] yet few would disagree with the assertion that it is the locus for many crucial decisions. As William Pederson notes in one of only a handful of studies to examine the organizational dynamics of rulemaking, "The Administrative Procedure Act is only a statute; it is not the source of all agency procedures. Commentators who focus too narrowly on the APA may forget what lies behind it, and the long paths an agency rule may have to trace before even being proposed for comment."[50] Notices of proposed rulemaking usually articulate detailed plans, and are frequently accompanied by book-length reports citing thousands (and sometimes tens of thousands) of pages of evidence. As a result, interested parties must often focus their attention on the pros and cons of one clearly defined course of action rather than on the relative merits of competing approaches.

Again, Congress, and in some cases agencies themselves, have occasionally sought to provide for earlier input in policy formulation through supplementary means such as advisory committees. Agencies also occasionally use advance notices of proposed rulemaking to solicit early public input concerning the nature and severity of alleged problems and the advisability of different policy strategies.[51] The technique of negotiated rulemaking even allows contending interests to develop their own policies under agency supervision.[52] Procedures such as these remain the exception rather then the norm, however, and usually provide for only hortative comments from a restricted group of participants where they are employed.[53]

The limitations associated with the timing of participation, per se, are normally reinforced by the fact that agency plans submitted for public comment represent substantial investments of time and organizational resources. The development of a proposed rule or an application decision having broad policy effects involves months and frequently years of work. It usually entails extensive research as well as a good deal of communication and consensus building among various types of administrative professionals and political appointees within and outside the agency. Sunk costs are sufficiently great by the end of this process that administrators are often disinclined to change their minds in response to public comment, especially with regard to basic policy choices. The extension of more rigorous due process to rulemaking, which has ironically been intended to ensure effective participation, has added to the incentive for agencies to formulate tight, fully developed policies in anticipation of challenges from affected interests and close scrutiny by the courts.

It bears reemphasis that the process of bureaucratic policy development is poorly understood, and that the degree to which administrators are receptive or unreceptive to comment undoubtedly varies considerably from one setting to another.[54] As might be expected, agency officials almost universally indicate that they respond appropriately to intelligent public input. At the same time, other observers frequently offer the assessment that participation in rulemaking has little effect other than perhaps to render the process more legitimate. As one notes, "Hearings themselves serve some useful and important purposes. However, one of these purposes does not seem to be changing the viewpoints of any of the participants."[55] As another states, "Hearings are not the basis for decision making. Rather, project plans are placed on the docket as a *fait accompli* by agency managers who challenge the competence of laymen to find fault with their documents."[56]

Finally, practical limitations on the accessibility of administrative procedures often limit their effects as well. Even to the extent that opportunities exist for input at a meaningful stage in the decision-making process, and even to the extent that agencies are inclined to be receptive to public comment, many of those with a stake in administrative actions simply lack the wherewithal to participate effectively. For instance, Jerry Mashaw argues that the ability to request a pre-termination hearing may be a relatively ineffective means of ensuring fairness in the application of a program such as AFDC, where most recipients lack the education and sense of efficacy needed to challenge agency officials.[57] Heavy reliance on informal dispute resolution in regulatory adjudication can be explained in part by the fact that even business firms are inclined to avoid the expense and anxiety that accompany their right to formal due process.

Participation in administrative policy decisions can be especially demanding. Although the ability to offer meaningful input is conditioned by contextual factors that have received relatively little systematic attention,[58] the resources needed for viable participation in rulemaking and other types of policy decisions often prohibit effective comment by individuals and by some groups. The standard means of providing notice of proposed rulemaking—the *Federal Register*—is a document that few citizens know about, much less read. In addition, viable participation is often contingent on the ability to marshal convincing legal and empirical analysis. Again, it is ironic that the institution of hybrid procedures has made participation in rulemaking more costly by placing a higher premium on legal expertise and the ability to support policy positions with rigorously substantiated arguments. The imposition of economic analysis as a criterion for agency actions has reinforced this tendency. Although the diversity of decision making precludes generalization, the price of competent participation in some areas of rulemaking (and certainly in many important proceedings) often begins at several hundred thousand dollars.

The Impact of Structural Constraints

Yet if administrative procedures and judicial review are far from comprehensive in their purview, and if the 1980s witnessed a rescission in the scope and rigor of such controls, it remains that the process of implementing statutes is much more highly structured today than it was thirty years ago. Evidence further suggests that, if they are limited in important respects, the constraints described above have had a substantial impact.

At the very least, adjudicatory due process provides opportunities for those with adequate resources to challenge administrative actions. Although there are strong incentives to settle regulatory disputes through informal negotiation, the APA's formal constraints are still brought to bear in a substantial proportion of cases. Perhaps a more important point is that reliance on informal techniques reflects the fact that agencies, too, are motivated to avoid the rigors and the organizational costs of due process. The availability of trial-like proceedings and opportunities to challenge final decisions under strict standards of judicial review in regulatory adjudication thus serve as underlying constraints and bargaining resources that affected interests can use to influence decisions that are reached informally.

Nor is it accurate to assume that the extension of due process to non-regulatory adjudication is rendered nugatory by practical limitations on the ability of individuals to participate. Some have suggested that, apart from any instrumental value of due process, its mere availability is an important source of legitimacy. Beyond this, evidence indicates that a surprisingly high proportion of individuals from even the most disenfranchised elements of society avail themselves of opportunities to challenge adverse decisions if the stakes are sufficiently high. For example, requests for hearings to review the termination of AFDC benefits roughly doubled nationwide in the wake of *Goldberg.* To put this in perspective, of the 12,000 individuals who received advance notices of termination or reduction of their AFDC benefits each month in New York City, 2,000 requested hearings.[59] Although the topic has not received much attention, it is reasonable to expect that government employees and other classes of individuals protected by the courts' redefinition of property and liberty interests are more apt to be aware of and willing to assert their rights than welfare recipients.

The effects of procedural constraints on agency policy making have been especially significant. In contrast to the pessimistic views offered by some, Cornelius Kerwin feels that "There is little question that agencies take public comment seriously."[60] He bases this conclusion on a number of observations, including his examination of agency responses to comments contained in rules' explanatory preambles. His most convincing evidence is a survey in which many interest groups indicate that participation in rulemaking holds its own in competition with other strategies for influencing government. Presumably these insiders would not waste scarce resources on a futile cause.

There is no doubt that the institutional developments described above have had a substantial impact in this regard. As judges have become more willing to review policy decisions on both substantive and procedural grounds, it has come to be taken for granted in many areas that significant agency initiatives will be challenged before the courts. At least 80 percent of all EPA rules are so contested, for example.[61] Given a natural aversion to having their actions remanded or nullified, agencies have made painstaking efforts to respond to comments offered during rulemaking. If such responses are sometimes exercises in justifying detailed and thoroughly researched alternatives already chosen, the anticipation of challenges from affected interests under hybrid rulemaking, as reinforced by the liberalization of standing and various statutory provisions, has increased the incentives for agencies to consider potential or actual objections from affected interests at earlier stages of policy development.

The anticipation of judicial review has also served the complementary goal of due process that decisions be based on accurate factual assertions and sound constructions of statutory intent. A number of observations attest to the heightened efforts of agencies to provide convincing justifications for their actions. One crude illustration is the growth of explanatory material accompanying regulations published in the *Federal Register*. A comparative analysis of eighty rules issued by four regulatory agencies in 1966 and 1986 shows that the length of the preambles justifying agency decisions almost doubled as a percentage of the total length of the regulations themselves.[62]

This is especially instructive in light of the earlier discussion concerning the Supreme Court's desire that judges accord greater deference to bureaucrats on questions of policy. Whatever the effects of *Vermont Yankee* (1978), *Chevron* (1984), and other decisions on the courts' willingness to take a "hard look," agencies still feel compelled to provide much more rigorous analyses in defense of their rules than they did before the 1970s.

The records generated under hybrid rulemaking procedures illustrate this point. For instance, the average length of Federal Trade Commission rulemaking records compiled voluntarily under the APA's notice-and-comment requirements was 3,123 pages. In contrast, the average length of rulemaking records increased to 64,850 pages after Congress imposed substantial-evidence review and other elements of formal due process in 1974. An especially revealing observation is that the portion of the records submitted by agency staff increased from 34 percent to 62 percent. Analogous developments have occurred in many other agencies.[63]

Just as it has led to more rigor in agency policy making, the growth of institutional constraints has had important consequences for the internal structure and efficiency of public administration. An organization's complexity and the dynamics of its decision making tend to mirror the complexity of the "task environment" in which it operates. Thus, whereas the development of rules was once dominated to a much greater extent by technical specialists with expertise directly in line with agencies' central missions (often scientists and engineers), lawyers, economists, and various other kinds of staff professionals have assumed more prominent decision-making roles in many areas of administration. The few existing analyses of administrative policy making as an organizational process clearly attest to this structural "differentiation." In case studies prepared for the Administrative Conference, for example, rules developed by the Federal Aviation Administration and the Environmental Protection Agency required sixty-nine and fifty-five internal clearance stages, respectively. Much of this communication involved conflict among professional specialists with distinctive policy-making orientations.[64]

A related consequence of the increased stringency of administrative procedures and judicial review is that the process of agency policy making has become more protracted. This is illustrated by the experience of the Federal Trade Commission. Under the informal, notice-and-comment procedures the commission had used before 1975, the average time between initial notice and the issuance of a final rule was 14.1 months. With the exclusion of one anomalous proceeding that lasted over six years, the figure drops to 10.6 months.[65] In contrast, most of the sixteen rules proposed under hybrid procedures in 1975 and 1976 have yet to be promulgated. The FTC is an extreme example, and there is no doubt that increased delay in its rulemaking has been due not only to more rigorous procedures but also to the ambitiousness and controversiality of many of its proposals. Still, the extension of formal due process to rulemaking has been a very significant source of delay, and the FTC's experiences have paralleled those of many other agencies.[66] Statistics such as these represent only part of the delay associated with judicialized rulemaking procedures, moreover. Equally if not more important is the additional time agencies spend formulating proposed rules that will withstand challenges from opponents and heightened scrutiny from judges.

Beyond delay, the requirement that actions be rigorously justified has led to the abandonment of some proceedings, and has had the effect of stifling other initiatives that would have been taken under the old system of less-demanding administrative procedures and judicial review. It has also sometimes affected the means by which administrators carry out their mandates. As rulemaking procedures have become more burdensome, for example, agencies have sometimes foregone the articulation of legally binding, general standards in favor of other forms of action. In this regard, the imposition of rigorous due process, which has been intended to render administration more accountable, has ironically induced agencies to rely more heavily on alternative means of developing and enforcing policy that are generally less open and visible than rulemaking. These have included the use of adjudication and reliance on threats and informal understandings.[67]

Conclusion

Administrative law is relatively new in the United States.[68] The reason for this is that public administration did not become an important locus of government authority until the twentieth century. The preceding discussion has described the most important dimensions of the formal administrative process as it has evolved in response to the growing role of bureaucracy in our political system. One trend has been the extension of due process as a means of protecting individual rights to new areas of administrative adjudication. Even more important has been the imposition of more rigorous procedural constraints and judicial review to many kinds of policy decisions.

This chapter has also sought to place these developments in perspective. If controls on agency discretion have generally become more demanding, recent years have seen a modest but notable reversal of this trend in deference to the values of bureaucratic expertise and efficient management. The impact of administrative procedures and judicial review on agency policy decisions is limited in a more fundamental way by the fact that they are designed primarily to test alternatives. Thus, they tend to have little direct impact on the processes of agenda setting and alternative formulation. The expansion of administrative procedures and judicial review has had important effects, nonetheless. Participatory opportunities have been strengthened in many cases, at least for some kinds of interests, and agencies have been forced to provide more rigorous justifications for their actions. This has often translated into substantial delay and resource costs in administration.

The transformation that has occurred can be explained by the fact that both the doctrinal premises and the political conditions that provided the bases for limited controls on bureaucracy have eroded over the past three decades. In the first instance, faith in the traditional view of bureaucracy as an efficient transmission belt has given way to less-flattering metaphors. Widely perceived shortcomings in the performance of agencies left to their own devices have, in turn, provided the impetus for doctrinal revision and for more stringent controls over bureaucracy. In the second instance, the environment of agency decision making has become more contentious in many areas, and administrative procedures and judicial review have thus become more salient as means of promoting different kinds of interests. In these regards, the overview presented above provides the basis for a more synoptic look at the causes and effects of administrative due process.

Notes

1. Kenneth Culp Davis, *Discretionary Justice: A Preliminary Inquiry* (Baton Rouge: Louisiana State University Press, 1969), p. 22.

2. For example, this is the official, if implicit, definition given to adjudication by the Administrative Procedure Act. See U.S. Statutes at Large 60 (1946); 237, as amended. U.S. Code, vol. 5, secs. 551–59, 701–6, 1305, 3105, 3344, 5372, 7521.

3. John P. Comer, *Legislative Functions of the National Administrative Authorities* (New York: Columbia University Press, 1927), p. 51.

4. See, for example, Kenneth F. Warren, *Administrative Law in the Political System,* 2d ed. (St. Paul, Minn.: West Publishing, 1982).

5. Davis, *Discretionary Justice.*

6. Presiding officers are often agency employees, but are typically segregated organizationally from agency officials who perform prosecutorial and policy-making functions. The techniques used to ensure their neutrality vary. In the FTC, for example, presiding officers are located in a separate office building blocks away from the rest of the agency.

7. Davis, *Discretionary Justice.*

8. *Administrative Procedure Act,* U.S. Code, vol. 5, sec. 551 (14); sec. 556 (d).

9. *Administrative Procedure Act.*

10. 397 U.S. 254 (1970).

11. The reasonableness of actions that infringe on individual rights has thus become a significant concern in areas where the privilege doctrine once preempted review of any kind. Courts have become attentive to the rationale for decisions making such things as public employment or the receipt of licenses, permits, or benefits contingent on the waiver of constitutionally protected rights. In one case, for example, the Supreme Court held that a teacher could not be dismissed for exercising his First Amendment right to criticize school board policy [*Pickering v. Board of Education,* 391 U.S. 563 (1968)]. Judges have also applied the concepts of equal protection and substantive due process to ensure that there is some rational connection between legislative or administrative policies and legitimate public ends. For a general discussion of these trends, see William Van Alstyne, "The Demise of the Rights–Privileges Distinction in Constitutional Law," *Harvard Law Review* 81 (1968): 1439–64.

12. The courts have looked to written contracts as well as to informal understandings in deciding whether tenure exists.

13. 419 U.S. 565 (1975).

14. 424 U.S. 319 (1976). For an excellent discussion of this case and the balancing test it imposes, see Jerry Mashaw, "The Supreme Court's Due Process Calculus for Administrative Adjudication in Matthews v. Eldridge: Three Factors in Search of a Theory of Value," *University of Chicago Law Review* 44 (1976): 28–59.

15. See, for example, Colin S. Diver, "The Wrath of Roth," *Yale Law Journal* 94 (1985): 1529–44; Rodney A. Smolla, "The Reemergence of the Right–Privilege Distinction in Constitutional Law: The Price of Protesting Too Much," *Stanford Law Review* 35 (1982): 69–120; Brigitte Fleishmann, "A Cultural Historian's Reading of Charles Reich's Impact on the Contemporary Discourse on 'Welfare'," *William and Mary Law Review* 31 (1990): 307–20.

16. Jerry L. Mashaw, *Due Process in the Administrative State* (New Haven: Yale University Press, 1985).

17. 412 U.S. 669 (1973).

18. *Warth v. Seldin,* 422 U.S. 490 (1975).

19. 461 U.S. 95 (1983).

20. For a brief and readable discussion of these concepts see Warren, *Administrative Law,* pp. 441–52.

21. *Office of Communications of the United Church of Christ v. FCC,* 359 F. 2d 994 (1966).

22. *Administrative Procedure Act,* U.S. Code, vol. 5, sec. 553.

23. Responses to a pair of congressional questionnaires on the subject indicated that administrators considered public notice and comment to be unduly burdensome, espe-

cially given that they communicated informally with relevant interests in developing rules as a matter of course. See Bruce Frederickson et al., *Facilitating Public Participation in Federal Agencies: Hearings before the Subcommittee on Administrative Practices and Procedures of the Senate Judiciary Committee*, 94th Cong., 2d sess., 1976.

24. Albert L. Nichols and Richard Zeckhauser, "Government Comes to the Workplace: An Assessment of OSHA," *The Public Interest* 49 (fall 1977): 39–69.

25. Although the APA allows interested parties to petition agencies to initiate rulemaking proceedings, it affords little guarantee that such requests will not be rejected out of hand.

26. For a thorough description and analysis of the participatory provisions of this statute, see Teresa M. Schwartz,"The Consumer Products Safety Commission: A Flawed Product of the Consumer Decade," *George Washington Law Review* 51 (November 1982): 32–95.

27. See, for example, Davis, *Discretionary Justice;* Jeffrey L. Jowell, *Law and Bureaucracy: Administrative Discretion and the Limits of Legal Action* (Port Washington, N.Y.: Dunellen Publishing, 1975); David L. Shapiro, "The Choice of Rulemaking or Adjudication in the Development of Administrative Policy," *Harvard Law Review* 78 (1965): 921–72.

28. *SEC v. Chenery Corp.*, 332 U.S. 194 (1947).

29. Davis, *Discretionary Justice,* pp. 56–57.

30. Colin S. Diver, "Policymaking Paradigms in Administrative Law," *Harvard Law Review* 95 (1981): 393–434; quotation pp. 409–10.

31. Antonin Scalia, "Back to Basics: Making Law Without Rules," *Regulation Magazine* (July/August 1981): p. 25.

32. Writing in 1972, Robert Hamilton estimated that formal procedures were confined to about a dozen relatively obscure areas of regulatory administration. See Robert Hamilton, "Procedures for the Adoption of Rules of General Applicability: The Need for Procedural Innovation in Administrative Rulemaking," *California Law Review* 60 (1972): 1277–1338.

33. See Hamilton, "Procedures for the Adoption of Rules"; Diver, "Policymaking Paradigms in Administrative Law"; Stephen DeLong, "Informal Rulemaking and the Integration of Law and Policy," *Virginia Law Review* 65 (1979): 257–356.

34. 401 U.S. 402 (1971).

35. 567 F. 2d 9, *cert. denied,* 438 U.S. (1977) 829.

36. For a thorough discussion of these developments, see DeLong, "Informal Rulemaking."

37. *Vermont Yankee Nuclear Power Corp. v. Natural Resources Defense Council,* 435 U.S. 519 (1978).

38. *Chevron, U.S.A., Inc. v. Natural Resources Defense Council, Inc.,* 467 U.S. 837 (1984); *Baltimore Gas and Electric Company v. Natural Resources Defense Council, Inc.,* 462 U.S. 87 (1983). An important case that reinforced *Chevron* was *Chemical Manufacturers Association v. NRDC,* 470 U.S. 116 (1985).

39. *Motor Vehicle Manufacturers' Association v. State Farm Mutual Automobile Insurance Company,* 463 U.S. 29 (1983).

40. Peter H. Schuck and Donald Elliott, "To the Chevron Station: An Empirical Study of Federal Administrative Law," *Duke Law Journal* (November 1990): 984–1077. See also Peter L. Strauss, "One Hundred Fifty Cases Per Year: Some Implications of the Supreme Court's Limited Resources for Judicial Review of Agency Action," *Columbia Law Review* 87 (1987): 1093–1136.

41. See, for example, William F. West and Joseph Cooper, "The Rise of Administrative Clearance," in George Edwards and Steven Schull, eds., *The Presidency and Public Policymaking* (Pittsburgh: University of Pittsburgh Press, 1985).

42. Michael S. Baram, "Cost–Benefit Analysis: An Inadequate Basis for Health, Safety, and Environmental Regulatory Decision Making," *Ecology Law Quarterly* 8 (1980): 473–532.

43. Ibid.

44. Kerwin's recent work provides an excellent overview of variation in rulemaking procedures. Cornelius M. Kerwin, *Rulemaking: How Government Agencies Write Law and Make Policy* (Washington, D.C.: Congressional Quarterly Press, 1994).

45. Author's conversation with NRC official, October 1992.

46. Herbert A. Simon, *Administrative Behavior,* 3d ed. (New York: Free Press, 1976).

47. *Heckler v. Chaney,* 470 U.S. 821 (1985).

48. Peter Woll's study of these techniques is dated in its illustrations but still a valuable description of the dynamics of "informal adjudication." See Woll, *Administrative Law: The Informal Process* (Berkeley: University of California Press, 1963).

49. See Kerwin, *Rulemaking,* for a good description of this process and of how its structure and culture vary among agencies.

50. William Pederson,"Formal Records and Informal Rulemaking," *Yale Law Journal* 85 (1975): 38–39; p. 51.

51. This input is used to formulate a proposed rule, which then becomes the subject for more public comment.

52. See Kerwin, *Rulemaking,* pp.185–91, for a concise discussion of negotiated rulemaking.

53. For a clear description of such devices, see Administrative Conference of the United States, *A Guide to Federal Agency Rulemaking,* 2d ed. (Washington, D.C.: Administrative Conference of the United States, 1991).

54. A systematic investigation of this subject would be an imposing and ultimately subjective task given the difficulties of assessing the causes and importance of changes in proposed policies. Such an undertaking would also require a close familiarity with the policy areas under investigation.

55. A. Lee Fritschler, *Smoking and Politics* (Englewood Cliffs, N.J.: Prentice-Hall, 1969), p. 90.

56. OMB official, interview by author, June 1986.

57. Mashaw suggests that the goal of avoiding arbitrary, capricious, or otherwise inaccurate decisions may be better served in some contexts by devoting scarce administrative resources to internal quality control, such as a system in which random samples of application decisions are examined for error. See Jerry Mashaw, "The Management Side of Due Process," *Cornell Law Review* 59 (1974): 772–824.

58. In one of the few efforts to address this subject in a rigorous way, William Gormley finds that the level of political conflict and technical complexity surrounding policy issues define the ability of different types of interests to participate effectively in decision making by state public utility commissions. His analysis suggests that, whereas state agencies created to represent the public interest are technically sophisticated, they are often immobilized by political conflict. In contrast, citizens' groups are free to commit themselves on controversial policy issues, but often lack the resources to analyze technically complex questions. See William Gormley, "Policy, Politics, and Public Utility Regulation," *American Journal of Political Science* 27 (February 1983): 86–105.

59. Mashaw, "The Management Side of Due Process."

60. Kerwin, *Rulemaking,* p. 67.

61. Administrative Conference of the United States, *Guide to Federal Agency Rulemaking.*

62. William F. West, "The Growth of Internal Conflict in Regulatory Administration," *Public Administration Review* 48 (July/August 1988): 773–82.

63. West, "Growth of Internal Conflict"; Hamilton, "Procedures for the Adoption of Rules."

64. Fred Emery and Associates, *Federal Agency Rulemaking as an Organizational Process* (Washington, D.C.: Administrative Conference of the United States, 1986).

65. These data exclude several rules that were delayed when the legality of FTC rulemaking was in question. The average time for all rules was 20.3 months. West, *Administrative Rulemaking: Politics and Processes* (Westport, Conn.: Greenwood Press, 1985).

66. Hamilton, "Procedures for the Adoption of Rules." See also Staff of the Senate Committee on Governmental Affairs, *Delay in the Regulatory Process,* 95th Cong., 1st sess., 1977, Committee Print.

67. Hamilton, "Procedures for the Adoption of Rules"; Scalia, "Back to Basics."

68. It is also relatively new as an area of academic concern. The first notable authority on the subject in the United States was Ernst Freund. Perhaps his leading work was *Administrative Powers Over Persons and Property* (Chicago: University of Chicago Press, 1928).

3

Politics, Ideas, and Administrative Procedures

This chapter seeks to gain a better appreciation of administrative due process by placing it in sharper theoretical focus. As discussed in chapter 1, empirical and normative concerns are inevitably tied together in evaluating institutional controls over the bureaucracy. Bearing this in mind, the following discussion examines two broad perspectives, both of which are necessary for understanding and assessing the systemic role played by administrative procedures. One focuses on the political implications of structural choice, while the other focuses on the relationship between institutional arrangements and normative theory.

Participatory opportunities, standards of rationality, and other "rules of the game" are seldom neutral with regard to those who stand to be affected by what agencies do. To some extent, therefore, they emerge from the same political cauldron as substantive policy. As discussed in the first section of this chapter, administrative procedures have become increasingly salient as means of furthering substantive policy interests as the political environment of program implementation has become more contentious and more uncertain. This, in turn, suggests that evaluation should be concerned with the kinds of interests promoted by different institutional constraints.

To some extent, structural controls on agency decision making can also be understood as efforts to ensure that bureaucracy conforms with our expectations about how administrative decisions ought to be made. This legitimizing function derives from the inherent tension between agencies' exercise of judicial and legislative authority, on the one hand, and the Constitution's specification of powers, on the other. As discussed in the second section of this chapter, its importance is underscored in many people's minds by the perception that agencies left to their own devices often fail to carry out their mandates in an accurate or equitable manner.

This latter perspective obviously has important prescriptive as well as descriptive implications. From the standpoint of constitutional design, the essential question that must be asked in evaluating due process has to do with the fit between its underlying goals and the actual character of administration. As with the doctrinal foundations of executive control and legislative oversight discussed in later chapters, normative justifications for structural controls on bureaucratic discretion reflect an ambivalence about the proper character of agency decision making and the process values that should guide it. At the most fundamental level, however, administrative procedures and judicial review are based on the assumption that bureaucratic actions are demonstrably correct or incorrect in terms of their factual and legal premises.

The use of due process to promote consistency and accuracy in agency adjudication was in keeping with the traditional view of administration as a transmission belt for attaining statutory objectives. This instrumental goal remains appealing, despite the tension that has always existed between it and the demands of effective management and despite reservations about the efficacy of adversary proceedings in some contexts. More problematic issues are raised by the extension of administrative procedures and judicial review beyond their traditional role in protecting individual rights in the application of policy to their use as constraints on policy formulation. Although objective rationality as enforced by the courts has been an appealing basis for holding non-elected officials accountable in their legislative capacities as well, it is frequently an unrealistic expectation that has pernicious consequences. The limitations of due process as a constraint on bureaucratic discretion can thus be identified primarily, though not exclusively, with the fuzzy line between politics and administration.

The Politics of Structural Choice

Given that the *how* of administration has important implications for what agencies do, procedural controls often reflect the interests of those who stand to be affected by bureaucratic action. As discussed in chapter 1, limited controls on administrative policy making at midcentury were consistent with the harmonious clientele relationships that characterized bureaucratic politics in many areas. In contrast, increased emphasis on the "autopilot" function of administrative procedures in recent decades reflects the continued expansion of delegated authority and the growing contentiousness and instability surrounding policy implementation. As a result of such developments, those potentially affected by administration have developed greater incentives to secure institutional arrangements that will perpetuate their interests as agencies address issues that were unanticipated or that were technically or politically intractable during the legislative process.[1]

The Substantive Implications of Structural Choice

The political dynamics of structural choice can be described by distinguishing between those who stand to win and those who stand to lose as legislative programs are carried out. Not surprisingly, the intended beneficiaries of regulatory programs frequently seek provisions that will enable them to play an active role in agency agenda setting. As discussed, such requirements are relatively uncommon. They are most notable in areas of social regulation, where public-interest groups have sometimes secured petitioning rights and other action-forcing mechanisms as a hedge against the possibility that changing political conditions will cause bureaucrats to become less aggressive in executing their responsibilities. Heightened opportunities to seek injunctions contained in some of the EPA's enabling statutes have proved especially valuable to environmentalists.

Program beneficiaries also frequently favor the use of rulemaking over adjudication, especially in regulatory settings. The relative explicitness and visibility of policy codified in rules and the broader participatory opportunities afforded by rulemaking have been appealing as ways of holding agencies accountable for carrying out their mandates. Rulemaking is similarly equated with aggressive regulation in many contexts. Rules may be vague or trivial, of course. By the same token, individual adjudicatory decisions may establish broad policy, either in a direct sense or through precedent. Rulemaking nevertheless encourages agencies to create general standards in a more precipitous way than they are likely to do through adjudication.

The rulemaking revolution can be partly understood in these terms. Agencies' aversion to rulemaking before the 1970s was due in part to the fact that, as a means of developing comprehensive standards, it was more likely than case-by-case administration to elicit opposition from powerful groups. A number of writers illustrated this thesis by citing instances in which political reactions from regulatees led to sanctions against agencies that deviated from their normal emphasis on adjudication.[2] Marver Bernstein even alleged that agencies' reliance on protracted adjudicatory proceedings against individual firms was a symptom of capture in that it enabled agencies to look busy while accomplishing little in the way of protecting the public from industry abuses.[3] The difficulty of discerning the direction of agency policy from case law may have provided a further motivation for reliance on adjudication under conditions of industry dominance.

Rulemaking thus became more popular, not only as a sound administrative practice, but as a response to growing demands for aggressive policy during the late 1960s and 1970s. Its appeal as an accountable and cost-effective means of achieving statutory objectives is clearly evident in the histories of much of the consumer, environmental, and health and safety legislation that requires its use. The same basic political considerations that spurred Congress to require rulemaking in many statutes also prompted established agencies, such as the FCC and the FTC, to adopt it voluntarily. The issuance of legally binding general standards became attractive and even indispensable as a way to cope with increased pressures to produce results. In marked contrast to the imperatives that had defined their political environments in earlier times, quiescence began to appear more costly than decisive action as the public-interest movement gained strength.

If provisions that encourage or require forceful action favor program beneficiaries, the imposition of rigorous criteria for testing agency proposals tends to favor program opponents. Obviously, the more stringent the terms of adjudicatory due process, the more difficult it is for agencies to impose regulatory sanctions or take away individuals' benefits. In the same vein, hybrid rulemaking procedures have frequently resulted from pressures by industry groups that wish to use adversarial hearings and the burden of justification associated with substantial-evidence review as ways to impede agency action. Thus, the extension of formal due process to agency policy decisions can often be understood from a political standpoint as a counterpoise to the increased use of rulemaking. As Robert Hamilton comments in an extensive survey of hybrid procedures:

> A person adversely affected in some way by a proposed rule may find little solace in the opportunity to submit written comment. . . . On the other hand, agency personnel and others desiring a prompt implementation of a regulatory program . . . suggest that formal procedures are proposed to create delay in rulemaking rather than to improve the end-product of the rulemaking process. Congress becomes the battleground for these opposing views when a new statute granting rulemaking authority is being considered. To a surprising extent, Congress has become sympathetic to the fears expressed by persons who may be subject to regulation under a broad grant of rulemaking authority.[4]

Opponents of agency action have also generally advocated policy analysis. Many allege that the logic of economic analysis contains intrinsic biases that inhibit the faithful pursuit of program goals. A frequent charge is that the computation of social costs and benefits in terms of market values is biased in favor of the existing distribution of resources in society. It follows that the goal of economic efficiency may be at odds with the implementation of policies that are intended to redistribute resources among groups or from one generation to the next. Critics have claimed in this regard that cost–benefit analysis is an inappropriate standard on which to judge agency decisions in areas where Congress has sought to redistribute economic resources, either directly or through the redefinition of legal rights. The impressionistic accounts of many of those who have used it also suggest that economic analysis inevitably tends to place disproportionate weight on policy effects that can be quantified with confidence as opposed to values that must be described qualitatively or assigned "shadow prices" based on more speculative assumptions.

These claims are debated, and hinge to a substantial degree on competing philosophical positions. At any rate, different types of interests have aligned themselves in predictable ways on the issue of policy analysis according to the issues at stake. In the implementation of public works and energy-development programs, for example, economic analysis has been advocated as a way of incorporating the consideration of environmental and other concerns as a counterbalance to developmental goals. In contrast, environmental, consumer, and health and safety interests have opposed the use of cost–benefit analysis and related techniques in areas of social regulation, while business groups and conservatives have endorsed it as a sensible way to ensure that agency policies promote economic health. In general, policy analysis is often favored by opponents of agency action because it subjects proposals to a higher burden of justification, and because it confers legitimacy to a broader range of policy concerns that compete with program goals.

The political implications of structural choice may not always be as straightforward as the preceding discussion suggests. For example, Kenneth Davis and others argue that regulatees should favor rather than oppose the use of rulemaking. This is because the articulation of general standards provides greater certainty as to agencies' future actions, and is thus conducive to planning and investment.[5] In a related vein, James Wilson implies that those potentially subject to administrative sanctions should favor rulemaking because it limits the power bureaucrats would otherwise derive from the ability to act arbitrarily.[6] Several scholars have also observed that judicialized constraints on policy making have been favored by those who stand to benefit from programs. Richard Harris and Sydney Milkis maintain that advocates of social regulation lobbied for hybrid rulemaking requirements in the belief that, by ensuring the viability of public comment and by publicizing the bases for agency actions in a record, these provisions would provide effective opportunities to challenge agency decisions that strayed from legislative intent.[7] As such, they were perceived as a hedge against capture by special interests.

These alternative interpretations are not without merit. The fact that competing coalitions may favor the same constraints can be attributed to a misunderstanding of procedural effects in some instances. In the case of the Federal Trade Commission, for example, agency officials strongly opposed the hybrid rulemaking procedures that business interests wanted to attach to a new delegation of rulemaking authority. They felt, justifiably as it turned out, that such constraints would be a substantial source of delay, defeating Congress's avowed intent to strengthen consumer protection. Yet some leading advocates of aggressive action, such as Ralph Nader and Congressman Bob Eckhart, supported the imposition of such requirements. As lawyers, they were comfortable with the judicial process and had used it effectively in the past to block business and government actions that were inimical to consumer interests.[8] What they apparently failed to appreciate was that the context of consumer protection had changed to one of promoting policy change.

To some extent, however, different assessments of the political causes and effects of administrative procedures are indicative of the fact that a particular constraint can pose advantages as well as disadvantages for a particular type of interest. Terry Moe's plausible but contradictory assertions about the implications of formal due process illustrate this point. On the one hand, he states that the "judicialization of agency decision making" is a means by which "currently advantaged" groups seek to objectify administration and thus render it more difficult for actors in the two political branches of government to intervene in agency affairs in response to opponents of administrative programs. On the other, he notes that opponents of programs "push for cumbersome, heavily judicialized decision processes."[9] In fact, both of these characterizations contain elements of truth.

What Moe and others fail to note is that the calculus of structural choice sometimes involves a tradeoff, where the relative magnitudes of costs and benefits are defined by contextual factors such as the specific nature of what an agency does and the environment in which it operates. In the case of hybrid rulemaking procedures, for instance, the heightened accountability and participatory opportunities they provide may outweigh the impediments of formal hearings and a higher burden of proof where mandates are relatively specific and where proponents of aggressive action fear agency capture. This may have been true with regard to the design of some environmental programs, where clearly articulated legislative goals would facilitate the formulation of means–ends justifications and where program advocates were especially concerned about the potential effects of ex parte communications from industry officials.

Competing Theoretical Perspectives

A more basic issue concerns the underlying political dynamic of structural choice. While most analyses stress the role of groups in securing favorable institutional arrangements, some view administrative procedures as instruments of legislative control. Mathew McCubbins, Roger Noll, and Barry Weingast (MNW) provide the most recent and fully developed version of this "congressional-dominance" thesis.[10] In their analysis, the delegation of authority stems primarily from legislative uncertainty regarding the particular issues agencies will confront. The dilemma this creates from Congress's perspective is that bureaucratic discretion might produce policies that are inimical to the constituent interests of members of the coalition responsible for the program's passage, and thus may undermine future electoral support. Administrative procedures can be appreciated under this logic as tools that legislative "principals" use to ensure that administrative "agents" will promote coalition goals. This argument is appealing because of its elegance and because it extends an influential body of work over the past two decades that emphasizes careerism as the dominant motive behind congressional behavior. Indeed, bureaucracy's instrumental relationship to the need for legislators to be reelected has come to be viewed by many as a defining feature of American government.

MNW argue that administrative procedures promote legislators' electoral interests in two ways. Some, such as notice-and-comment rulemaking and freedom of information requirements, facilitate the role affected interests play in alerting politicians to controversial actions. Given that comprehensive oversight is infeasible, a system of "fire alarms" provides a rational way to allocate limited resources to administrative policy areas that are most salient to elected officials. A second and perhaps more important function performed by administrative procedures from a principal–agent standpoint is to "stack the deck" in favor of an existing set of legislative interests. Uncertainty regarding uncontrolled discretion leads Congress to impose decision-making criteria and opportunities for participation that favor the winning coalition's constituents.

One might question the significance of the distinction between MNW's principal–agent model and the traditional interest-group perspective given that the programs favored by legislators are tied to the interests of the constituents that keep them in office. Upon closer examination, however, the two approaches differ as to who ultimately controls and is served by structural constraints. An explanatory model based on group pressures simply assumes that administrative procedures reflect an accommodation of the forces that exist when a statute is passed. Although this is also consistent with the notion of deck stacking, such political responsiveness is only instrumental to legislators' overriding electoral (or other) interests insofar as the configuration of forces surrounding the administration of a program remains static.

The principal-agent model's contractual metaphor is critically flawed in this regard. If political environments change, as they almost inevitably do, the judicially enforced participatory rights and decision-making criteria embodied in administrative procedures will necessarily subvert the interests of winning coalitions at later points in time. Fire-alarm oversight allows Congress to promote the goals of changing coalitions, to be sure. Whether the legislature consciously institutes administrative procedures for this purpose and whether it does so pursuant to its own interests as distinct from immediate group pressures are interesting but extremely difficult questions.[11] In any case, oversight by future coalitions is logically inhibited by deck stacking. This fact is illustrated by statutory provisions that impose formal due process on rulemaking. Given the heightened standards of justification and judicial review associated with such requirements, courts have been less willing than in informal rulemaking to tolerate ex parte influences from Congress (and other sources).[12]

Although the relationship between specific structural constraints and group interests is not fully understood, therefore, the best political explanation for administrative procedures is consistent with the traditional pluralist model. Legislators impose procedural constraints, not as principals strategically promoting their long-term electoral interests or institutional power, but primarily as conduits for group pressures. Procedural constraints may thus reinforce or offset substantive program objectives, as well as each other, in accordance with the dictates of majority building. This is consistent with the observation that many statutes combine provisions designed to facilitate agency action with provisions designed to make administration more difficult.

The Magnuson-Moss Act of 1974 illustrates the role of procedural choice as an element of mutual partisan adjustment. In response to pro-regulation forces, Congress sought to encourage aggressive action by the FTC through a new delegation of rulemaking authority. The statute also included an "intervenor funding" program that was designed to enable consumer representatives to participate in agency proceedings on a more equal footing with business groups. As mentioned above, however, Congress also constrained the FTC by attaching hybrid rulemaking procedures to its new delegation of authority. The latter provision, which was promoted by industry groups and opposed vehemently by agency officials, was ultimately necessary if the bill was to emerge from the House Commerce Committee and succeed on the floor.

It is important to add that many legislatively imposed constraints on bureaucratic discretion are not attached to particular programs, but cut across agencies and policy areas. The Administrative Procedure Act is the most notable example here. Congress no doubt realized in 1946 that the APA would affect the implementation of many programs not yet contemplated. Other statutes such as the National Environmental Protection Act fit into this category as well. These kinds of constraints are obviously difficult to explain as efforts to promote the goals of coalitions responsible for particular programs. As such, they are difficult to reconcile with MNW's conception of deck stacking, as well as with interest-group explanations such as those offered by Moe. Recent efforts to explain administrative procedures by so-called neoinstitutionalists have relied heavily for their illustrations on programs in social regulation—an area where "designer" statutes are unusually prominent.

To say this is not to deny that a broader type of pluralist politics can play an important role in the enactment of generally applicable procedures. In the case of the APA, there was substantial conflict between conservatives, who favored the imposition of formal due process on a broad range of agency actions (including rulemaking), and liberals, who saw such proposals as a threat to New Deal programs that depended on delegated authority.[13] Although some have characterized the APA as a victory for advocates of positive government, the statute also contained important concessions to business and its allies in the legal community. The most notable of these was the retention of formal due process as a constraint on regulatory adjudication. Unlike the explanations offered by rational-choice perspectives, however, the political interests surrounding the passage of the APA were defined as much by ideology and by vague anticipation of future benefits as by concrete interests in substantive policy outcomes.

If the pluralist version of the politics of structural choice is not particularly elegant, it does have important implications for how we evaluate administrative structure. For instance, the most popular perspective in the "policy implementation" literature views institutional arrangements as instruments that are either well or poorly designed for achieving program objectives.[14] Although bureaucratic effectiveness in the pursuit of legislative goals is a legitimate concern where clear substantive goals can be discerned,[15] the premise that structural constraints help to *define* Congress's objectives complicates any effort to evaluate policy implementation in terms of legislative intent. Given that procedural and substantive provisions are sometimes mutually negotiable, the selection of the latter as evaluative criteria can be somewhat arbitrary.

To the extent that it reflects pluralist politics, therefore, one might evaluate the formal structure of administration by simply noting that it "is what it is." As Moe observes, the administrative process is not designed for efficiency to the extent that it reflects the accommodation of competing interests.[16] The delay that sometimes characterizes agency decision making might be justified as well as explained in such terms. The fact that efficiency is subordinate to other goals in American government is, after all, clearly evident in the Constitution's prescription that policy should be made through a system of separated and shared powers exercised by different institutions representing different constituencies. Given this, structural features that promote relevant political interests at the expense of efficiency in agency decision making may not be out of line insofar as policy-making authority has devolved from the constitutional branches to the bureaucracy.

Administrative Design and Normative Theory

At the same time, it would be a mistake to focus on material self-interest as the sole or even the predominant source of structural constraints on agency discretion. An obvious fact that the rational choice perspective and some other analyses sacrifice on the altar of theory building is that the formal administrative process is attributable as much to the courts as it is to Congress. Judges may be motivated to strengthen their own power to review and influence agency decisions. Their thinking may also be responsive to broad public sentiment or may ultimately be grounded in cultural assumptions about the roles and status of various groups. In addition, many of the cases that allow courts to shape administrative law are brought by organized interests. Yet in any event, there is little evidence to suggest that judicial decisions are driven by group pressures in a direct or easily demonstrable way. Even in the case of statutorily prescribed requirements, to say that group interests often influence the choice of procedures is not to accord exclusive control to such factors. Congress must at least justify procedural requirements in terms of normative premises. Beyond this, it is cynical to deny that legislators are motivated to some extent by considerations of good government. In these regards, administrative procedures can also be explained in terms of the problems of legitimacy posed by a large and powerful bureaucracy, and the corresponding need to institutionalize desired process values in agency decision making.

An understanding of the normative foundations of administrative procedures is also central to the tasks of evaluation and prescription. To many, at least, the fact that substantive goals are embedded in the structure of policy implementation to some extent does not render questions of intelligent institutional design irrelevant. Without delving into the murky relationship between administrative procedures and legislative intent, one can evaluate the constraints described above in a more general sense by considering the fit between the qualities they seek to promote in administration and the reality of what agencies are called upon to do. If a good deal of the delay and inefficiency that characterize policy implementation can be attributed to the influence of politics on institutional design, they can also be attributed to inaccurate and confused assumptions about the character of administration.

Richard Stewart's "traditional model of administrative law" provides a reference point for understanding the normative foundations of the institutional developments described in this chapter. Derived from the same instrumental perspective that informed classical public administration theory, this paradigm stressed constraints that would ensure the "accurate, impartial, and rational application of legislative directives to given cases or classes of cases" in regulatory administration.[17] At the same time, it prescribed few procedural controls on nonregulatory adjudication or on agencies' policy-making discretion under the popular assumption that bureaucracy, guided by its expertise and good will, would serve as an efficient transmission belt for achieving legislative goals. These precepts were generally embodied in the procedures that existed through the passage of the APA. As Stewart and many others have argued, however, the growth of bureaucratic power, coupled with widespread disillusionment concerning the quality of agency performance, has had profound theoretical and practical implications.

One response to the administrative state has been to expand the traditional model by extending the protections afforded by due process to new types of individual interests. This development has been portrayed most plausibly as a systemic adaptation to the growing role of bureaucracy in American life. As government has become a major dispenser of economic opportunity and security by providing jobs, occupational licenses, welfare benefits, subsidies, and other controls and services, it has become increasingly unrealistic to restrict constitutionally protected property and liberty interests to relationships that exist wholly within the private sector.[18] For example, an administrative decision to revoke the security clearance of an aerospace engineer may substantially limit his or her opportunities for employment given the dependency of the industry on defense contracts. The pervasiveness of government in many areas of economic and social activity has thus dictated an increased need for due process as an assurance of fairness in nonregulatory adjudication.

Charles Reich's classic interpretation of this trend in its early stages (primarily with regard to the issuance of licenses and permits during the 1950s) may well have promoted the extension of procedural rights to new areas of administrative adjudication in the 1960s and 1970s. As Reich noted in 1964, "today more and more of our wealth takes the form of . . . status [granted by government] rather than of tangible goods."[19] Given this, it followed that "those forms of largesse which are closely linked to status must be deemed to be held as of right. . . . The presumption should be that the professional man must keep his license, and the welfare recipient his pension. These interests should be 'vested.' "[20] Reich's concept of "New Property" was cited in more than forty Supreme Court cases between 1968 and 1978.[21]

If the New Property can be viewed as a modification of the traditional model's prescriptions for accuracy and consistency in the application of statutory provisions to individuals, the other developments described in chapter 2 reflect an abandonment of its premise that administrative policy making should be left to bureaucratic discretion. Yet just what values have motivated these constraints has been the subject of disagreement. Some scholars have stressed the importance of political responsiveness as the underlying goal of administrative procedures. In contrast, others have viewed recent developments as a reformulation of the traditional model's goal of objective rationality. In fact, while efforts to structure agencies' policy-making discretion reflect both of these goals, the latter is ultimately controlling in important respects. This, in turn, has important implications for explaining and evaluating the effects of due process.

Perfecting the Pluralist System

Many have sought to explain structural constraints on agency policy making as a reaction to the belief that bureaucrats will be insensitive to relevant interests when left to their own devices. Stewart's influential work thus describes the courts' redefinition of interests entitled to participate in agency policy making as an effort to institutionalize and perfect the pluralist model that he feels had come to dominate prescriptive (as well as descriptive) thinking about American government by the 1960s. Stewart argues that the expansion of standing can be understood as a departure from the earlier view of bureaucracy as a technically efficient transmission belt, as well as from the subsequent faith that bureaucrats themselves would adequately consider all the elements of the public interest they were typically instructed to serve. As an antidote to this problem, representatives of environmentalists, consumers, and other diffuse, statutorily protected interests were given opportunities to participate on equal footing with intense and well-organized economic interests that had allegedly come to dominate agencies' environments.

Many legislative requirements can be ascribed to this same desire to correct inequities in the process of agency decision making. In a broad assessment of administrative procedures and other institutional features of regulatory administration created during the 1960s and 1970s, for example, Richard Harris and Sydney Milkis stress the importance of citizen participation and empowerment as antidotes to capture, clientelism, and other pathologies alleged to afflict agencies.[22] Whether they can be attributed to the ascendancy of New Left ideology, as the authors claim, statutory provisions such as heightened petitioning opportunities, intervenor funding programs, advisory committees, freedom of information requirements, and the like obviously evince a desire to ensure effective access and participation in the development of administrative policy. The use of rulemaking has also been justified as a policy-making strategy that allows all affected interests to participate in agency decision making, and hybrid rulemaking procedures have been appealing to some as an assurance that such input will be taken seriously. In these regards, the expansion of interest representation in regulation paralleled developments in other areas, such as the Great Society programs of the 1960s.[23]

Analyses that stress the goal of responsiveness as an explanation for administrative structure necessarily assume that agency decision making has come to be viewed as a political process by the elites who make and influence institutional policy. Stewart argues in this regard that the popularity of interest representation as a normative theory of bureaucracy stems from the realization among scholars and judges that the traditional administrative value of technocratic efficiency makes little sense to the extent that broad mandates fail to reconcile competing social values. As he states:

> The application of legislative directives requires the agency to reweigh and reconcile the often nebulous or conflicting policies behind the directives in the context of a particular factual situation with a particular constellation of affected interests. The required balancing of policies is an inherently discretionary, ultimately political procedure.[24]

Institutionalizing Rationality

Stewart's interpretation of the assumptions behind increased standing undoubtedly contains a good deal of truth that can be extended to a variety of other institutional developments. At the same time, the linkage between administrative law and interest representation breaks down in a crucial respect. If many constraints on agency discretion seem designed to ensure that agencies accommodate relevant interests, participation is also structured by the assumption that decisions can be justified in terms of existing goals. In this regard, other scholars have come to the very different conclusion that recent developments in the administrative process have been driven, not by the assumption that agency decision making is inherently political, but by the desire to promote objective, comprehensive rationality.[25]

As the enforcers of procedural requirements, courts apply an instrumental perspective in evaluating agency actions. Judges may overturn adjudicatory orders and rules because agencies did not accommodate those entitled to participate in decision making, and some scholars have stressed the importance of such procedural considerations as ends in themselves. Yet the logic of political interest representation as a doctrinal basis for administrative procedures and judicial review is contradicted by the fact that interests, as such, are not supposed to be relevant considerations when courts review the substance of agency actions. Most constraints that seek to guarantee effective participation in administration and accountability to the courts are therefore ultimately designed to ensure that decisions are technically correct—that they are based on sound factual evidence and accurate interpretations of legislative intent. It is in this sense that Lon Fuller refers to due process as the "institutional embodiment of rationality."[26]

The pluralist ideal of balanced representation in administration is necessarily subordinate in this sense to the traditional model's goals of accurate policy implementation. Thus, although the extension of more rigorous due process to agency rulemaking has been described as an effort to guarantee effective interest representation, and to some extent has been intended as such, it has also been justified by Congress and the courts as a way of ensuring that agency decisions are instrumentally sound. Consider the following congressional testimony supporting hybrid rulemaking procedures, for example:

> To assure the integrity of the decision-making process, the decision maker should be required to consider the facts, to expose those facts to the crucible of cross-examination, and to be held to a decision based on the weight of the evidence and logic.[27]

The desire for comprehensive rationality has been the animus behind other important developments in administrative law as well. Economic analysis obviously seeks to promote analytical inclusiveness and to reduce decision making to an objective exercise of identifying and measuring probable policy effects. Rulemaking has similarly been viewed as a technique that encourages agencies to approach policy development synoptically. Reliance on case-by-case implementation was frequently criticized in this regard as a reactive and incremental approach that failed to make explicit linkages between administrative actions and statutory objectives, and that often ignored important policy considerations by focusing on the facts of individual cases.

The Question of Coherency

The tendency to portray recent developments in the administrative process as means of promoting either interest representation or instrumental rationality is understandable given the tension between these goals, coupled with the natural bias among academics for logically consistent explanations. Indeed, almost all efforts to account for the structure of public administration as the result of ideas have assumed that coherent normative theories of bureaucracy have dominated institutional policy making at particular points in our history. In a classic article, for example, Herbert Kaufman explains trends in institutional design as a function of the ebb and flow in popularity of competing models of neutral competence, executive leadership, and representativeness.[28] Harris and Milkis's more recent work similarly argues that the structure of regulatory administration at any point in time is the residue of intellectual/institutional "regimes," such as the Progressive Movement and the New Deal, each of which embodied its own distinctive premises about the proper basis of agency accountability.[29] In reality, however, constraints on agencies' policy-making discretion over the past three decades have sought to promote both political responsiveness and objectivity in important respects.

Perhaps one should not jump too readily to the conclusion that these goals are incompatible. Searching for a coherent intellectual foundation behind recent developments in judicial review of agency policy making, Martin Shapiro has moved from an earlier view of representative and instrumental norms as cyclical, competing forces to the argument that academic elites and ultimately courts have come under the influence of a philosophy that seeks to integrate participation and substantive rationality by redefining their purposes.[30] This theory views the participatory dimensions of administrative law, not as means of registering the naked force of competing coalitions, but as means of promoting rational discourse on the ethical and factual premises behind agency actions. The purpose of administrative procedures and judicial review under this model is not to arrive at decisions that are demonstrably correct in terms of existing statutory goals, for it recognizes that such goals often do not exist. Nor is the truth viewed as something that can be attained in any final or absolute sense. Rather, this theory assumes that morally correct action can be *pursued* through reasoned discourse, and that participation structured through the adversary process can therefore lead to policies that are superior in a vaguely objective sense to those that would otherwise have been made under open-ended mandates.

Whether or not, or the degree to which, rational analysis is useful for defining public values is a difficult question far beyond the scope of this discussion (and the capabilities of this author). Shapiro, himself, is critical of the intellectual trend he describes, which he feels has provided the justification for judges to assume the role of philosopher kings. In any case, it seems unlikely that many judges or even a substantial proportion of legal academics have been directly influenced to a great extent by the abstruse and somewhat mystical principles of "postconsequentialist ethics" that Shapiro views as the foundation for recent developments. One should never rule out the possible effects of intellectual osmosis, of course, and one should never interpret things too literally. It is also undeniable that judges have sometimes imposed their own values on agency policy making. Yet there is little in recent judicial opinions to suggest that the goal of discovering ethical truths through rational analysis has supplanted the traditional expectation that actions be justified objectively in terms of legislative intent as an explicit basis for administrative procedures and judicial review.

At the same time, the fact that the latter task is even more daunting than the former in many contexts has important implications for evaluating as well as describing the evolution of administrative law as a control on agency policy making. The lack of a coherent intellectual foundation for administrative law may support realists' contention that ideas are merely handmaidens for political interests.[31] To a considerable extent, however, it simply reflects a confused attempt to reconcile two attractive but contradictory values in public administration. In either case, the simultaneous pursuit of rationality and political responsiveness has important implications for agency policy making.

Practical Significance

To observe that due process can be a source of delay and blockage in administration is a commonplace. As already discussed, the determination of "what process is due" in administrative adjudication has long been conceived of as a matter of balancing greater assurances of viable participation and accurate decision making, on the one hand, against the state's interest in efficient administration on the other. The imposition of more rigorous constraints on agency policy making might be assessed according to a similar equation. Thus, for instance, the delay and other resource costs associated with hybrid rulemaking procedures must be balanced against the assurances they provide that agency decisions will be based on sound factual assertions and accurate constructions of statutory intent. By the same token, one might assess economic analysis in terms of the marginal "costs and benefits" of an increasingly rigorous investigation of the probable effects of policy alternatives.

Reasonable people can obviously disagree about the relative weights that should be assigned to these competing considerations. Yet a more basic issue has to do with the fact that the tradeoff between the instrumental goal of due process, on the one hand, and administrative efficiency or expediency, on the other, is not germane to procedural choice in many contexts. Some have suggested, for example, that adversary proceedings are a poor forum for considering "legislative" (as opposed to "adjudicative") facts.[32] Rules and other administrative policies tend to be based in large measure on broad assertions regarding their probable effects that frequently evoke disagreement among experts. While such issues are empirical in nature, many feel that they are best resolved in an informal setting that permits the modification of views and the building of consensus based on a free exchange of information.

A more fundamental point is that many other key issues in administrative policy making are not even theoretically subject to proof or disproof. Whether it is bounded or comprehensive, the concept of rationality presumes that clearly defined objectives already exist. Thus, the pursuit of accurate or instrumentally sound decisions makes little sense to the extent that Congress has failed to resolve competing values. In this regard, much of the delay that has come to characterize agency policy making can be viewed, not as either warranted or excessive attempts to perfect decisions, but as futile efforts to develop tight means–ends justifications for actions where none are possible. The operational definitions of "deceptive practice," "unreasonable risk," and many other statutory terms inevitably lie in the eye of the beholder, and typically they imply the need for agencies to balance competing interests. Again, although administrative due process as enforced by judicial review is also designed to ensure the viability of participation, it excludes values, per se, as relevant input. The polarizing effect of adversary proceedings exacerbates this tendency by restricting not only the ability of but the incentives for participants in policy making to arrive at mutually acceptable solutions through negotiation and compromise.

It bears further emphasis that the political saliency of bureaucratic policy making has grown in recent decades in keeping with the trends discussed in chapter 1. Agency decision making has become important to a larger and more diverse array of groups and governmental actors in many areas of administration. This trend has both contributed to and resulted from key institutional changes in the administrative process. Thus, the conflict and complexity inherent in many agencies' substantive mandates have been amplified by the expansion of standing, by enhanced statutory rights of participation, by the increased use of rulemaking, and by other judicial and congressional efforts to promote broader participation. The net result of recent efforts to structure agencies' policy-making discretion has been to render their decision-making environments more legislative, while simultaneously restricting their ability to rely on legislative modes of interest accommodation and conflict resolution.

The U.S. Forest Service represents in microcosm what has occurred in many areas of administrative policy making. Once dominated by the interests of businesses reliant on timber resources, the agency's decision making has been opened up to a much broader range of concerns since the 1960s. Indeed, this has occurred, not only within the agency's environment, but within the organization itself, where different factions have emerged to promote the competing goals of "maximum sustainable yield" and "ecosystems management." In an excellent study of Forest Service policy making, Julia Wondolleck observes that the structural constraints imposed on land-management decisions have not been conducive to resolving conflict within the agency and its environment. As she notes, interest "airing" is not the same thing as interest "accommodation." Thus, while the agency

> . . . now confronts a political resource-allocation task in addition to the traditional scientific land-management task to which it is accustomed, [the] . . . decision-making process . . . remains one based in technical expertise. It provides no means of resolving the disputes that inevitably arise. It cloaks political problems in technical analysis.[33]

This same basic characterization can be applied to many areas of administrative policy making.[34]

Conclusion

As discussed, two perspectives are useful in understanding the expanded role of procedural constraints on agency discretion. In part, they can be explained as an extension of politics. As the stakes in administration have increased, so have efforts by affected interests to secure institutional arrangements that will promote the substantive policy outcomes they desire. In part, administrative procedures also reflect the force of ideas. As bureaucracy has become more powerful, we have sought to legitimize its actions by ensuring that they conform with precepts regarding the proper character of administration.

Whether the doctrinal sources of institutional structure ultimately have a life of their own that is independent of material interests is a vexing issue not soon to be resolved. Among the most important obstacles confronting such an effort is the fact that self-interest is an exceedingly flexible concept that is difficult to separate from norms in many contexts. The distinction between ideology or group interests seems to be somewhat arbitrary in explaining the participatory institutions resulting from the consumer and environmental movements, for example. Even to the extent that one can discriminate between them conceptually, alternative explanations that stress one or the other are often exceedingly difficult to separate empirically. As Jerry Mashaw observes:

> These two perspectives not only look at different data—idealists at expressed purposes; realists at implicit (sometimes hidden) interests or ideology, but they have dramatically different methodologies for the interpretation of behavior, and conflicting ideas of what would count as reasons for action. Given this radical disjunction between the two approaches . . . , mediation of their rival claims may be impossible. If the methodology determines both evidence and its interpretation, then to ask who has the best explanation of administrative processes may simply pose an issue of taste.[35]

Suffice it to say, however, that although normative arguments clearly seem to be rationalizations for self-interest in some cases, this linkage is remote and not readily observable in others.

Whatever their teleological status, doctrinal considerations are central to the tasks of evaluation and prescription. In this regard, a fundamental ambivalence about what administration is and what it should be has prevented the emergence of a coherent theory to replace the traditional model of public administration, which viewed bureaucracy in instrumental terms. This ambivalence is clearly reflected in the institutional developments described above. Given the obvious fact that agencies' mandates frequently require them to balance competing demands on scarce resources, we have sought to ensure that they take all relevant interests into account. But given our discomfort with the exercise of legislative discretion by nonelected officials (coupled with the fact that most agency decisions are based to a considerable extent on technical considerations), we have also sought to extend the goal of objectivity from its traditional role in protecting individual interests affected by individual application decisions to agency policy making as well. The dominance of instrumental rationality as the ultimate basis for judicial review defines the limitations of due process as a constraint on agency discretion. As discussed in chapter 8, a crucial challenge facing the theory and practice of administrative law is to accommodate the fact that agencies do different things that require different kinds of constraints. Although scholars have certainly not ignored this reality, much remains to be done in the way of categorizing administrative actions.

The inherent rigidity of due process naturally suggests that we look to oversight by the two political branches of government as alternative means of controlling agencies' policy-making discretion. As discussed in the following chapters, the same ambivalence and confusion about the essential character of implementation that is evident in the theory and practice of administrative law permeates thinking about executive and legislative oversight. Ironically, however, while the idea that the formal administrative process facilitates participation by affected interests has sometimes led scholars to neglect its more basic demand that agency actions be demonstrably rational, the assumption that the purpose of executive and legislative oversight is to ensure faithful and efficient compliance with statutory objectives has inhibited a realistic assessment of presidential and congressional motives and capabilities in controlling the bureaucracy.

Notes

1. There is a burgeoning literature attributing the institutional character of administration to politics. Students of bureaucracy have long been concerned with the political dimensions of organizational choices, such as the decision to create an independent or an executive-branch agency or the decision to place the latter within a department friendly or hostile to its mission. Students of government and administrative law have also long been aware of the political determinants and effects of procedural requirements and judicial review. The idea that the constitutional features of public administration can be explained in terms of their substantive effects has more recently been appropriated by public choice theorists. Although their claim to have rediscovered the significance of formal structure (allegedly long neglected by behavioralists) ignores a good deal of scholarship in public administration and elsewhere, these so-called new institutionalists have gone beyond previous work in their efforts to develop general propositions about the political significance of administrative procedures.

Bound together by the primacy accorded to self-interested behavior, political perspectives are nevertheless far from uniform in their assumptions about the determinants of administrative structure. Important questions arise, not only from competing theories, but from the ambiguities and internal contradictions that mar individual accounts. In the latter regard, the use of deductive, microeconomic analysis to explain procedural choice has not yet produced the conceptual clarity and logical consistency claimed by its practitioners. While it is laudable for its attempt at theory building, much of the recent work on administrative institutions is characterized by plausible but conflicting propositions about their significance, analogous to the "proverbs" of classical, prescriptive organization theory criticized by Herbert Simon.

2. See William L. Cary, *Politics and the Regulatory Agencies* (New York: McGraw-Hill, 1967); J. Skelley Wright, "Beyond Discretionary Justice," *Yale Law Journal* 81 (January 1982): 575–97; A. Lee Fritschler, *Smoking and Politics* (Englewood Cliffs, N.J.: Prentice-Hall, 1969).

3. Marver Bernstein, *Regulating Business by Independent Commission* (Princeton, N.J.: Princeton University Press, 1955).

4. Robert Hamilton, "Procedures for the Adoption of Rules of General Applicability: The Need for Procedural Innovation in Administrative Rulemaking," *California Law Review* 60 (1972): 1314.

5. See Kenneth Davis, *Discretionary Justice* (Baton Rouge: Louisiana State University Press, 1969).

6. James Q. Wilson, "The Dead Hand of Regulation," *The Public Interest* 25 (Fall 1971): 39–58.

7. Richard A. Harris and Sidney M. Milkis, *The Politics of Regulatory Change: A Tale of Two Agencies* (New York: Oxford University Press, 1989). In their eagerness to explain all institutional features of social regulation as means of empowerment, Harris and Milkis simply ignore the fact that hybrid rulemaking procedures have often been opposed by public-interest representatives and have been strongly favored by opponents of regulation. The authors are clearly guilty of this in their discussion of the Magnuson-Moss Act, for example. Their argument is more valid in the case of the Environmental Protection Agency, however.

8. Committee staff, interview by author, June 1980.

9. Terry Moe, "The Politics of Bureaucratic Structure," in *Can the Government Govern,* ed. John 'Chubb and Paul Peterson (Washington, D.C.: Brookings Institution, 1989), p. 275, p. 276, respectively.

10. Mathew McCubbins, Roger Noll, and Barry Weingast, "Administrative Procedures as Instruments of Political Control," *Journal of Law, Economics, and Organization* 3 (Fall 1987): 243–677; idem, "Structure and Process, Politics and Policy: Administrative Arrangements and the Political Control of Agencies," *Virginia Law Review* 75 (1989): 431–82. See also Jonathan R. Macy, "Organizational Design and Political Control of Administrative Agencies," *Journal of Law, Economics, and Organization* 8 (March 1992): 93–110.

11. I am dubious that administrative procedures are envisioned by Congress as fire alarms. Yet the problem confronting an empirical examination of this proposition is that fire alarms may reflect currently dominant interest groups' uncertainty regarding their future influence, but they might just as easily reflect the legislature's need to respond to future coalitions. Identifying instances in which legislative majorities do things that are inimical to the desires of currently dominant constituent interests is a very difficult (and some might say nonsensical) task.

12. This is clearly evident in *Sierra Club v. Costle,* 657 F. 2d 298 (D.C. Cir. 1981), which is perhaps the leading precedent dealing with ex parte communications. A fuller discussion of this issue is presented in chapter 8.

13. Dominant elements within the legal profession favored the institution of court-like procedures, partly out of professional bias and sincere conservatism, but also because it would raise the premium on their expertise within the administrative process. Their most important clients in the business community favored formal due process as a means of impeding agencies' ability to act. These pressures eventually led to the passage of the Walter-Logan Bill, which President Roosevelt vetoed for obvious reasons. For a comparison of this legislation with the APA, see Foster H. Sherwood, "The Federal Administrative Procedure Act," *American Political Science Review* 41 (April 1947): 271–80. See also Attorney General's Committee, *The Administrative Procedure Act: A Legislative History* (Washington, D.C.: U.S. Government Printing Office, 1946), S. Doc. 248, 79th Cong., 2d sess. For a recent discussion of the politics surrounding the enactment of the APA, see Cornelius M. Kerwin, *Rulemaking: How Agencies Write Laws and Make Policy* (Washington, D.C.: Congressional Quarterly Press, 1994).

14. See, for example, Daniel A. Mazmanian and Paul A. Sabatier, *Implementation and Public Policy* (Glenview, Ill.: Scott, Foresman, 1983).

15. A glaring inconsistency found in many of these studies is their explanation of failure to achieve legislative goals as a function of vague statutory directives.

16. Terry Moe, "The Politics of Bureaucratic Structure."

17. Richard B. Stewart, "The Reformation of American Administrative Law," *Harvard Law Review* 88 (June 1975): 1667–1814.

18. See, for example, William Van Alstyne, "The Demise of the Rights–Privileges Distinction in Constitutional Law," *Harvard Law Review* 81 (1968): 1439–64.

19. Charles A. Reich, "The New Property," *Yale Law Journal* 73 (1964): 733–87; quotation p. 738.

20. Ibid., p. 785.

21. Michael B. Levy, "Illiberal Liberalism: The New Property as Strategy," *The Review of Politics* 45 (1983): 576–94.

22. Richard A. Harris and Sydney M. Milkis, *The Politics of Regulatory Change: A Tale of Two Agencies* (New York: Oxford University Press, 1989).

23. As Schulman observes, "One of the major causal components associated with the poverty cycle [was] a deficiency in political authority, efficacy, and legitimacy on the part of the poor." See Paul R. Schulman, *Conquering Space and Poverty: Implementation as Success and Failure* (New York: Elsevier Science Publishing, 1980).

24. Stewart, "The Reformation of American Administrative Law," p. 1682.

25. Colin Diver, "Policymaking Paradigms in Administrative Law," *Harvard Law Review* 95 (1981): 393–434.

26. Lon Fuller, "The Forms and Limits of Adjudication," *Harvard Law Review* 91 (December 1978): 353–409.

27. Winston H. Pickett on behalf of the Chamber of Commerce of the United States, Hearing on the Product Warranties and FTC Improvement Act of 1971, Before the Senate Commerce Committee, S. 986, 92d Cong., 1st sess. Comm. Ser. No. 92–8 (March 22, 1971).

28. Herbert Kaufman, "Emerging Conflicts in the Doctrines of Public Administration," *American Political Science Review* 50 (December 1956): 1057–73.

29. Harris and Milkis, *The Politics of Regulatory Change*.

30. For an expression of the first view, see Martin Shapiro, "On Predicting the Future of Administrative Law," *Regulation Magazine* (May/June 1982): 18–25. For an expression of the second, see idem, *Who Guards the Guardians? Judicial Control of Administration* (Athens: The University of Georgia Press, 1988). To my knowledge, Shapiro does not explicitly recognize this transformation of his thought in his works, and he may well disagree with my interpretation.

31. Jerry L. Mashaw implies this in "Explaining Administrative Procedures: Normative, Positive, and Critical Stories of Legal Development," *Journal of Law, Economics, and Organization* 6 (Special issue 1990): 267–98.

32. Kenneth Culp Davis, *Administrative Law and Government* (St. Paul, Minn.: West Publishing, 1975).

33. Julia M. Wondolleck, *Public Lands Conflict and Resolution: Managing National Forest Districts* (New York: Plenum Press, 1988), p. 154.

34. See, for example, West, *Administrative Rulemaking: Politics and Processes* (Westport, Conn.: Greenwood Press, 1985).

35. Mashaw, "Explaining Administrative Procedures."

4

The Administrative Presidency

The most widely prescribed control over bureaucratic policy making is to strengthen the president's administrative powers. The appeal of this prescription is easy to understand, both in terms of the Constitution's apparent division of responsibilities and in terms of the incentives that would logically seem to determine executive behavior. In the latter regard, it is frequently claimed that, as the one official elected by a national constituency, the president is uniquely motivated to rationalize the bureaucracy pursuant to broad national objectives. As such, strong executive control is viewed as the natural counterpoise to the fragmentation and parochialism frequently alleged to characterize the administrative state.[1]

As a prelude to discussing and evaluating these claims in the next chapter, this chapter describes the resources in personnel administration and direct, centralized management that define the president's relationship to the bureaucracy. These powers are substantial, and indeed the president's capabilities for shaping administrative policy through the appointment process and through the Executive Office have expanded dramatically since the New Deal. At the same time, the president's role as chief executive is limited by the sheer size of the bureaucracy, by a necessary sharing of power with the legislature, and by the inherent tension between line and staff as alternative means of control.

Presidential Powers

The president can employ two basic strategies as chief administrator. One is to use prerogatives as a personnel manager to staff agencies with effective and loyal executives. The other is to centralize supervisory and decision-making power in the Executive Office. Although they often conflict with one another, and although different presidents might pursue and balance them in different ways, both of these strategies are important ingredients of effective performance in the White House.

The resources available to the president for controlling the bureaucracy have grown steadily since the Second World War. This has occurred in part through the amplification of existing powers, such as the ability to appoint political executives and prepare a budget. In addition, recent administrations have sought to extend and refine their control over administration through innovative new devices that allow the president (or executive agents) to monitor and influence individual agency decisions. The enhancement of executive control over the bureaucracy in these various ways has occurred through the evolution of a large "institutional presidency." As with the various means of congressional oversight discussed in chapter 5, many of the president's administrative tools are central to his or her legislative activities as well. Indeed, the president's roles as chief legislator and chief administrator are often so closely interrelated as to be indistinguishable.

Presidential Personnel Administration

The personnel process is the logical place to begin discussing executive control of agencies. The ability to fill the top several layers of the federal bureaucracy with competent political executives is the single most important tool by which the president can control administrative policy. Presidential authority in this area derives from Article II, Section 2 of the Constitution, which states that the president, "Shall nominate, and by the Advise and Consent of the Senate, shall appoint Ambassadors, other public Ministers and Consuls, Judges of the Supreme Court, and all other Officers of the United States. . . ." The extent of the president's appointment power is also defined by statutory law as the legislature exercises the authority to create agencies and programs, and to define their organizational structure. Congress thus determines how many political executives agencies are to have, as well as whether "inferior officers" are to be chosen by the president or by department heads (who must be presidential appointees). Enabling legislation requires the most important, or at least the most politically sensitive, appointive positions to be confirmed by the Senate. Roughly a thousand appointees to cabinet departments, independent agencies, and the Executive Office are subject to this legislative check.

The most powerful and visible presidential appointments fall under the "executive schedule," a system of five levels of "nonprotected" positions and pay grades that is distinct from the various classifications that make up the career civil service. Cabinet secretaries, undersecretaries, assistant secretaries, agency and bureau heads, commissioners, and most other top officials are included among the roughly seven hundred executive schedule appointments. Typically, a president and his or her immediate staff might play some direct role in filling five hundred or so of these positions, with the remainder of the selections being made by appointees in the cabinet departments and the White House.[2] Presidents can also fill roughly 1,650 "Schedule C" positions, most of which provide direct staff support for higher-level political appointees. Although these appointments are used primarily as a source of patronage, they are hardly devoid of policy influence.[3]

Personnel management by the White House cannot be described neatly in terms of the distinction between political officials and the civil service. Indeed, these two categories run together at the margins. As Hugh Heclo observes, "A conventional image of pyramid-like structures in the executive branch, with a neat division of politicians above and bureaucrats below, is badly misleading. Rather than picturing a single, clearly defined boundary line, one should think instead of an erratic smudge."[4] Some executive schedule positions are traditionally given to career bureaucrats, for example, while up to 10 percent or about seven hundred of the jobs in the Senior Executive Service may be filled by political appointment. In addition, presidents are not without influence over the career bureaucracy. Perhaps their most important power in this regard is the ability to transfer SES careerists within and among agencies. Presidents can also use the Office of Personnel Management to help establish standards, such as recruitment criteria and guidelines for classification and pay, that influence the character of the lower-level civil service.

Although the Constitution does not address the issue, it has come to be understood that the president has unilateral removal power over political executives that can be exercised for any reason (or without giving a reason). This principle was solidified by the Supreme Court in *Myers v. the United States*,[5] a 1926 case involving a suit for backpay by a postmaster who had been discharged without cause by President Wilson. The central issue in *Myers* was the constitutionality of a statute that required senatorial consent for the suspension or removal of a postmaster. Writing for the majority, Chief Justice (and former President) Taft argued that the ability to fire appointees at will was necessary if the president's authority was to be commensurate with his responsibility to ensure that the laws be faithfully executed. Taft also argued that, in light of the Senate's explicit power in the appointment process, the Constitution's silence regarding its removal authority indicated that the Framers did not intend it to play such a role.[6]

A limitation on the executive's removal power is that it does not extend to independent boards and commissions, whose enabling statutes generally provide that their members be appointed by the president but thereafter generally serve for fixed and overlapping terms. The constitutionality of this arrangement was upheld by *Humphrey's Executor* in 1935, a case that involved an effort by President Roosevelt to remove a member of the Federal Trade Commission whose policy views conflicted with his own.[7] The Court ruled that commissioners of independent agencies could be removed for reasons such as incompetence or malfeasance, but not for political reasons. This was justified by the fact that such regulatory bodies performed quasi-judicial and quasi-legislative (as opposed to executive) functions that Congress could legitimately seek to insulate from influence by political officials. As a practical matter, however, the separation of independent boards and commissions from the executive is mitigated in most cases by the president's ability to remove and redesignate their chairpersons. Although the powers of the chairperson vary from agency to agency, these officials often have substantial influence in establishing policy agendas and in hiring key staff.[8]

Centralized Management

In conjunction with executive appointive and removal powers, which can be used to establish the general direction of administrative policy, the president has a variety of other tools to control the bureaucracy in a more direct and specific way. One is reorganization authority. The function of creating, abolishing, combining, and defining the duties of government agencies was exercised exclusively through statutory law until 1932, when Congress first delegated broad reorganization authority to the executive. The president has possessed this power almost continuously since then, although Congress has redefined its substantive boundaries and the terms under which it may be exercised on a number of occasions. One important addition has been a grant of authority to establish new units within the Executive Office. In contrast, presidential authority to create or abolish cabinet-level departments was taken away in 1964. Power to reorganize independent agencies was originally given to the president, rescinded in 1939, reinstated in 1949, and rescinded again in 1977.[9]

Like administrative procedures discussed in chapter 3, organizational arrangements often have important policy and political implications. The decision to place an agency in a friendly or a hostile department can have a substantial effect on how aggressively it pursues its mandate. A function's institutional locus can also help determine the degree to which decisions reflect the interests or direct input of the president. Understandably, then, although giving the president authority to restructure the bureaucracy has been appealing in the interest of effective management, the legislature has also viewed it as a source of advantage for a potential competitor. This ambivalence has been manifested in the use of temporary rather than permanent authorizations in granting such power. As a further limit, all such delegations included either one- or two-house legislative vetoes until the Supreme Court's decision in *INS v. Chadha* invalidated those options in 1983.[10] Since then, presidential reorganization power has been confined yet more closely by the requirement that plans be approved by joint resolution.

Reorganizations and other presidential actions are often implemented through executive orders and proclamations.[11] Like the substantive rules issued by agencies, some of these statements create policy in a direct sense (although they are not arrived at through public notice and comment). Others are analogous to procedural rules in that they help define agencies' internal management practices or seek to facilitate executive review of bureaucratic decisions. Executive orders and proclamations can be based on specific or implied delegations of authority from Congress, and indeed they are normally justified in such terms. In addition, although the Constitution does not mention such devices, their use has long been accepted as an adjunct to executive authority under certain circumstances. Like presidential prerogatives generally, the statutory and constitutional foundations of this power are poorly defined and subject to a good deal of debate. In any case, the president's constitutional authority to issue executive orders has provided the vehicle for a variety of important managerial and policy initiatives.[12]

The president's fiscal powers are perhaps foremost in the arsenal of resources that can be used for centralized management. Although it is a legislative rather than an administrative responsibility, budget preparation encourages the president to engage in the basic oversight functions of auditing and assessing the effects of program implementation. Executive budget preparation entails extensive communications with agencies concerning their performance as a matter of course. It also allows the president to establish priorities among agency programs that compete for scarce resources in light of the administration's objectives. The legislature makes final spending decisions, but at the very least the president's exclusive responsibility for submitting a budget recommendation permits him or her to establish the agenda for debate. Formally, if not always in practice, it also precludes most agencies from taking appropriations requests directly to Congress.[13] These prerogatives are important, not only as means of establishing policy, but as implied or explicit threats that the president can use to extract information from and influence administrators.

The president also has discretionary controls over the use of money that has been appropriated. One is the authority to transfer budgeted funds within and among agencies. The most familiar and perhaps the most important of executive spending prerogatives is impoundment, a general power that includes the processes of deferral (reserving appropriated funds for a later point in time) and rescission (blocking the expenditure of funds entirely). Impoundment has been a controversial tool. It is needed in the interest of sound management, given that agencies execute their budgets within constantly changing environments. At the same time, it affords the president an opportunity to subvert legislative programs pursuant to his or her own political agenda.

Largely in response to Richard Nixon's liberal use of this technique for the latter purpose, the Impoundment Control Act of 1974 enabled either house of Congress to disapprove deferrals and required the president to obtain the approval of both houses for rescissions within forty-five days. Notwithstanding these limitations, presidents can delay or stop program spending in a variety of ways that are beyond the legislature's direct control. As Louis Fisher notes, "quasi-impoundments" may be effected through "slow processing of applications, frequent change of agency regulations, rejection of applications for minor technical deficiencies, and many other administrative actions (or inactions)." Such techniques can be especially effective because they are difficult to distinguish from normal administrative actions and thus may effectively disguise presidential motives.[14]

A variety of other tools enhance executive influence over the substance of administrative policy. Like budgetary powers, the ability to formulate, submit, and veto enabling legislation is not an administrative activity, per se, but it is intertwined with the president's ability to control the implementation of laws. In a sense, the inverse of this power is the executive's ability to screen any voluntary or requested communications from agencies to Congress concerning substantive policy and its implementation. "Legislative clearance" enables the president to intercept hearing testimony and reports submitted for the conduct of legislative oversight, and to interdict bureaucratic proposals for new programs that might be antithetical to administration objectives. It can also enable the president to stop agencies' efforts to secure legislation that would allow them to resist executive control of existing programs. Finally, what might be termed "administrative clearance" refers to the executive's ability directly to screen and control the exercise of bureaucratic discretion. This technique requires agencies to submit proposed rules and other actions to the president for review before they go into effect.

These various means of centralized control are brought to bear through the institutional resources of the Executive Office of the President. As Fisher observes, this set of staff organizations is indispensable as a "counterbureaucracy to control unruly departments and agencies."[15] Along with the White House Staff, the Office of Management and Budget is the most important organization within the EOP. Presidents rely heavily on OMB, not only in budget preparation, but to perform other functions that relate directly or indirectly to the control of bureaucracy. The agency is composed of divisions for budgeting and for management, as well as a number of smaller offices responsible for such things as legal affairs, legislative liaison, and economic policy. On the fiscal side of OMB, budget examiners are given responsibility for particular agencies, or perhaps particular programs within agencies. These officials provide much of the specialization, experience, and manpower needed to evaluate agencies' funding requests intelligently in light of White House priorities. As James Pfiffner observes, budget examiners are OMB's "workhorses," the "people with green eyeshades who scrutinize carefully all agency expenditures."[16]

Variation in Executive Control

The Chief Executive's administrative role is far from uniform across the federal bureaucracy. Although the subject has been given little systematic attention (perhaps because it defies systematic generalization), both the institutional powers and the incentives of the president vary a great deal from one agency and program to another. They also vary over time in accordance with the interests and needs of individual presidents, and with the orientations of Congress and other actors that have a stake in the administrative process.

A number of institutional factors help to define variation in the president's administrative capabilities. For example, the fact that some executive-branch agencies may have several tiers of political appointees while others of similar size may be headed by careerists has obvious implications in terms of the president's ability to exercise control through the personnel process. Such variation in the president's appointment prerogatives is partly attributable to politics. As Heclo observes:

> Not all top posts in the federal executive branch are of equal salience all the time. How far down political appointments go in a given agency typically registers the degree of political interest and controversy attached to the particular activities at the time of its creation. The location of these political hot spots naturally changes over time.[17]

Other structural features that are partly or wholly beyond the president's control can also have an important bearing on the executive's ability to achieve desired goals in administration. These include the organizational location of agencies, the specificity of enabling legislation, and the presence or absence of opportunities for interest groups and courts to participate in implementation. As discussed in chapter 3, for example, statutory opportunities for environmentalists to seek action-forcing injunctions undermined Ronald Reagan's efforts to cut back on EPA regulation through the selection of conservative appointees and through OMB review.

Aside from institutional capabilities, the president's interest in what agencies do is likely to vary substantially from one area to the next. As James Anderson observes, for example, Lyndon Johnson devoted considerable energy to monitoring and influencing the implementation of several programs, some of which he favored and some of which he opposed, yet he paid little attention to others.[18] Variation in the president's attention to different types of administration results in part from the demands of the office. Thomas Cronin notes that chief executives tend to devote more attention to the administrative and legislative affairs of the "inner cabinet," partly because those departments (State, Defense, Treasury, and Justice) are more closely associated with the president's established roles in foreign affairs and macro-level domestic policy, and partly because of Congress's proprietary interest in the clientele agencies that largely comprise the "outer cabinet."[19] At the same time, presidents have hardly been predictable or consistent in their administrative priorities. Each has pursued different sets of goals, and has done so with different levels of force and coherence. Whereas Carter and Reagan actively sought to impose their priorities on regulatory agencies, for example, Johnson lacked a coherent regulatory agenda and often avoided dealing with regulatory issues when he could.[20]

Executive management has also varied substantially in its style and institutional structure from one administration to the next. Different presidents have stressed different criteria in the appointment of political executives, for example. Thus, whereas President Kennedy sought to recruit "action intellectuals," Johnson placed a higher premium on government experience (perhaps in keeping with mentor Sam Rayburn's uneasiness about the fact that none of the best and brightest had so much as run for sheriff).[21] Presidents have also applied very different organizational strategies to the task of management. Consistent with his military background, Dwight Eisenhower favored a clear delineation between line and staff responsibilities, and relied heavily on his cabinet as a means of direct communication with and control over the bureaucracy. In contrast, other modern presidents have placed much greater emphasis on the Executive Office in their efforts to monitor and influence agency performance.

Frequent changes in the features of the Executive Office are further indicative of the variation in political circumstances, interests, and personality that define the president's relationship to the bureaucracy. More than eighty different entities have belonged to the Executive Office at one time or another, with units being added and deleted in accordance with changing preferences in the White House and Congress. Furthermore, agencies within the Executive Office that have survived over several administrations have been put to different uses in accordance with the objectives and operating styles of different chief executives. For example, the legislative clearance role of BOB/OMB was expanded under Roosevelt, Truman, and Eisenhower, and then cut back to varying degrees in favor of White House staff review under subsequent administrations. As discussed later, the composition of BOB/OMB has changed a good deal over time, as well. Other Executive Office agencies such as the Council of Economic Advisors and the Office of Program Development have experienced similar changes in organization and usage.

The Expansion of Executive Capabilities

Despite the idiosyncratic advances and retreats of individual administrations, presidential capabilities for controlling the bureaucracy through the personnel process and through centralized management have both expanded in important ways since the New Deal. Although presidents have always been concerned with the need to recruit qualified executives for the key positions in their administrations, the appointment process was typically carried out in an ad hoc fashion until the latter half of the twentieth century. It was also driven to a large extent by considerations of patronage as opposed to competence. To the degree that there was an active search for executive talent, moreover, it tended to be confined to a narrow sample of Washington insiders and to other individuals known personally by the president and his advisors. G. Calvin MacKenzie observes that, in a broad sense, the Truman administration was the first to consider personnel management as something crucial to the president's success. It was not until then that the appointment process came to be viewed on balance as a matter of finding the right people to fill positions rather than as a matter of finding appropriate positions for people who must be rewarded.[22]

The process of selecting political executives has become increasingly systematic and institutionalized since the late 1940s. Thus, for example, Truman was the first president to designate an aide whose primary responsibility was to screen potential appointees. Although the Eisenhower White House was initially inclined to revert to the old unstructured system of identifying and evaluating potential appointees as needs arose, it soon became apparent that a more formal apparatus was needed. Kennedy, in turn, doubled the recruitment staff of his predecessor, and subsequent administrations have devoted ever larger numbers of White House personnel to this task. They have also developed increasingly sophisticated techniques, adapted in some cases from the private sector, for identifying potential appointees from across the nation and from various walks of life.[23]

The growth in the number of political appointments is to some extent both a cause and an effect of the president's increased interest in personnel administration. Heclo illustrates this trend by tracing the layering of political appointees above the bureau level in several departments. Whereas the Department of Labor had a secretary and two assistant secretaries in 1933, for example, by 1960 it had a secretary, an undersecretary, and four assistant secretaries. By 1976, it had a secretary, an undersecretary, three deputy undersecretaries, and six assistant secretaries. Many of these additional appointive positions are associated with offices created to perform staff functions such as planning and policy analysis.[24] Similar developments have occurred with respect to Schedule C positions, which increased by more than 50 percent during the late 1970s and early 1980s despite a corresponding reduction of about one hundred thousand career personnel in civilian agencies.

Some recent presidents have also taken an increased interest in personnel management within the civil service. Frustrated by the liberal orientations of senior bureaucrats, the Nixon administration made extensive efforts to circumvent civil service requirements in filling sensitive career positions. These attempts were widely perceived to be abuses of the system, and were countered by provisions in the Civil Service Reform Act of 1978. At the same time, they highlighted what many had come to feel was a legitimate need for more presidential control over the career bureaucracy, especially at the upper levels. This was reflected in the creation of the Office of Personnel Management, an agency of about 5,700 people headed by an individual appointed and subject to removal by the president. Until that point, the effectiveness of the old Civil Service Commission as a personnel agent of the president had been undermined to some extent by its other role as guarantor of neutral competence in the selection, retention, and promotion of career bureaucrats. Indeed, its structure as an independent commission clearly reflected the latter goal.[25] The 1978 legislation also created the Senior Executive Service, phasing out the existing system of "supergrade" classifications. Among other things, this was designed to give the president and his subordinates more freedom in assigning personnel to policy-making positions within the career bureaucracy.

The president's resources for centralized management have expanded as well. As originally constituted in 1939, the Executive Office consisted of the Bureau of the Budget (about forty employees transferred from the Treasury Department) and a few advisers. Since then, it has grown to include over seventeen hundred personnel in eighteen agencies (although different accounting practices yield quite different figures in both these regards). Among the more important of its components are the White House Staff, the Office of Management and Budget, the National Security Council, the Council of Economic Advisors, the Central Intelligence Agency, the Office of Policy Development, the Domestic Policy Council, and the Office of the U.S. Trade Representative.

The expansion of presidential staff resources has not been steady or irrevocable. Again, the features of the Executive Office have changed many times. An especially important observation is that, although the current set of organizations dwarfs the entity that was created in 1939, the Executive Office was actually larger in 1960 (about 2,700 personnel) than it is today. After peaking at about 4,000 employees in the early 1970s, it has fluctuated between 1,500 and 1,900 personnel over the past two decades. In a similar vein, the BOB/OMB experienced most of its growth during the 1940s, and appears to have "stabilized" roughly within a range of from 500 to 700 employees.

Yet if the Executive Office has not grown in size in recent years, it has been put to new uses. A basic element in the evolution of the presidency has been the rise of policy analysis as an intellectual tool for centralized control over government. Used in the Second World War for purposes of strategic and tactical planning, a variety of increasingly sophisticated techniques that might be loosely classified under the headings of "systems" or "economic" analysis became more and more popular as aids for decision making beginning in the 1960s. This development was facilitated by the increased availability of economic and other policy-relevant data, and by the continued improvement of computers that could be used to process such information. Lyndon Johnson sought to extend the president's ability to evaluate agency programs and to influence the allocation of expenditures through the application of program budgeting to the activities of the entire federal government. As discussed later, subsequent presidents have relied heavily on cost–benefit analysis and related techniques as means of evaluating administrative actions.

Much of the executive's capacity for centralized policy control is an adjunct to the "legislative presidency" that has expanded so dramatically since the New Deal. Indeed, although its roles in the legislative and administrative processes are frequently difficult to distinguish from one another, the former undoubtedly consumes most of EOP's resources. In many ways, the most interesting development in the expansion of the president's administrative power, per se, has been the creation of an increasingly strong institutional capability for direct intervention in agency decision making by the White House and the Executive Office. Most of the management techniques discussed to this point only allow the president to influence the general contours of policy implementation rather than specific actions. In contrast, a series of initiatives under recent administrations have allowed the Executive Office to screen individual bureaucratic policies in much the same way that it exercises central clearance over agency communications with Congress.

Presidents have always devoted some energy to monitoring and influencing the activities of the bureaucracy. For instance, Lyndon Johnson required and reportedly read periodic memoranda from his cabinet secretaries outlining the major policy activities of their departments.[26] Accounts from his aides further reveal that Johnson would sometimes respond to executive summaries with penetrating questions about program implementation.[27] Until the 1970s, however, presidential awareness of and involvement in specific agency decisions tended to be haphazard and was circumscribed by limited White House resources.

As with many innovations in the expansion of presidential power, the first step in the evolution of a more systematic process of administrative review occurred during the Nixon administration. All proposed environmental regulations were required by executive order to be submitted for comment to other agencies in the federal government as well as to affected state governments. (In practice, this requirement was enforced only for EPA rules.) Unresolved differences between the EPA and another agency or agencies would result in a meeting between the conflicting parties, with a representative from OMB acting as a mediator. Although EPA was free to issue regulations over anyone's objections, this so-called "Quality of Life Review" program created a systematic mechanism for the executive to identify environmental policies that might adversely impinge on other agencies' programs and constituents.[28]

Gerald Ford's Executive Order 11821, as later amended by E.O. 11949, expanded on Nixon's relatively modest efforts at centralized review of agency regulations, both in terms of the substantive scope and the rigor of Executive Office involvement. It required that any agency proposing a "major regulation" (defined as one having a projected economic impact in excess of $100 million per year) must prepare an Inflation Impact Statement justifying its action. These reports, which were essentially cost–benefit analyses, were later subjected to review by the Council on Wage and Price Stability, an entity created by Congress at the president's behest and placed within the Executive Office. COWPS's formal position in relation to agencies was ultimately advisory, but IIS review did create a systematic mechanism by which an agent of the president could screen important regulations from across the federal bureaucracy pursuant to a clearly established policy criterion.

The main features of Ford's program were extended under Jimmy Carter. After a number of fits and starts and a good deal of negotiation within the administration, a complex system was devised in which major rules were required to be justified by Regulatory Analyses (again, cost–benefit analyses). These, in turn, were to be reviewed by a number of entities within the Executive Office and by a Regulatory Analysis Review Group comprising representatives from executive-branch agencies. Carter later required agencies to review existing regulations and to publish semiannual agendas of all policies under development.[29]

The most far-reaching initiatives in centralized review of administrative rulemaking were instituted by Ronald Reagan. E.O. 12291, issued in February 1981, required that cost–benefit analyses be prepared for all regulations proposed by executive-branch agencies. It specified that major rules be justified by a formal analysis that quantified probable effects "to the maximum extent feasible," and that other rules be accompanied by what was presumably a less-rigorous analysis. In either case, agency policies and their supporting analyses were to be submitted to OMB at two different points in their development: immediately before they were to be published in the *Federal Register* as proposed rules, and again before their promulgation as final regulations (after the conclusion of public comment). Reviewing authority within OMB was vested in the Office of Information and Regulatory Affairs, a unit that had been created by Congress in 1980 to implement the Paperwork Reduction Act.[30] OIRA was staffed by about eighty "desk officers" who, like their counterparts on the budgeting side of OMB, divided responsibilities along agency lines. These provisions were augmented in 1985. E.O. 12498 thus required agencies to prepare yearly "calendars" describing all ongoing regulatory actions, ranging from policies nearing completion to those merely contemplated but not yet begun.[31]

The Reagan program was clearly designed to be a more comprehensive and forceful system of centralized review than its predecessors. It did not give the executive explicit authority to overrule agencies. As discussed in the final chapter, whether an agency within the Executive Office or even the president can do this is a controversial legal issue. It did, however, give OMB the power to question agencies and to require that rules be justified by additional analysis. The architects of E.O. 12291 further reasoned that OMB would enjoy substantial de facto power by virtue of its proximity to the president and of its ability to sanction recalcitrant agencies through its budgetary power, its ability to set personnel ceilings, and other prerogatives at its disposal. As James Miller put it, OMB's influence over agencies would be ensured by its status as the "toughest kid on the block."[32] In the event that a dispute between an agency and OMB could not be resolved, it was to be appealed to the Vice President's Task Force on Regulatory Relief (a group that was also charged with reviewing existing regulations). This group was disbanded in the middle of the Reagan administration. A similar body called the Vice President's Council on Competitiveness emerged in the Bush administration under the leadership of Dan Quayle.

As the latest installment of executive clearance, President Clinton signed an executive order in September 1993 that replaced E.O. 12291. Changes contained in the Clinton program are designed to prevent what many have perceived to be abuses of executive oversight by previous administrations, such as secretiveness in OMB–agency communications, back-door access by special interests, and excessive involvement by White House officials. In the last regard, it abolishes the Vice President's Council on Competitiveness. At the same time, Clinton's E.O. 12866 evinces the skeptical orientation toward regulation of earlier programs, and it retains the most salient elements of centralized review under Reagan and Bush. OIRA still has responsibility for assessing the social and economic consequences of existing regulations and of significant proposed rules.[33] The new order also expands the role of the vice president. Among other things, Al Gore is empowered to intervene in the review process at the request of a cabinet member or OMB, presumably in response to unsettled agency–Executive Office disputes that might occur. Adopting a feature of the Nixon and Carter programs, moreover, the Clinton order requires that the director of OIRA distribute proposed regulations among other federal agencies in order to identify possible conflicts.[34]

Executive Power in Perspective

Notwithstanding the considerable resources at the executive's disposal, it remains to be asked how effective the president is or can be in controlling the administrative process. The inherent limitations of presidential personnel administration are frequently recited. Although the recruitment process has become increasingly systematic and centralized, it is hardly perfect. New administrations are flooded with job seekers, yet there is always a limited pool of talented and loyal executives who are willing to serve in government (and often take a substantial pay cut). The allure of the private sector also makes it difficult to retain competent political executives, as well as the talented young Schedule C appointees and careerists that they must rely on.[35] There are further limits on the president's personal knowledge of appointees, and White House staff sometimes err in their assessment of individuals and of executive preferences in the context of particular positions. Numerous instances can be cited in which presidents have been surprised by the policy orientations of their appointees. Most such mistakes may be corrected by removal, of course, but the use of this technique is often construed as a sign of disarray within the administration and may have other political costs as well.

Nor has the president been freed from considerations of patronage and political symbolism. Although loyalty and competence have become increasingly important considerations, the need to reward supporters and to select individuals who are acceptable to Congress, party factions, interest groups, and the bureaucracy itself is still very much a part of the appointment process. Some presidential administrations are more homogeneous than others, and this has important implications for the style and effectiveness of executive management.[36] The ideological purity of the Reagan presidency does much to explain its impact on the administrative process. All presidents are elected by and accountable to numerous, often conflicting constituencies, however, and their administrations must inevitably reflect this to some extent. Bush's appointments were more diverse than Reagan's, perhaps because of his own preferences or because of the emerging need to appease disaffected moderates within the Republican Party. An early assessment suggests that Bill Clinton is driven by an especially strong obligation to represent diverse interests in his appointments, sometimes at the expense of selecting people whose views are consistent with his own. As one commentator observes, Clinton has approached the appointment process as a matter of "picking a cabinet in which women had to be balanced with men, blacks with whites, statists with progressives, growth-boosters with deficit-cutters."[37]

Even to the extent that a president can find the right people for the right positions, this management team is very small in relation to the career bureaucracy and can only supervise a fraction of what it does. This limitation is exacerbated by the ability of careerists to insulate themselves from unwanted interference through their control over information. Moreover, even the most talented appointees frequently lack the personal contacts and the familiarity with the details of specific programs that are demanded for effective leadership. As transients with an average tenure of about eighteen months, political executives often leave their agencies just as they have begun to grasp the nuances of their jobs.[38]

Finally, the president's ability to control bureaucracy through the personnel process is constrained by the fact that appointees must respond to a variety of competing pressures. The phenomenon whereby executives become coopted by their agencies (or "marry the natives," to use John Erlichman's picturesque metaphor) is inevitable to some extent. Like most people, presidential appointees are inclined to attach special importance to the functions they and their organizations perform, and this tendency is reinforced by the fact that they are exposed to bureaucracy's way of looking at things on a day-to-day basis. More important than such psychological forces, perhaps, the need to maintain morale and loyalty among their subordinates frequently requires political executives to make concessions to their agencies that may be at odds with the president's agenda. Effective management also frequently demands that concessions be made to the other branches of government and to the groups they represent.

Largely because of these constraints, some recent presidents have sought to centralize control over the bureaucracy in the White House and the Executive Office. Yet this strategy has important limitations as well. The most obvious are that the Executive Office is relatively small in comparison with the bureaucracy, and that it frequently lacks the expertise needed to participate intelligently in agency decisions. Even under Reagan's program of regulatory review, which again was the most ambitious effort at direct centralized control of the bureaucracy to date, roughly eighty OIRA desk officers were given responsibility for reviewing more than two thousand rules per year (in addition to their other duties under the Paperwork Reduction Act). In addition, most of these individuals did not have training or extensive prior experience relevant to their areas of responsibility. Understandably, oversight was far from comprehensive, and it was often not technically well-informed when it did occur.

As discussed in the preceding chapter, moreover, agencies exercise policymaking discretion in ways that are far less visible and less amenable to centralized review than rulemaking. In general, an expansion of staff sufficient to permit anything approaching comprehensive review of administrative actions would entail the creation of a very large Executive Office, indeed. The statistics cited earlier are instructive in this regard. The fact that the key components of the Executive Office have remained fairly stable in size, despite a clear desire by recent presidents to extend and centralize their power, can be explained in part by Congress's occasional reluctance to act as an accomplice in undermining its own ability to control the administrative process. At the same time, it suggests that the creation of an ever-larger Executive Office has diminishing and eventually negative returns in terms of the ability to control the bureaucracy pursuant to presidential goals.

The natural limits of the Executive Office as an instrument of centralized management are defined partly by the fact that, as it grows, the "president's bureaucracy" necessarily becomes unwieldy, just like the executive branch it helps to monitor and control. Just as line agencies, moreover, its organizational components develop their own institutional perspectives, embedded in procedures, organizational arrangements, recruitment practices, and informal norms, that are distinct from those of the president. Aside from the arrested growth of the Executive Office, these facts help to explain frequent changes in its composition and the inconsistent use of agencies such as OMB and CEA from one administration to the next. As discussed in the following chapter, the tension between presidential goals and organizational routines also helps to explain the politicization and "deinstitutionalization" that has occurred in some staff agencies, as well as the tendency of recent presidents to transfer important functions from other Executive Office organizations to the White House staff.

Aside from the balance that must be struck between the need for adequate staff capabilities and loyalty to presidential goals, the limits of centralized control are also defined by its uneasy relationship with cabinet government. To say that the appointment process is far from perfect as a means of bringing presidential priorities to bear in administration is not to deny its importance as a management tool. Given this, presidents must be (or at least should be) wary of allowing the Executive Office to undermine the authority of political appointees and careerists within the departments. Excessive centralization can damage agency morale and can create a climate of hostility that impedes efforts by the president's staff to extract information from and influence the departments.

Insofar as centralized management permits the president or presidential agents in the Executive Office to identify important issues in the administrative process, executive power to affect desired outcomes is also limited by important legal constraints. Presidential abilities to audit agency expenditures and activities and to prepare budget recommendations are obviously limited by Congress's final authority in the appropriations process. In addition, Congress almost always delegates discretionary policy-making authority to departmental secretaries or agency heads rather than to the president. It does so under the assumption that the former are likely to be more responsive to its wishes. Although the issue is a controversial one, many and probably most scholars feel that it is illegal for the president directly to usurp such authority.[39] In practice, agencies have occasionally issued rules over the objections of the Executive Office and even the White House under the central clearance programs initiated by recent presidents. As the final interpreters of statutory commands, the courts can also enjoin agencies to take actions opposed by the executive and can disapprove actions that the president favors. On a number of occasions, judges have intervened against Executive Office attempts to block agency regulations or to pressure agencies to deregulate.[40]

The president's institutional capabilities are thus limited in a variety of respects. Our system of separation of powers ensures that the president lacks the kind of hierarchical authority needed to manage the bureaucracy like a business firm or a military command. Richard Waterman argues in this regard that Neustadt's general characterization of presidential power applies as well to administrative management as it does elsewhere. To a large extent, the president's influence over the bureaucracy is tied to the ability to persuade—to convince others of the rightness or political expediency of actions the president desires.[41] Given this, executive influence depends largely on the qualities of the individual in office.

At the same time, one should take care not to exaggerate the limitations on the president's administrative power. As Neustadt also observes, the chief executive is not without important resources for use in efforts to convince or negotiate with other actors. These include "informal" assets, such as the prestige of office and the unparalleled opportunity to shape public opinion, as well as the formal powers conferred by the Constitution and statutory law. The president cannot rely too heavily on the latter for fear of appearing weak or precipitating retaliatory action by others with their own sources of power. Nevertheless, presidential appointment and removal powers and prominent roles in budgeting and in the enactment of enabling legislation are substantial sources of leverage in executive efforts to influence administrators as they interpret and carry out their mandates. Research conducted by Dan Wood in recent years demonstrates the effectiveness of these prerogatives in areas where the president has taken a strong interest in the direction of bureaucratic policy. Looking at the performance of a number of regulatory agencies over time, Wood finds that policy output is affected significantly by changes in political personnel and by the exercise of other executive powers.

Recent initiatives in centralized clearance have also proven to be a source of substantial influence over policy implementation in areas of interest to the president. If agencies have remained legally free to disregard executive preferences under such programs, and if they have occasionally exercised this option, they have normally acceded or at least made concessions to pressures from OMB and the White House. As a matter of perspective, Reagan's E.O. 12291 led to a withdrawal of 2.7 percent of all rules submitted to OIRA for review between 1985 and 1989, and to a modification of 22.2 percent over the same period.[42] Although the latter figure represents minor as well as significant changes, this qualification is offset by the anticipatory effects of OMB review (as reinforced by informal communications in some cases).

Conclusion

This chapter has provided a general overview of the institutional powers and capabilities that define the president's relationship to the bureaucracy.

It has given special attention to the expansion of resources for personnel management and centralized management through the Executive Office in recent years—developments that would seem to indicate an increasingly important linkage between what the bureaucracy does and the incentives that drive the modern presidency. At the same time, the president is limited in the role of chief executive by the size of the bureaucracy, its inertia embedded in organizational structures and habits, and its capacity to resist outside direction. These limitations, which confront political executives in all developed nations, are reinforced by our system of separation of powers.

Just how much control the president has over the bureaucracy is a complex issue that has elicited very different responses. Whereas some stress the power of the presidency in administration (and other areas), others emphasize the inherent limitations of the office. The truth in describing the president's ability to control administration lies somewhere between these assessments. Its location is not only dependent on an examination of presidential resources, moreover; as discussed in chapter 5, it is also relative to one's assumptions about what the president's goals in the administrative process either are or ought to be. A consideration of presidential motives and behavior in light of these expectations brings the developments discussed above into sharper focus. Scholars have often evaluated the president's administrative capabilities against the traditional model of coordinative management facilitated by clear lines of authority. If presidential powers are not equal to this idealized conception of the executive function, there is also little to suggest that the president's interest in administration is defined by traditional managerial concerns.

Notes

1. For a cogent expression of this view, see Terry M. Moe, "The Politicized Presidency," in *New Directions in American Politics,* ed. John E. Chubb and Paul E. Peterson (Washington, D.C.: Brookings Institution, 1985).

2. Richard W. Waterman, *Presidential Influence and the Administrative State* (Knoxville: University of Tennessee Press, 1989).

3. Patricia W. Ingraham, "Building Bridges or Burning Them? The President, the Appointees, and the Bureaucracy," *Public Administration Review* 47 (September/October 1987): 425–35.

4. Hugh Heclo, *A Government of Strangers* (Washington, D.C.: Brookings Institution, 1977), p. 36.

5. 272 U.S. 52 (1926).

6. For an excellent (and critical) discussion of *Myers,* see John A. Rohr, "Public Administration, Executive Power, and Constitutional Confusion," *Public Administration Review* 49 (March/April 1989): 108–14.

7. 295 U.S. 602 (1935). See Rohr, "Public Administration."

8. In the case of the Federal Trade Commission, for example, Ronald Reagan's

designation of James Miller to replace Michael Pertschuck as chairman resulted in the tabling of a number of initiatives that had been under development for years, and in the institution of a higher burden of evidence for justifying new policies. For an excellent study of the powers and influence of chairpersons in several independent commissions, see David Welborn, *Governance of Federal Regulatory Agencies* (Knoxville: University of Tennessee Press, 1977).

9. For a discussion of these developments, see Peri E. Arnold, *Making the Managerial Presidency: Comprehensive Reorganization Planning 1905–1980* (Princeton, N.J.: Princeton University Press, 1986); Harold Seidman, *Politics, Position, and Power: The Dynamics of Federal Organization* (Oxford: Oxford University Press, 1980).

10. *Immigration and Naturalization Service [INS] v. Chadha*, 462 U.S. 919 (1983).

11. The distinction between an executive order and a proclamation is somewhat fuzzy, but the latter is often understood to be a hortative statement while the former is thought to be legally binding. Although proclamations are sometimes used for policy purposes, they are more commonly associated with "head-of-state" functions such as formal statements honoring particular individuals or groups.

12. The president's authority to issue executive orders and proclamations has received surprisingly little attention from scholars. For an excellent discussion of various forms and purposes of these devices, and of the legal and normative issues surrounding their promulgation, see Philip J. Cooper, "By Order of the President: Administration by Executive Order and Proclamation," *Administration and Society* 18 (August 1986): 233–62.

13. A few agencies, such as the National Cancer Institute, must submit their budgets directly both to Congress and the president.

14. Louis Fisher, *The Politics of Shared Power* (Washington, D.C.: Congressional Quarterly Press, 1981), p. 86.

15. Ibid., p. 141.

16. James A. Pfiffner, "OMB: Professionalism, Politicization, and the Presidency," in *Executive Leadership in Anglo-American Systems,* ed. Colin Campbell and Margaret Jane Wyszomirski (Pittsburgh: University of Pittsburgh Press, 1991), p. 196.

17. Heclo, *A Government of Strangers*, p. 44.

18. James E. Anderson, "Presidential Management of the Bureaucracy and the Johnson Presidency: A Preliminary Exploration," *Congress and the Presidency* 1 (Autumn 1984): 137–64. See also David Welborn, *Regulation in the White House: The Johnson Presidency* (Austin: The University of Texas Press, 1993).

19. Thomas E. Cronin, *The State of the Presidency* (Boston: Little Brown, 1980). According to Cronin, the inner cabinet consists of the departments of Justice, Treasury, State, and Defense.

20. David Welborn provides a very interesting and thorough treatment of this subject in *Regulation in the White House.* Contrary to many impressionistic accounts, which associate Johnson's limited interest in policy implementation with Great Society programs, Welborn finds that LBJ did take an active interest in some areas of regulation. Yet his participation was not informed by a comprehensive philosophy, and White House interest was often motivated by a desire to avoid involving the president in regulatory decisions.

21. See, especially, G. Calvin MacKenzie, *The Politics of Presidential Appointments* (New York: Free Press, 1981).

22. G. Calvin MacKenzie, *The Politics of Presidential Appointments*; idem, "The Paradox of Presidential Personnel Management," in *The Illusion of Presidential Government,* ed. H. Heclo and L. Salamon (Boulder, Colo.: Westview Press, 1981).

23. MacKenzie, "The Paradox of Presidential Personnel Management."

24. Heclo, *A Government of Strangers;* idem, "Issue Networks and the Executive Establishment," in *The New American Political System,* ed. Anthony King (Washington, D.C.: American Enterprise Institute, 1978).

25. Like many other independent commissions, its members served for fixed and overlapping terms, and could only be removed for "cause." It was also required to be bipartisan in that only two of its three members could belong to the same political party.

26. Anderson, "Presidential Management of the Bureaucracy and the Johnson Presidency."

27. Welborn, *Regulation in the White House,* p. 13.

28. For a discussion of this program and its successors in the Ford and Carter administrations, see Paul R. Verkuil, "Jawboning Administrative Agencies: Ex Parte Contacts by the White House," *Columbia Law Review* 80 (June 1980): 943–89.

29. Ibid. For an excellent description of the Carter program and an analysis of the motives that underlay it, see James E. Anderson, "The Carter Administration and Regulatory Reform: Searching for the Right Way," *Congress and the Presidency* 18 (1991): 121–45.

30. The Paperwork Reduction Act was also a significant extension of executive power, giving OMB the authority to review and approve all agency requests for information from the public. The OIRA was largely composed of staff from the recently abolished COWPS.

31. William F. West and Joseph Cooper, "The Rise of Executive Clearance," in *The Presidency and Public Policy Making,* ed. George Edwards, Stephen Schull, and Norman Thomas (Pittsburgh: University of Pittsburgh Press, 1985).

32. James Miller, quoted in "Deregulation HQ," interview with Murray L. Weidenbaum and James C. Miller, *Regulation* (March/April 1981): p. 21.

33. A significant rule is defined as one having an annual economic effect of $100 million, or one that otherwise adversely affects "the economy, a sector of the economy, productivity, competition, jobs, the environment, health or safety, or state, local, or tribal governments or communities."

34. *Federal Register* 58, no. 190 (October 4, 1993): p. 51735.

35. Indeed, Washington has become the most attractive territory in the nation for corporate "headhunters."

36. See, for example, John Kessel's comparison of White House staffs in the Carter and Reagan administrations in John Kessel, *Presidential Parties* (Homewood, Ill.: Dorsey Press, 1984).

37. "Clinton Picks a Cabinet," *The Economist,* January 23, 1993, p. 15.

38. Heclo, *A Government of Strangers;* Ingraham, "Building Bridges or Burning Them?"

39. For a good discussion of the nuances of this issue, see Verkuil, "Jawboning Administrative Agencies."

40. Eric Olsen, "The Quiet Shift of Power," *Virginia Journal of Natural Resources Law* 4 (1984): 1–80.

41. Richard W. Waterman, *Presidential Influence and the Administrative State* (Knoxville, Tenn.: University of Tennessee Press, 1989); Richard E. Neustadt, *Presidential Power: The Politics of Leadership from FDR to Carter* (New York: John Wiley, 1980).

42. Executive Office of the President, *Regulatory Program of the United States Government* (Washington, D.C.: U.S. Government Printing Office, 1991).

5

The Politics of Presidential Management

Presidential management has often been justified as a rationalizing force in public administration. Under the traditional version of this argument, the executive function was portrayed in instrumental terms as something that would promote accuracy and efficiency in the implementation of individual statutes as well as government-wide coordination among agency programs. Although it coincided neatly with a simple conception of separation of powers, this apolitical conception of the president's relationship to the bureaucracy was never realistic and was probably never taken very seriously by its exponents. More recently, scholars have explicitly prescribed strong executive control over administration as an institutional arrangement that naturally integrates an incentive for sound management with focused political accountability to a national constituency.

The curious thing about this latter model of executive leadership is that it has remained so popular in the abstract despite the consistent failure of chief executives to conform with its precepts. Although generalization across and even within administrations is difficult, there are several important respects in which the administrative presidency often deviates from expectations. The least surprising observation is that presidents are not strongly motivated to manage the bureaucracy in a traditional sense. The pursuit of economy and efficiency in program implementation and issues of coordination, per se, do not occupy much of the president's personal attention, nor do they command a large share of the institutional resources of the presidency. In addition, while executive influence can have an important centralizing and rationalizing effect on administration, its potential as a counterweight to the fragmentation of power and the horizontal relationships that characterize bureaucratic politics is frequently exaggerated. The administrative presidency is, of necessity, more amorphous in terms of its institutional structure and more pluralistic in its dynamics than commonly recognized. By the same token, it is frequently responsive to special as well as general interests.

Two Models of Presidential Management

Executive control has long been a popular response to the administrative state. Its appeal lies in the perception that the president is the logical person to hold the federal bureaucracy accountable and to manage its activities. In this regard, one can identify two alternative models of presidential management based on different sets of assumptions concerning the nature of administration as its relates to presidential goals. A strong administrative presidency has traditionally been justified by the expectation that it will promote economy and efficiency in the attainment of legislative objectives. An alternative justification for executive control that is more plausible, if more troublesome from a constitutional standpoint, is that it will rationalize the administrative process pursuant to broad national concerns reflected in the president's own policy agenda.

The Traditional Model

The Constitution says little about the means to be used, but its enjoinder for the president to take care that "the laws be faithfully executed" seems to be a clear statement of what his or her goals should be in the administrative process. Thus, the president's role in managing the bureaucracy has traditionally been conceived of as ensuring that statutes are interpreted correctly and carried out efficiently. Beyond the effective implementation of individual programs, the traditional conception of executive management also encompasses the task of coordinating the activities of different agencies. Scholars have frequently inferred this broader constitutional role as general manager from the Framers' apparent dissatisfaction with the lack of centralized control under the Articles of Confederation. Although there was considerable debate as to how powerful he should be, there was widespread agreement at the Constitutional Convention about the need for a stronger executive to order the affairs of government.

The premise of the traditional model is the assumption that administration is an instrumental process that can and should be divorced from politics. It follows from this that one can clearly delineate between the legislative function and administrative/executive activities (which are one in the same under the traditional model), and that these two powers can be formally divided between Congress and the president, respectively. The appeal of the traditional model can thus be attributed in large measure to the fact that it circumvents the messy issues that arise under the alternative premise that executive and legislative powers are mixed together in the administrative process.

The expectation that the president not only should but will manage the bureaucracy effectively has enjoyed widespread popularity in the twentieth century as a response to an ever-larger and more diverse administrative state. Some Progressives of the late 1800s and early 1900s viewed the president and other elected executives as threats to neutral competence, and were responsible for structural arrangements that inhibited centralized control of administration. The most notable of these institutions at the federal level were the civil service system and the independent commission form of regulatory agency. As it developed, however, the "science of administration" that sprang from the Progressives' concern with efficiency came to emphasize the importance of unified, hierarchical control as a fundamental principle of effective public administration at all levels of government.

The assertion that strong presidential management was needed to ensure the faithful, economical, and coordinated execution of legislative objectives had become prevalent by the 1930s, and it has remained a common theme since then in the works of political scientists, law scholars, and students of public administration. It has also served as the central premise behind the prescriptions of a series of commissions appointed in the twentieth century to study the administrative process and offer recommendations for its reform.[1] Consider, for example, the following excerpts from the reports issued by the Brownlow Committee (1937), the first Hoover Commission (1949), and the Ash Council (1971):

> The President is the general manager of the United States. The very purpose of an Executive Department under the Constitution is to center upon a unified and powerful Executive responsibility for a coordinated policy of administration and its efficient execution.[2]

> On the President . . . falls the crushing burden of bringing all the units of the executive branch into harmony, and of fitting them together so that a unified program may be carried out.[3]

> The President is responsible under Article I of the Constitution to "take care that the laws be faithfully executed." That duty extends to the activities of the regulatory agencies to assure that the laws enacted by Congress are carried out effectively and fairly.[4]

These and other commission reports have recommended organizational changes within the federal bureaucracy designed to centralize administrative power in the presidency. Among their most frequent prescriptions have been to consolidate and reorganize departments along rational, functional lines, to place the independent regulatory commissions under the president's direct control, and to augment the responsibilities and capabilities of the Executive Office.

Executive Leadership and the Bureaucracy

As discussed in earlier chapters, the traditional model is obviously limited insofar as administration involves value judgments as opposed to instrumental concerns. Whether or not the legislature articulates clear goals, moreover, it is naive to expect that presidents should be content simply to ensure that statutes are faithfully and efficiently executed. Presidents are politicians with interests and constituencies that are independent from those of Congress. As such, they are judged by historians and voters according to their effectiveness as political leaders—not on their performance as custodians charged with carrying out congressional objectives. The imperative for executives to control public administration pursuant to their own political ends has become stronger in direct relation to the growth of bureaucracy as a source of policy discretion.

The fact that the president is naturally motivated by political considerations in relations with the bureaucracy has evoked two general reactions. As Terry Moe observes, the ideal of neutral competence has retained a good deal of currency as a criterion for executive management, notwithstanding the widespread abandonment of the politics/administration dichotomy as a description of reality.[5] This perspective has remained especially popular among public administrationists. Scholars as sophisticated as Hugh Heclo, Frederick Mosher, and James Pfiffner have thus criticized the politicization of the executive's relationship with the bureaucracy as a development that undermines responsible and effective government. Few of these critics deny that the president has a policy agenda, but at least some analyses seem to imply that the president should confine political activities to the legislative process.

At the same time, many scholars have recognized a legitimate relationship between the bureaucracy and the executive's political goals. Although their logic is vague, even most recent critics seem to object, not to the proposition that the president should pursue his own policy objectives through administrative management, but to the politicization of executive institutions as a means of achieving those objectives. Indeed, a closer examination of the traditional model of executive management reveals that its leading exponents were ambivalent and probably disingenuous regarding the proper basis for the president's administrative role. Theorists such as Gulick and Leonard White were hardly as ignorant concerning either the political dimensions of administration or the political motives of the president as has been assumed in countless attacks on their work.[6]

Beyond their recognition of the limitations of the politics/administration dichotomy, advocates of the traditional model were undoubtedly aware of the internal contradiction of their argument. The reason that executive control was so badly needed according to the Brownlow Report and other representative works of the era was that the federal bureaucracy had become a mess, with different agencies promoting redundant or conflicting objectives.[7] To the extent that executive coordination might serve as an antidote to this problem, it necessarily forced the president to modify program objectives or to choose some legislative goals over others. As such, it was at odds with the accurate and effective implementation of individual statutes.

In these regards, the portrayal of presidential management as bearing an instrumental relationship to congressional goals has, to some extent, always been a ritual necessitated by the ambiguous constitutional status of delegated authority and by the corresponding need to avoid the controversial issue of who should control it. As Peri Arnold observes:

> To address the Constitution's failures head-on would have left administration's intellectuals as mere external critics of government. But an apolitical-technical model of good administration deflected politically based conflict over presidency-strengthening reforms, and it justified a role for scholars of public administration within government as neutral experts with skills to make government work better.[8]

Herbert Kaufman's description of the model of "executive leadership" that came to the fore during the New Deal (and at earlier points in our history) suggests a normative view of presidential management, not as a caretaker function, but as a nationally accountable institution for both developing and carrying out coherent policy. Kaufman notes that, although justifications for executive management such as those offered by the Brownlow Report "were tied to the peg of separation of powers," at some level there was always an awareness of the tension between presidential control and neutral competence. Gradually, this tension gave way to an abandonment of the latter goal in favor of "the doctrine of the continuity of the policy-formulating process ... [that was] better suited to the aims of executive leadership."[9]

If traditional administrative theorists avoided confronting the issue head-on, many recent advocates of strong executive control have explicitly endorsed the proposition that effective presidential management must be integrated with presidential politics. For instance, Richard Nathan bluntly asserts that "a political executive should be just that—*political and executive.*"[10] Nathan and many other scholars in law and political science have sought to legitimize this prescription by arguing that members of the Constitutional Convention intended for the president to impose his policy preferences on the bureaucracy in cases where Congress failed to resolve political issues in the enactment of statutes. Whether the Framers had such foresight, politically based management has been readily justified by the argument that the implementation of many statutes requires discretionary value judgments, and that these should be made by the president (and the president's political agents) rather than by unelected and unaccountable bureaucrats.

In addition to its academic proponents, some members of the Supreme Court have become increasingly receptive to this appealing view of the administrative presidency. As Justice Rehnquist noted in support of the Reagan administration's efforts to persuade the National Highway Traffic Safety Administration to rescind an airbag rule promulgated under Carter, for example:

> The agency's changed view of the standard seems to be related to the election of a new President of a different political party. It is readily apparent that the responsible members of one administration may consider public resistance and uncertainties to be more important than their counterparts in a previous administration. A change in administration brought about by people changing their votes is a perfectly reasonable basis for an executive agency's reappraisal of the costs and benefits of its programs and regulations. As long as the agency remains within the bounds established by Congress, it is entitled to assess administrative records and evaluate priorities in light of the philosophy of the administration.[11]

The expectation that the president's political discretion will be circumscribed by legislative intent is, of course, problematic. Again, coordinative management of the federal bureaucracy necessitates the selection of overarching goals that take precedence over individual agency programs. And again, there is little reason to believe that, aside from the legal constraints they face, presidents should be particularly attentive to congressional goals that differ from their own. If many contemporary advocates of a strong and politically motivated administrative presidency are reluctant to acknowledge these facts, it is fair to say that most of them are unconcerned with the possibility that its policy influence will spill over the "bounds established by Congress." Many are no doubt enthusiastic about this prospect because they view centralized control by the president as an antidote to the policy fragmentation produced by the legislature's decentralized structure and its receptiveness to special interests.

The appeal of the administrative presidency among modern scholars thus lies in the expectation that its natural tendency is to fuse political leadership and management. Because executive power is theoretically focused in one individual who is chosen by the entire electorate, its effect is to rationalize the administrative process (and policy making in general) pursuant to broad national objectives. As James Sundquist expresses this sentiment, "the executive branch is equipped with a powerful Executive Office of the President that can offset parochial pressures and try to arrive at a concept of the broader national interest."[12] Similarly, David Welborn notes that "the perspective of the presidency is thought to be uniquely government-wide in scope. This leads to a necessary preoccupation with problems in organizational interrelationships and policy integration. . . ." Later, Welborn adds that "there is an enforced integration of concerns at the presidential level that enfolds executive leadership in the president's basic business of national leadership."[13]

To portray this revised model of the administrative presidency as established orthodoxy would be misleading. If executive control pursuant to the president's own policy objectives has its detractors, however, it enjoys broad approval among those who believe that a prescriptive theory of bureaucratic control should begin from the premise that agencies must inevitably make political choices in carrying out their mandates. Kaufman notes that "the years from 1910 to 1950 were characterized by the rise of the quest for executive leadership to a place of pre-eminence in administrative thought and action."[14] Although the popularity of forceful executive leadership in the administrative process and elsewhere suffered in the wake of Vietnam and Watergate, the presidency has since re-emerged as the most widely prescribed antidote for subgovernment politics and similar maladies alleged to beset the bureaucracy. As discussed in the final chapter, the Supreme Court's adoption of this model has had important institutional effects in recent years.

The Character of Presidential Administration

Assuming that executive control does rationalize bureaucratic performance pursuant to the interests of a national constituency, its desirability cannot be divorced from a consideration of the relationship between the administrative process and the legitimate goals and prerogatives of Congress and the courts. Leaving such constitutional issues aside until the final chapter, a more immediate concern is the empirical premises behind arguments for a powerful administrative presidency. How strongly is the control of public administration related to the imperative for executive leadership? To the extent that it is, what are the president's managerial and political goals? These are important questions, not only as reality checks for prescriptive analysis, but as bases for describing the impact of presidential influence over the bureaucracy.

As observed in chapter 4, it is difficult to generalize about the presidency because it is so personalized.[15] Every president comes to office with a unique set of priorities and a leadership style that reflect life experiences, personality, and the political circumstances under which that individual must operate. Given this, the degree to which, the ends for which, and the manner in which chief executives have sought to manage the bureaucracy have varied a great deal. In general, though, presidents have become increasingly conscious of the need to control the administrative process as a means of furthering their programmatic ends, and this has had a centralizing effect on agency policy. At the same time, the increasingly important linkage between bureaucracy and the president's goals has not been translated into systematic efforts to improve the internal management of programs or to coordinate the activities of different agencies pursuant to a consistent set of pre-established, hierarchically ordered policy objectives. Nor is executive influence always guided by overarching national concerns.

Politics and Management

The idea that a powerful executive should be inclined to integrate the desire to shape policy with a concern for sound public administration is both plausible and appealing. If they have done so implicitly in many cases, most advocates of a strong administrative presidency have thus conceived of executive management as a sequential process of top-down planning and control. The executive defines policy objectives that can be attained through legislation and through the exercise of bureaucratic discretion, and then sees to it that those goals are carried out effectively and perhaps efficiently. It is in this sense that the authors of the Brownlow Report and many subsequent theorists have assumed that presidential politics is or can be compatible with the precepts of sound administration. Indeed, attributing to the presidency its own policy goals supplies a unity of purpose, essential to rationalization, that is missing under a strict separation of executive and legislative powers founded on the politics/administration dichotomy.

In fact, all presidents have endorsed economy and efficiency, and most have commissioned studies to determine how these goals can be better achieved. Some have also been familiar with and have sought to institute the latest management techniques. President Johnson was responsible for the governmentwide adoption of program budgeting, Nixon embraced management by objectives, Carter was a devotee of zero-based budgeting, and Clinton appears to be convinced that the nebulous injunctions of Total Quality Management can pay dividends in the public sector. There are obviously many competing demands on presidential time and resources, however, and a number of observations suggest that the systematic management of the bureaucracy is a relatively low priority for chief executives. Although formal job designations can be misleading, for instance, only one out of eighty-one assistants, deputy assistants, and special assistants in George Bush's White House Office had a title suggesting that administrative management was his or her primary responsibility.[16]

Indeed, some authorities have argued that sound management of agency programs has become a less-important priority under recent administrations. As Ronald Moe observes, for instance, OMB's Reorganization and Management Division—whose job it is to promote organizational efficiency in the executive branch—has suffered severe cutbacks. Ironically, this has occurred since the agency was renamed in the Nixon administration as an ostensible signal of its increased emphasis on those functions. Whereas its management staff consisted of 224 employees in 1970, it had dropped to 47 by the latter part of the Reagan administration. Commenting on the decline of executive management represented by these figures, Moe notes that

> the staff of the management side of the old BOB had once been an elite corps of civil service generalists committed to protecting the institutional interests of the President and increasing the capacity of agency management to perform its missions. As the 1970s progressed, however, the staff withered, management functions were transferred to budget analysts, and organizational issues gradually ceased to be considered relevant to the management portfolio.[17]

Nor does available evidence suggest that presidents and their staffs have given much attention to the broader managerial task of reviewing and coordinating policy implementation by different agencies. In his account of the Johnson presidency, James Anderson notes that cabinet meetings were seldom used to identify and eliminate redundancy and conflict among programs. Even the most extensive system of centralized executive review instituted to date was notable for its inattention to policy coordination in a direct and active sense. As the GAO noted in an extensive study of Reagan's E.O. 12291:

> OMB does not appear to exercise its powers under E.O. 12291 to reduce conflicts among regulations or to ensure consistent application of the regula-

tory analysis process. . . . OMB officials told us that they make no systematic effort to uncover potential conflicts among proposed regulations, or between proposed rules and existing rules, and that they are addressing the issue in only an ad hoc way.[18]

A common theme in the literature is that the will and the capacity of the executive to perform effective management have suffered as the institutional apparatus that largely defines presidential performance has become more politicized. According to Heclo and others, whereas the dominant ethic within OMB was once to provide objective staff assistance, the agency has become more conscious of promoting the president's political agenda in recent decades.[19] This change in orientation has resulted from the increased importance attached to political criteria in selecting OMB directors, as well as from the creation of appointive positions to control the agency's two operating divisions and to perform a variety of other functions. It has also resulted from related, often subtle changes in the recruitment patterns and performance incentives that determine the behavior of career officials. This was clearly the case in the Reagan administration's implementation of E.O. 12291, for example, where the OIRA "desk officers" responsible for reviewing agency regulations were highly attuned to the preferences and constituent interests of their superiors.[20] Similar changes have occurred in some other Executive Office agencies, such as the National Security Council.

Some feel that, as presidents have elevated partisan considerations over neutral competence as a basis for recruitment, evaluation, and organizational structure, OMB and other staff organizations have lost the expertise needed to understand administrative issues and the credibility needed to communicate effectively with the bureaucracy. This trend has allegedly been manifested in a variety of ways. For example, Margaret Wyszomirski argues that the "deinstitutionalization" that has naturally accompanied the politicization of OMB and some other Executive-Office agencies has limited the memory of program details and the personal contacts with agency officials needed for effective presidential management. Indeed, some have argued that the relationship between OMB and the bureaucracy has degenerated into one of mutual suspicion and even hostility.[21]

The emphasis on partisanship to the detriment of professional management in departmental agencies has not been so clear cut, perhaps. If the layering of presidential appointees atop the bureaucracy Heclo describes has increased the potential for politicization, he also notes a postwar trend toward an emphasis on substantive expertise as a basis for choosing political executives. Writing in the late 1970s, he observed that being a "professional policy watcher" had largely replaced patronage as a basis for appointment as administrative policy making had become increasingly complex and increasingly reliant on objective analysis.[22]

One should not infer too much about the president's motives from Heclo's impressions, however, for the profiles of political appointees in terms of previous government experience, schools attended, age, and various other characteristics have remained strikingly similar since the 1930s (and perhaps since before that).[23] If a premium was placed on substantive knowledge and experience during the Carter administration, moreover, Nixon's emphasis on "political personnel administration" within both the appointive ranks and the career bureaucracy suggests that professional competence was not an overriding priority during his tenure. Nor would most observers accuse the typical Reagan appointee of being a "technopol." Although some were experienced and competent public executives, many were chosen primarily on the basis of political loyalty and philosophical correctness.[24] Writing a decade after Heclo, Pfiffner argues that, as the selection of political appointees has become increasingly centralized in the White House, partisan considerations have naturally become more important in filling lower-level jobs such as the deputy assistant secretaries in cabinet departments and the direct subordinates to agency heads. Many of these positions have always been presidential appointments, but previously tended to be given to career bureaucrats as a concession to agency demands for experienced managers.[25] The Reagan White House also assumed a consultative role in the selection of noncareer SES personnel and Schedule C appointees, positions that had also normally been filled at the discretion of higher-level cabinet and subcabinet officials in previous administrations.

Of course, the Reagan administration may well have been anomalous in its emphasis on ideological purity. Conversely, however, to the extent presidents have found it necessary to sacrifice political loyalty in favor of substantive knowledge and managerial expertise in selecting departmental officials, this has probably contributed to the centralization of power within the Executive Office. As discussed in chapter 4, although the appointment of political executives remains the single most important means by which the president can influence administration, the ability to choose people who are both technically qualified and committed to executive goals, as well as their ability to control the career bureaucracy once in office, are subject to important limitations. Thus, recent executives have relied increasingly on their staffs to perform legislative and oversight functions that are closely related to presidential interests. Growing emphasis on legislative clearance and the institution of administrative rule review are two of the more obvious manifestations of this trend. The centralization of authority within the Executive Office at the expense of departmental discretion has accompanied the politicization of staff agencies as an effort to ensure that policy making is responsive to the president's needs.[26]

Just as politicization has undermined neutral competence as a basis for executive personnel administration, centralization has allegedly been inimical to the complementary organizational principle that line and staff functions should be clearly delineated. One frequent claim has been that the presence of Executive Office staff in operational areas has alienated departmental appointees from the president. Another is that it has created confusion within the bureaucracy by subjecting agencies to multiple sources of authority and conflicting objectives. Yet another is that centralized control is destined to be sporadic and ineffectual given the relatively small size and limited expertise of the Executive Office.

Administration and Executive Leadership

In general, then, although what constitutes sound management is in the eye of the beholder, recent presidents have de-emphasized the kinds of staffing and organizational arrangements that many associate with economy and efficiency. As noted earlier, some scholars deplore this apparent neglect of traditional administrative values. For example, Ronald Moe argues that a renewed intellectual emphasis on concerns such as those that guided the work of Luther Gulick and Charles Merriam might rekindle a practical tradition of sound executive management that has been lost since the administration of Franklin Roosevelt.[27] The currently fashionable notion of "process management" prescribes that the president and senior advisers forego direct involvement in agency policy making, confining themselves to issues of coordination and to facilitating a "more orderly and systematic" expression of relevant interests.[28] Again, although their premises concerning the relationship between politics and administration are often fuzzy or simplistic, such critics are generally concerned, not with the fact that the president has political goals, but with the fact that the president uses political means to achieve them. Thus, students of public administration view neutral competence and the rational organization of responsibilities, authority, and communications as principles by which executives can further their own policy objectives within the administrative process. Heclo cites the ethic of dispassionate loyalty by British civil servants to the ends of whatever government happens to be in power as a role orientation for presidential staff organizations that would enhance the effectiveness of executive leadership.[29]

If it ever existed outside the realm of prescriptive theory, however, there is little reason to believe that such a tradition could be compatible with the incentives that drive the modern presidency. Despite the nostalgic yearnings of some scholars, most accounts suggest that the management of agency programs failed to consume much of Roosevelt's attention. The preferences this prototypical modern president displayed for political expedients such as overlapping functional responsibilities, redundant channels of communication, and alphabet agencies were sharply at odds with the principles of rational administration advocated by his Brownlow Committee. Even the organization created by the president to plan a coherent industrial strategy for the Second World War (a source of national unity if there ever was one) was headed by two individuals so as to represent the conflicting views of labor and management. Brownlow himself observed that Roosevelt's organizational practices "shocked every student of public administration to the marrow of his bones."[30]

In contrast, the high priority that Jimmy Carter reportedly gave to organizational management may have been symptomatic of his oft-noted failure to grasp the realities of presidential politics. Scholars have seldom portrayed Carter's "managerial mind" as having been an asset to his presidency. Moreover, even Carter's actions as chief administrator were often sensitive to the political demands of his office at the expense of traditional managerial considerations. Although he came to office vowing to restore cabinet government, he eventually instituted a number of measures designed to strengthen the influence of the Executive Office over administrative policy. Similarly, Carter's practical ambivalence about the advantages of technical expertise and professional management informed his contribution of a new layer of presidential appointees to OMB, as well as his selection of a longtime Georgia associate with little federal government experience to head that agency (notwithstanding ample precedent at the time for appointing an experienced careerist).[31]

Some would argue that the slighting of managerial values by most presidents reflects the fact that administration is not closely related to their success in office. According to Erwin Hargrove, Lyndon Johnson's exceptional success in the legislative process was accompanied by a relative lack of interest in the bureaucracy. Generalizing from this, he notes that

> President Johnson and his aides were more interested in legislative victories than in program implementation. The competition of politics drives a President to define achievement as a good legislative box score with Congress. All the obstacles to Presidential leadership have been seen on the input side, and this is where the energies and the plaudits have gone.[32]

Hargrove's characterization is clearly exaggerated, for LBJ did take an active interest in the implementation of some programs.[33] It is true, however, that Johnson, Roosevelt, and other presidents have often given priority to their legislative agendas, and have only later if at all given serious thought to comprehensive administrative strategies for consolidating their gains.[34] A fact worth noting is that most of the losses in OMB's management staff discussed above have been converted to new slots on the budgeting side of the agency, a unit whose responsibilities are more directly related to the president's role in formulating policy as opposed to overseeing its implementation.[35] Even within the latter division, the trend in recruitment and reward structures has been away from the development of the kind of detailed knowledge needed for program evaluation to the emphasis of broader analytical and political skills that can be used to promote the president's policy agenda.[36]

Yet if much day-to-day administration is not closely related to the president's goals, to equate a lack of interest in the details of program management and the systematic coordination of agency activities with a lack of interest in *what* the bureaucracy does increasingly misses the mark. The expansion of the executive's capabilities described earlier can thus be explained in terms of the growing importance of the bureaucracy as a source of legislative advice and as a locus of policy-making authority, and of the corresponding need to influence the exercise of bureaucratic discretion in those areas that are salient to the president. The factors that precipitate executive involvement in administration are idiosyncratic to some extent, depending on personal interests and constituency needs that are peculiar to individual presidents. In a broad sense, however, increased incentives for executive control of the administrative process are largely a function of the conflict that has come to attend agency decision making in many areas. It is hardly surprising that the most notable efforts to expand executive control over policy implementation since the early 1970s have focused primarily on regulatory administration, where the political salience of actions has become especially high. As an Executive Office memorandum explaining the Carter administration's oversight strategy observed, "Almost every regulatory decision is sharply contested and has a loser."[37]

An important point here is that executive influence over the bureaucracy does not have to be comprehensive or even systematic to promote the president's objectives. The implementation of Reagan's E.O. 12291 illustrates this fact. As discussed above, OMB made little if any conscious effort to eliminate redundancy and conflict in the output of regulatory agencies. Instead, it generally confined its scrutiny to proposed regulations that evoked significant conflict. As one staffer put it, various "bells and whistles" were employed by OIRA desk officers to identify rules that were politically salient. These cues included articles in trade journals and communications from lobbyists, congressmen, the White House, and other agencies with a stake in regulatory proposals.[38] While review was far from comprehensive, this strategy allowed the Reagan and Bush administrations to allocate limited organizational resources and political capital to administrative issues that were especially relevant to the president and his key constituents. As noted in chapter 4, it led to the withdrawal of 2.7 percent of all agency rules submitted for review between 1985 and 1989, and to a modification of 22.2 percent over the same period.

The politicization and centralization of the administrative presidency can be appreciated in these terms. As administration has become more conflictual and thus more salient to presidents, traditional management has become less important in relation to political responsiveness. Heclo and others are correct in their observation that the institutional manifestations of this development have limited presidential control over the bureaucracy in some respects. Yet the prescription for neutral competence and rational organization is more realistic in a parliamentary system of fused powers, where conflict can be resolved and goals articulated to a greater extent in the legislature. The American system of shared and separated powers increases the likelihood that the administrative process will become an arena for politics and that agencies will be subjected to competing influences. This, in turn, places a premium on political loyalty among the president's team.

In the same regard, the dynamics of our constitutional system dictate a relatively high emphasis on administration, as well as relatively high levels of politicization and centralization, where presidents disagree with Congress concerning the direction policy should take. Influence over the bureaucracy can compensate for the executive's inability to attain desired objectives in the legislative process. Presidents may also be motivated to ensure that agencies carry out goals that both they and Congress endorse, but the need for corrective action is relatively low under such circumstances. Although agencies may pursue agendas that differ from those of their political masters, the realities of bureaucratic politics suggest that this tendency should be at a minimum where the president and Congress are in alignment.

Like many hypotheses about presidential behavior, a "small n" makes it impossible to test these propositions in any rigorous way. Still, it is not surprising that the most dramatic advances in the evolution of the administrative presidency since the Second World War occurred under Nixon and Reagan—activist executives confronted with uncooperative legislatures. One can cite numerous instances in which both these administrations sought to influence the bureaucracy in ways that contradicted any reasonable construction of statutory intent or the current preferences of legislative majorities.[39] By the same token, although every recent president has shown some inclination toward centralized and politicized control of the bureaucracy, the Nixon and Reagan administrations were notable for the degree to which they instituted these qualities. In contrast, if his disinterest in program implementation has been exaggerated, no one has suggested that Lyndon Johnson applied his considerable energy and talent to the development of an "administrative strategy." This, despite every indication from his earlier career in the legislature and as a New Deal bureaucrat that Johnson was eager to immerse himself in the most mundane details of administration when it suited his ends.[40]

Although its strategy has not matured as of this writing, there has been at least a hint of this same dynamic within the Clinton administration. Controlling the bureaucracy appears to have been a relatively low priority for Clinton during his first two years in office. Immediately after the Republican congressional victories of 1994, however, key presidential advisers began to promote the administrative process as an alternative means of developing policy. In contrast to previous administrative strategies, which sought primarily to curb bureaucratic activism, Clinton aides suggested an increased emphasis on executive orders and rulemaking by agencies such as OSHA, EPA, and the Department of the Interior as ways of keeping the president's coalition intact.[41]

Centralization and Coordination

If the administrative presidency is not driven primarily by traditional managerial concerns, it can still have an important coordinating effect so long as a consistent set of preferences inform initiatives in personnel administration, central clearance, and other areas. A more modest claim for executive leadership can be based on the expectation that rationalization will occur as a by-product of presidential control or influence over important political issues that arise in the administrative process. This certainly occurred during the Reagan administration, where like-minded departmental appointees and Executive Office personnel implemented a consistent agenda across a wide range of administrative policy areas. The successful efforts of political executives such as James Watt and Thorne Auchter to promote business interests over competing "social" concerns are well documented.[42] These efforts were reinforced by the conservative perspective brought to bear by OMB as it reviewed agency rules.

Reagan's attempt to promote a coherent set of policy goals through the administrative process was historic in its extensiveness and its success. Nevertheless, the effect of any presidential influence is, almost by definition, to introduce more unity of perspective in the administrative process than would otherwise be the case. Without minimizing the importance of this dynamic, however, it is also important not to exaggerate the degree to which executive control of the bureaucracy reflects clearly ordered goals. To make the point that presidential administrations are more homogeneous in their orientations than the federal bureaucracy or Congress is not to say that they are free of internal conflict or of the need to accommodate inconsistent preferences. To a considerable extent, the kind of coordination associated with the administrative presidency is pluralistic and bottom-up rather than hierarchical and top-down.

How one describes the presidency depends largely on where one chooses to draw its boundaries. As discussed earlier, one might view the diversity of perspectives and the dispersion of power that characterize all administrations to one degree or another as a limitation on executive management rather than as one of its defining characteristics. There can be little doubt, for instance, that President Nixon would have appointed someone other than George Romney to be HUD Secretary if not for the need to appease moderate and liberal Republicans. As it turned out, Romney proved to be a substantial impediment to Nixon's efforts to cut back on social programs through the implementation process.[43] Yet however one decides to label them, concessions to party factions, agency clientele, influential legislators, and other conflicting interests are important means by which presidents seek to build and maintain the majority coalitions needed for success in office. A fact often overlooked in justifications for executive management is that the need for such concessions is a defining feature of presidential politics that is ordained by the decentralization of institutional and political power in our system.

Even to the considerable extent that subordinates are chosen on the basis of political loyalty, members of an administration frequently have conflicting perceptions of the president's and the nation's interests. In fact, astute executives may find it advantageous to surround themselves with individuals whose viewpoints reflect society's different interests (or at least the varied perspectives of policy-making elites). Franklin Roosevelt and John Kennedy are reputed to have had a passion for cultivating diversity and conflict among their inner circles, for example, and evidence suggests that Bill Clinton prefers to operate in much the same way. Even the Reagan White House had its share of conflict, albeit on a less-frequent basis and within narrower parameters. Like the demands of patronage, the need to promote such diversity may be inimical to the president's personal preferences at some level. At the same time, it is often functional in relation to the broader goal of effective governance. To borrow a term that Kaufman uses to describe an essential component of public-sector leadership, it defines an administration's "institutional embodiment of purpose"—the structural features of an organization or a regime that determine how plans will be made and how specific issues will be dealt with as they arise.

The need to accommodate competing interests is not, in itself, inimical to the control of administrative action for unified ends. It is theoretically possible to establish a coherent set of goals through the reconciliation of different interests, and then to rationalize administration pursuant to those criteria. Yet although this process occurs to some extent, it is undermined by constraints on time and other resources, and by the inevitable fusion of politics and administration. As noted earlier, much of the president's influence over administration occurs in response to policies generated by agencies as they carry out congressional mandates in light of their own perspectives, legislative pressures, and a variety of other influences. Most of the questions addressed in this manner are new ones that require administrations to add to or refine their agendas by resolving new conflict rather than by applying existing policy standards to specific cases. The politics of presidential coalition building do not end on election day, but continue throughout an administration as it confronts new issues.

The Clinton administration's reaction to a staff proposal that emerged from the Commerce Department in the spring of 1993 is illustrative of much executive oversight. Alerted by Detroit, Mickey Kantor led a coalition of administration officials who questioned the wisdom of extending a "foreign trade zone" tax advantage to a Nissan plant in Smyrna, Tennessee. Their efforts were countered by Ron Brown, Laura Tyson, and others who argued that the action would protect U.S. jobs, that it would foster a better relationship with Japan, and that it was consistent with many previous department decisions aiding U.S. companies (that were made routinely in most cases). The ultimate choice to approve the tax break clearly involved an elaboration of the administration's trade policy rather than an application of existing principles.[44]

The pluralistic dimensions of executive control have been abundantly evident in efforts since the Nixon administration to screen agency regulations. As have other recent presidents, for example, Carter based his initiative for centralized review of administrative rules on the general proposition that too much government intervention in the private sector had driven up consumer prices and had otherwise undermined economic efficiency. This premise, which had become increasingly popular in academic and government circles, served as an important unifying theme that guided Executive Office scrutiny of agency proposals. At the same time, much of the regulatory review that occurred could hardly be characterized as a matter of evaluating agency proposals in terms of hierarchically ordered goals. Anderson observes that the institutional structure of the review process and the fate of individual regulations within it was determined in the arena of bureaucratic politics, where "players within the Executive Office of the President and the executive branch generally ... possess differing interests, ideologies, goals, and priorities."[45]

Review of agency rules in the Carter administration often pitted the needs of industry, as represented by economists within the Executive Office, against regulatory goals, which were championed by political executives and careerists from the departments. Many departmental appointees shared with the Executive Office the abstract belief that much regulation was economically inefficient, but were frequently supportive of the specific regulations developed by their agencies. There were also cleavages within Carter's Executive Office itself. In describing the relationship between his Domestic Policy Staff and OMB, for example, Stuart Eizenstadt notes that "there were very few things on which we agreed."[46] Differences between the two organizations were partly attributable to the fact that the former was composed of policy generalists with political orientations, while OMB careerists applied a more technocratic and specialized perspective.[47]

The rhetoric surrounding regulatory review in the Clinton administration evinces similar kinds of tension, and the process itself has been designed to secure the approval of such diverse interests as the Sierra Club and the U.S. Chamber of Commerce.[48] Although centralized review of agency rulemaking reflected more homogeneous goals under Bush and (especially) Reagan, one can cite similar anecdotes from their administrations. There was substantial conflict between the Vice President's Council on Competitiveness and the EPA during the latter stages of the Bush administration, for example, and—true to form, perhaps—it is difficult to say where the president himself stood on most of the specific issues at stake.

In these regards, centralized review of administrative policies by recent executives has often not been a matter of top-down control, but a process in which conflict has percolated up through the bureaucracy and the Executive Office until it has reached a level where it could be resolved. Thus, for example, much of the communication that took place regarding administrative policies under the Reagan administration's program of central clearance involved OIRA desk officers and agency staff specialists responsible for developing regulations. The former representatives of the president were typically bright, ambitious, inexperienced, and highly self-confident men and women in their late twenties who had recently earned professional degrees in fields such as law, business administration, economics, and public affairs. Although review under E.O. 12291 did not formally occur until a

proposed rule had been completed, it was not uncommon for dialogue between desk officers and their agency counterparts to begin much earlier in
the development of controversial policies. Substantial modifications often
resulted from these staff-to-staff contacts, and it was often only where
agency–OMB conflict could not be resolved at this low level that issues
escalated through the parallel hierarchies of OMB and the departments, and
eventually into the White House.[49]

As might be expected, very few controversies regarding individual
agency actions rise all the way to the president. Indeed, subordinate executive officials view such a rare event as a failure in the performance of their
duties. There were few if any instances in which President Reagan personally became involved in the process of regulatory review, and Carter's
direct intervention in agency decision making was probably confined to his
vacillating efforts to secure a compromise on OSHA's famous cotton-dust
standard.[50] Rather, issues have normally been settled through negotiation
among various lower-level officials whose relative bargaining power has
been a function of their propinquity to the president, their office and personal reputation, and a variety of other considerations, including the expectations of Congress and the judiciary, and the need to maintain agency
morale. Decisions have sometimes reflected unilateral concessions, but
have often been reached through compromise among different factions
within the administration.

By airing different viewpoints and constituent interests, the political accommodation that frequently characterizes the administrative presidency
promotes a type of coordination that is often salutary. The need to facilitate
such accommodation was a prime motive behind the first program of centralized regulatory clearance established under Nixon. Infighting over the
organization of environmental responsibilities was intense as the inevitabil-
ity of federal involvement in that area became increasingly apparent, and it
had become clear by the time EPA was created that its functions would
impinge on programs administered by other agencies. Thus, Quality of Life
Review was instituted at the urging of the Department of Health, Education,
and Welfare, the Department of Housing and Urban Development, and
Atomic Energy Commission, among other agencies, and it was subsequently used to identify and reconcile conflicting interests within the executive branch.

Again, however, this is not the kind of control normally envisioned by
advocates of a strong executive. Indeed, the Nixon administration instituted
Quality of Life Review as an alternative to the creation of a Department of
Natural Resources that would have consolidated environmental-protection
and energy-development functions performed by various agencies. Al-

though the latter option was clearly more rational in an administrative sense, it was rejected because of fears that it would have attenuated the pursuit of popular environmental goals.[51] The divergence that often exists between the administrative presidency and principles of rational organization is captured by Mark Gearan's characterization of Clinton's White House as a soccer league of ten-year-olds: "No one is stuck to his part of the field during a game. The ball—any ball—would come on the field, and everyone would go chasing it downfield."[52]

As is true of reactive, incremental policy making in general, there is little guarantee of consistency across decisions to the extent that centralized executive clearance involves the resolution of conflict on a case-by-case basis. Again, presidents themselves only occasionally intervene in disputes over agency policy, and competing factions within the executive may well settle their differences by logrolling across issues. The following excerpt from a White House staff memorandum suggesting the need to placate EPA administrator Douglas Costle describes a process of review under the Carter administration that could hardly be characterized in terms of hierarchically ordered goals:

> Apart from the merits, I think we are bound to defer to Doug unless he does something which is very clearly wrong. First, he is head of the Regulatory Council, and the President and you should appear to give his judgment deference on that account. Second, he is in fact carrying water for us in selling regulatory reform to his regulatory colleagues . . . ; we do not want to anger Doug unnecessarily. Third, ozone is only the first of many EPA regulatory review issues for 1979. . . .[53]

The view of executive control as a source of coherency must be further qualified by noting that the configuration of individual perspectives, formal authority, and informal understandings that defines the administrative posture of the presidency can vary over time. This fact is illustrated well by the revitalization of regulatory review under President Bush. His administration initially pursued a course in the area of regulation that helped to reverse trends established by its predecessor. Thus, whereas rules and other kinds of agency output were curtailed sharply under Reagan, the bureaucracy's rate of production rose to an all-time high under the new president. Although the magnitude of this change was quite startling, some moderation was to be expected given the image conveyed by Bush's claim to be the "Environmental President" and other rhetoric. Late in its tenure, however, the administration assumed a much more critical posture on regulation. Bush's unleashing of Dan Quayle, his moratorium on new regulations, and other efforts to constrain bureaucracy were undoubtedly responses to the growing disenchantment among conservative Republicans that was perceived (correctly) as a threat to his reelection.

Constituent Interests

A related issue in describing and evaluating the administrative presidency concerns the types of political forces that it represents. The notion that the president should promote broad national concerns is plausible and contains a good deal of truth. If the public interest proves to be an ephemeral concept in the context of most specific issues, the president is accountable to a national constituency. Indeed, although it may not always serve to rationalize administrative policy in the way envisioned by defenders of executive power, the kind of pluralistic conflict resolution described above is defensible precisely because it serves the public interest in a procedural sense by accommodating a broad range of concerns that transcend subsystem politics.

By the same token, however, the administrative presidency is hardly immune from the kinds of inequities alleged to characterize pluralist politics generally. For example, many accounts of regulatory review under the Reagan and Bush administrations suggest that intervention in the administrative process was often if not usually precipitated by industry complaints. In fact, a key member of the Vice President's Task Force on Regulatory Relief explicitly invited such input in a 1981 speech to the National Chamber of Commerce, stating that the White House would act as an appeals board for business groups that had failed to influence policy at the agency level.[54] Vice President Quayle's Council on Competitiveness came to play a similar role during the latter stages of the Bush administration. Included among its actions were well-publicized attempts to narrow the EPA's definition of wetlands at the behest of developers. As noted earlier, the process of central clearance under Reagan and Bush institutionalized these kinds of concerns through the system of cues used by OMB staff to identify those rules that should be given close scrutiny.

Lobbyists have had a significant effect on bureaucratic oversight by other administrations as well. Such contacts were common under President Nixon. In one instance that has recently come to light, Nixon intervened to block passive restraint regulations being developed by the Department of Transportation after personal conversations with leaders of the auto industry. Although such dynamics may have been less pervasive under Jimmy Carter, they existed nonetheless. Perhaps the most notable instance of responsiveness to intense producer interests by the Carter administration was when its Council of Economic Advisors objected to a strip-mining regulation after accepting data and off-the-record arguments from members of the industry. As a general commentary on centralized oversight of the bureaucracy, Gerald Ford's secretary of transportation has argued that narrow, short-term considerations are often brought to bear precisely because of the political incentives that exist within the White House. As he observes:

> Even more ominous is the so-called White House political advisor, whose role is never clearly defined in public but whose bias may simply be the position that will most ensure reelection of the President. His advice will be tailored to achieve the support of a particular constituency at a time when politically desirable or to enhance the President's appeal in a region of the country. Such an advisor—immune from public scrutiny and congressional accountability, free from the constraints of agency decision-making procedures, and removed from the advice of experts in the bureaucracy—is not in a position to make a meaningful balancing choice among competing national goals.[55]

This is not to deny that the president also frequently represents broad national concerns in his efforts to control administration. Yet an equally important point, developed at more length in chapter 8, is that the distinction between special and general interests is often highly subjective. Whereas some would interpret Carter's creation of a separate Department of Education and his appointment of numerous consumer advocates as efforts to promote the public welfare, for example, others would describe these actions as efforts to please special-interest groups that were critical elements of his electoral coalition. Similarly, if the Reagan administration's efforts to cut back on environmental, consumer, and health and safety regulations were criticized by "public-interest" advocates, defenders of such actions argued that the desire of business groups to avoid or eliminate government restrictions corresponded with the overarching goal of economic efficiency. They could add that regulatory reform was an important element in the platforms of Republican (and Democratic) presidential candidates in recent years.

At a more abstract level, however, there is little reason to expect the president consistently to represent broad majoritarian interests in the administrative process. Two points are relevant here. The first is that the president's electoral appeal is based on policy positions in a wide variety of areas (and on other factors as well), and that different voters have different issue priorities and value structures. There is no guarantee that executive policy oversight on any particular issue will reflect a national mandate as a result. It may, for example, reflect the intense preferences of a minority at the expense of a more diffuse majority. This is especially apt to be the case if that minority comprises an important element of the president's constituency. A revealing observation about the centralized clearance of agency rules under Carter, Reagan, and Bush is that public opinion polls have shown enduring support for the social regulatory programs that have been the main targets of review.[56]

A second observation is that, because much executive management is necessarily reactive, most of the specific issues that must be dealt with arise between elections. As a result, access to executive officials as administrative policy is being made tends to be much more crucial than electoral decisions as a linkage between public preferences and the character of oversight. In this regard, executive management will be influenced, not necessarily by broad majoritarian interests, but by groups that are powerful, intense, and close to the president. The probusiness orientation of review under E.O. 12291 is again instructive. An industry attorney and former EPA official succinctly described the character of much executive oversight when he noted that "anybody representing a client who didn't [seek to influence OMB review] would be damn negligent."[57]

Conclusion

The executive's role was traditionally conceived of (or at least presented) as an instrumental, managerial function. Although some still cling to this normative model in a vague way, it was never very realistic and has become less so as the administrative process has come to bear an increasingly close relationship to the president's political needs. In this regard, many have come to view the president's political relationship to the bureaucracy as being not only inevitable, but desirable and worthy of encouragement. This revised conception of executive management is based on disillusionment with bureaucratic politics and on a pair of interrelated assertions about the character of executive influence. One is that it has a centralizing effect on administrative policy. The other is that it is motivated by broad national concerns as opposed to special interests. These propositions are not accepted universally, either as descriptions of reality or as justifications for strong executive control, but they are sufficiently plausible and they enjoy sufficiently widespread support to serve as a basis for evaluation.

The reality of executive influence over administration is much more complex than the revised model suggests. Presidential behavior defies neat generalization. The individuals who occupy the White House vary considerably in their orientations toward the bureaucracy, just as they do in other respects. An equally if not more important caveat is that the level and nature of involvement in administration by any particular president varies considerably from one department or agency to the next.

Beyond this, the results of any assessment of the administrative presidency depend largely on how one defines its boundaries. Is it confined to the president and his immediate staff? Does it include the Executive Office bureaucracy? Does it include political appointees in the executive branch and independent agencies? Given that the president can spend little time on the details of administration, the determination of where his or her team of agents ends and where the bureaucracy begins is of crucial analytical importance. Inconsistency on this basic definitional question, both among and within studies, has produced much confusion among scholars.

As a broad assessment of the administrative presidency, however, few would disagree with the assertion that executive resources are not equal to the task of systematic management of policy implementation. While some would be quick to redress this situation, there is not much evidence to indicate that presidents are especially interested in economizing and coordinating agency activities. If anything, in fact, the evolution of the presidency suggests an inverse relationship between chief executives' desire to influence bureaucracy and their commitment to traditional administrative values. The obvious if frequently overlooked explanation for this is that the president's stakes in the administrative process are defined largely by its political salience and by the corresponding need for responsiveness. This imperative also defines the natural limits of a large Executive Office bureaucracy as a means of controlling agency action.

If top-down management and coordination are not a priority for the administrative presidency, responding to politically important bureaucratic actions can enable the executive to allocate limited attention, staff resources, and political capital to issues that are most closely tied to his or her political needs. This, in turn, can promote consistency in the administrative process. In general, recent presidents who have placed the highest emphasis on administration are the ones that have gone the farthest in promoting a coherent set of policy objectives through centralized control over the bureaucracy. At the same time, scholars have often stressed the unifying effects of executive management to the neglect of its pluralistic and reactive dimensions. Few labor under the illusion that presidential administrations are monolithic, of course, yet many accounts assume that the need to accommodate different interests and viewpoints within the executive impedes the attainment of managerial goals that the president would otherwise be inclined to implement. In fact, administrative issues are frequently not amenable to resolution by the application of policy criteria that have already been formulated, and it is often meaningful to view conflict and negotiation among various representatives of the president as a procedural expression of executive goals necessitated by the decentralization of power in American government. This process may well result in the consideration of a more comprehensive range of decisional criteria than would otherwise be the case, but it often does not produce the type of hierarchically driven consistency within and across administrative policy areas that is frequently associated with presidential influence.

Whether a strong executive presence in administration promotes national objectives is an especially complex issue. Although the argument that it should is compelling in the abstract and contains a good deal of truth in reality, just what constitutes the public or national interest is often highly subjective. In any case, the fact that the president is elected by a national constituency does not insulate the office from influence by the same kinds of interests that are allegedly reflected in the mandates and orientations of the bureaucratic agencies. Well-organized groups are naturally adept at monitoring the administrative process and bringing problematic actions to the attention of the White House or Executive Office, and a brief reflection on any campaign for the White House will quickly dispel any illusion that the support of narrow and intense interests is not important to the president.

Beyond the consideration of presidential motives, per se, an evaluation of executive control over the bureaucracy cannot be divorced from a consideration of its relationship to Congress's ability to shape policy through legislation and oversight pursuant to its own institutional interests. Again, presidential efforts to influence public administration are often motivated by disagreement with Congress over the direction policy should take. In a general sense, perhaps the single most fundamental constitutional issue facing American government today concerns the rise of bureaucracy as a locus of political authority and the implications of this development for the balance between executive and legislative power. Leaving this aside until the final chapter, the discussion turns now to the consideration of congressional motives and capabilities in the administrative process.

Notes

1. For an excellent history of these commissions, their intellectual orientations, and their recommendations, see Peri E. Arnold, *Making the Managerial Presidency: Comprehensive Reorganization Planning 1905–1980* (Princeton, N.J.: Princeton University Press, 1980).

2. The President's Committee on Administrative Management, *Report with Special Studies* (Washington, D.C.: U.S. Government Printing Office, 1937), p. 219.

3. *General Management of the Executive Branch: A Report to the Congress.* The Commission on Organization of the Executive Branch of the Government (Washington, D.C.: U.S. Government Printing Office, 1949), p. 11.

4. The President's Advisory Council on Executive Organization, *A New Framework: Report on Selected Independent Regulatory Agencies* (Washington, D.C.: U.S. Government Printing Office, 1971), p. 16.

5. Terry M. Moe, "The Politicized Presidency," in *New Directions in American Politics,* ed. John E. Chubb and Paul E. Peterson (Washington, D.C.: Brookings Institution, 1985).

6. Luther Gulick and L. Urwick, *Papers on the Science of Administration* (New York: Institute of Public Administration, 1937); Leonard D. White, *Introduction to the Study of Administration* (New York: Macmillan, 1926).

7. The President's Committee on Administrative Management, *Report with Special Studies.*

8. Arnold, *Making the Managerial Presidency,* p. 17.

9. As Kaufman observes, "The sharp conceptual cleavage between politics and administration, which gained currency during the years when neutral competence was ascendant, and which served as a useful philosophical prop for the machinery favored in those years, became an impediment to the justification of executive leadership. For one thing, chief executives, in whom administrative responsibility and power were to be lodged, were also partisan politicians. Moreover, one of the main reasons advanced for seeking integration was elimination of the fragmentation resulting from the acceptance of the idea of separability of politics and administration." Kaufman, "Emerging Conflicts in the Doctrines of Public Administration," *The American Political Science Review,* 50 (December 1956): 1057–73; quotation p. 1067.

10. Richard Nathan, *The Administrative Presidency* (New York: Wiley, 1983), p. 7.

11. *Motor Vehicle Manufacturers Association v. State Farm Mutual Auto Insurance Co.,* 403 U.S. 29 (1983).

12. James L. Sundquist, *The Decline and Resurgence of Congress* (Washington, D.C.: Brookings Institution, 1981), p. 451.

13. David Welborn, *Regulation in the White House: The Johnson Presidency* (Austin: University of Texas Press, 1993), pp. 8–9, 10–11.

14. Kaufman, "Emerging Conflicts," p. 1067.

15. John H. Kessel, *Presidential Parties* (Homewood, Ill.: Dorsey Press, 1984).

16. Based on the author's interpretation of table 2–2 in John P. Burke, *The Institutional Presidency* (Baltimore: Johns Hopkins University Press, 1992), pp. 29–31.

17. Ronald C. Moe, "Traditional Organizational Principles and the Managerial Presidency: From Phoenix to Ashes," *Public Administration Review* 50 (March/April 1990): 129–40; quotation p. 134.

18. Comptroller General, Report to the Chairman, Committee on Governmental Affairs, U.S. Senate, *Improved Quality, Adequate Resources, and Consistent Oversight Needed If Regulatory Analysis Is to Help Control Cost of Regulations* (Washington, D.C.: GAO/PAD–83–6, November 2, 1981), p. 53.

19. Hugh Heclo, "OMB and the Presidency—The Problem of Neutral Competence," *The Public Interest* 38 (Winter 1975): 80–98.

20. Author's interviews with OIRA officials, June 1985.

21. Margaret Jane Wyszomirski, "The De-Institutionalization of Presidential Staff Agencies," *Public Administration Review* 42 (September/October 1982): 448–58; see also Patricia W. Ingraham, "Building Bridges or Burning Them? The President, the Appointees, and the Bureacracy," *Public Administration Review* 47 (September/October 1987).

22. Hugh Heclo, "Issue Networks and the Executive Establishment," in *The New American Political System,* ed. Anthony King (Washington, D.C.: American Enterprise Institute, 1978).

23. Linda L. Fisher, "Fifty Years of Presidential Appointments," in *The In-and-Outers,* ed. G. Calvin MacKenzie (Baltimore: Johns Hopkins University Press, 1987).

24. This is borne out by the study cited in the preceding note. Thus, while Reagan

appointees did not differ appreciably from their predecessors in terms of crude measures of their technical qualifications, they were substantially more homogeneous in their ideological and partisan coloring than political executives under previous administrations.

25. Pfiffner offers the following quote from Elliot Richardson to make his case: "There didn't used to be anything like the degree of control exercised by the White House over presidential appointments in those days as we have seen recently. . . . I think this administration has tried to cut too deep into the system by turning jobs traditionally held by career people over to appointees." James P. Pfiffner, "Nine Enemies and One Ingrate: Political Appointments During Presidential Transitions," in *The In-and-Outers,* ed. G. Calvin MacKenzie (Baltimore: Johns Hopkins University Press, 1987), p. 66.

26. Moe, "The Politicized Presidency."

27. Moe, "Traditional Organizational Principles."

28. See Hugh Heclo, "Introduction: The Presidential Illusion," and Lester M. Salamon, "Beyond the Presidential Illusion—Toward a Constitutional Presidency," both in *The Illusion of Presidential Government,* ed. Hugh Heclo and Lester M. Salamon (Boulder, Colo.: Westview Press, 1981).

29. Heclo, "OMB and the Presidency."

30. Louis Brownlow, *A Passion for Anonymity* (Chicago: University of Chicago Press, 1958), pp. 323–24. Quoted here from Burke, *The Institutional Presidency,* p. 8. For a somewhat different interpretation of Roosevelt's administrative posture see Pfiffner, "OMB: Professionalism, Politicization, and the Presidency," in *Executive Leadership in Anglo-American Systems,* ed. Colin Campbell and Margaret Jane Wyszominski (Pittsburgh: University of Pittsburgh Press, 1991). Pfiffner implies that FDR essentially separated the task of management, which he regarded as an important Bureau of the Budget responsibility, from his political stakes in the administrative process, which he sought to protect through other means.

31. Carter chose banker and longtime associate Bert Lance.

32. Erwin C. Hargrove, *The Power of the Modern Presidency* (New York: Alfred A. Knopf, Inc., 1974), p. 23.

33. See, for example, James E. Anderson, "Presidential Management of the Bureaucracy and the Johnson Presidency: A Preliminary Exploration," *Congress and the Presidency* (Autumn 1984): 137–64; Welborn, *Regulation in the White House.*

34. Welborn observes, for example, that Johnson had become frustrated in his dealings with the bureaucracy by the end of his tenure, and that more systematic efforts to consolidate his control over administration might well have been a priority during a second elected term. See *Regulation in the White House.*

35. Moe, "Traditional Organizational Principles."

36. Pfiffner, "OMB: Professionalism, Politicization, and the Presidency."

37. Quoted from James E. Anderson, "The Carter Administration and Regulatory Reform: Searching for the Right Way," *Congress and the Presidency* 18 (Autumn 1991): 121–45; quotation p. 136.

38. Author's interviews, June 1985.

39. President Nixon's extensive efforts to attain domestic policy goals that Congress would not endorse through the administrative process are well documented. Although he was somewhat more successful as chief legislator, Reagan's efforts to control bureaucracy were also clearly designed to overcome a hostile Washington establishment of which Congress was an important part. The primary focus of his efforts was thus to counteract legislative initiatives in social regulation. Congress took strong actions to curb administrative initiatives taken by both Nixon and Reagan.

40. See, for example, Caro's discussion of Johnson as a congressional staffer and a New Deal bureaucrat in Robert A. Caro, *The Path to Power* (New York: Vintage Books, 1990).

41. OMB officials, interviews by the author, December 1994.

42. Robert F. Durant, *The Administrative Presidency Revisited: Public Lands, the BLM, and the Reagan Revolution* (Albany: State University of New York Press, 1992); Susan Tolchin and Mark Tolchin, *Dismantling America—The Rush to Deregulate* (New York: Oxford University Press, 1984).

43. See Richard W. Waterman, *Presidential Influence and the Administrative State* (Knoxville: University of Tennessee Press, 1989), especially chapter 3.

44. Keith Bradsher, "A Trade Policy Test at Tennessee Nissan Plant," *New York Times,* June 14, 1993, pp. C1, 8, 9.

45. Anderson, "The Carter Administration and Regulatory Reform," p. 124.

46. Stuart E. Eizenstadt, "Executive Office Agencies and Advisory Policy Units, " in *Executive Leadership in Anglo-American Systems,* ed. Colin Campbell and Margaret Jane Wyszominski (Pittsburgh: University of Pittsburgh Press, 1991), p. 253.

47. Ibid.

48. David Lauter, "Clinton Order Lifts Regulatory Review Secrecy," *Los Angeles Times,* October 1, 1993, p. 14A.

49. Authors interviews, June 1985. William F. West and Joseph Cooper, "The Rise of Administrative Clearance," in *The Presidency and Public Policy Making,* ed. George Edwards, Stephen Schull, and Norman Thomas (Pittsburgh: University of Pittsburgh Press, 1985).

50. Reversing his earlier position on the issue, Carter largely supported a cotton-dust standard proposed by his labor secretary over the objections of key advisors in the Executive Office.

51. Alfred A. Marcus, "EPA's Original Structure," *Law and Contemporary Problems* 54 (Autumn 1991): 5–40.

52. "National Affairs," *Newsweek,* June 13, 1994, p. 25.

53. Domestic Policy Staff memorandum written from associate director Simon Lazarus to director Stuart Eizenstadt, July 27, 1977. Quoted from Anderson, "The Carter Administration and Regulatory Reform," p. 143.

54. Boyden Gray before the National Chamber of Commerce, April 10, 1981. For an extensive discussion of the Reagan administration's solicitation of complaints from the business community, see Tolchin and Tolchin, *Dismantling America.*

55. Statement of William T. Coleman, ABA Commission on Law and the Economy, *Federal Regulation: Roads to Reform,* 157 (1979). Quoted from Paul R. Verkuil, "Jawboning Administrative Agencies: Ex Parte Contacts by the White House," *Columbia Law Review* 80 (1981): 951 (note 44).

56. Tolchin and Tolchin, *Dismantling America,* pp. 263–65.

57. Felicity Barringer, "Feud Tests OMB as Regulatory Watchdog," *Washington Post,* November 26, 1982. Quoted from George C. Eads and Michael Fix, *Relief or Reform: Reagan's Regulatory Dilemma* (Washington, D.C.: Urban Institute, 1984).

6

Legislative Oversight

As with the expansion of administrative due process and presidential controls, Congress has increased its efforts to review and influence policy implementation in direct proportion to the rise of bureaucracy as a locus of political authority. This chapter describes the resources and techniques that Congress relies on in performing oversight. As with the discussions of administrative due process and executive management, it gives special attention to institutional developments in recent decades that have enhanced Congress's ability to monitor and shape bureaucratic actions.

This chapter also discusses the effectiveness of Congress's efforts to supervise policy implementation. Scholars have often dismissed oversight as being insignificant. This assessment has been based in part on the assertion that the legislature lacks the time and the expertise to monitor and evaluate administrative performance in any meaningful way. In many accounts, the Congress's lack of resources is compounded by the fact that oversight is a low priority in light of the careerist incentives that drive legislative behavior. Beyond this, some authorities allege that the inherent fragmentation of committee-based oversight renders coordinative management of the bureaucracy impossible.

Although it retains a good deal of currency, the belief that legislative oversight is ineffective has eroded over the past two decades. A substantial augmentation of congressional resources devoted to oversight since the 1960s obviously belies the claim that the review of administrative programs has remained a low priority. Whether these resources are sufficient remains an open question, the answer to which depends on one's assumptions regarding what the goals of oversight are or should be. Oversight can never be a comprehensive management tool, yet this assessment of its effectiveness may reflect unrealistic assumptions regarding the relationship between policy implementation, on the one hand, and Congress's institutional needs and its representative function on the other. As with presidential management, oversight is an important, albeit imperfect, means by which Congress can influence policy in those areas of administration most important to it.

An Overview of Legislative Controls

Congress relies on a variety of formal powers, resources, and techniques to monitor and influence the implementation of its laws. Whether all of these devices constitute "legislative oversight" depends on which of several definitions of that term one chooses to apply. In this regard, the fact that many studies of oversight fail to define their subject is not an indication that there is an implicit consensus as to its meaning. Individual scholars sometimes use the term in vague and contradictory ways, and conceptions of what oversight is vary significantly where clear definitions are offered. Part of the confusion surrounding the meaning of *oversight* stems from the fact that some define it prescriptively, excluding what they consider to be illegitimate behavior by Congress, while some use it descriptively.

Functional Issues

A consideration of several related but partially independent definitional issues provides a useful foundation for considering the purposes and effects of the legislature's role in the administrative process. One issue concerns the substantive focus of oversight. In many instances, the term is reserved for review of the general direction and effectiveness of implementation. This is true of Dennis Riley's suggestion that oversight can be categorized as legislative (determining whether programs work), fiscal (making sure money is spent the way Congress wants it spent), or investigative (inquiring into government economy, efficiency, and effectiveness). Congress's interest in the administrative process is not limited to such considerations, however, and oversight may also refer to the review of particular administrative decisions articulating general standards through rules and other policy statements. In some of its applications, oversight further encompasses legislators' involvement in the relationship between agencies and individuals—what is commonly referred to as casework.

Another important distinction concerns the timing of legislative involvement. In an early and influential treatment of the subject, Joseph Harris defines oversight as "review after the fact."[1] For many others, however, oversight consists of congressional review during as well as after policy implementation. Some go even further, defining oversight as any type of legislative behavior that affects administration. For instance, Lawrence Dodd and Richard Schott discuss appropriations and enabling legislation as means of performing oversight.[2]

An underlying issue, related to that of timing, is whether the meaning of oversight should be confined to review or whether it should include direct influence by Congress in the administrative process. Review after the fact ensures conformity with the popular conception of the oversight function as passive supervision, whereas review during implementation is obviously necessary if oversight is to include direct influence over agency actions. In a similar vein, the distinction between monitoring and influence has important implications for the classification of institutional mechanisms. Formal means of congressional intervention in agency affairs such as the legislative veto obviously fall outside the realm of passive supervision but are compatible with definitions that include active involvement in administration. The argument that policy influence via oversight is functionally equivalent to and interdependent with legislation may also help account for definitions that include legislative actions before the fact. This reasoning lies behind Morris Ogul's definition of oversight as "behavior by legislators and their staffs, individually or collectively, which results in an impact, intended or not, on bureaucratic behavior."[3]

It is important to emphasize that definitions of oversight can reflect conceptions of Congress's actual or its proper role in the administrative process, a fact that helps explain the interrelationship between empirical and normative analysis alluded to earlier. The issues outlined here will reemerge later, but Christopher Foreman's description of oversight as "two interlocking congressional processes" will serve as a broad working definition. Thus, for the present purposes the term can be conceived of as "efforts to *gather information* about what agencies are doing and to *dictate or signal* to agencies regarding the preferred behavior or policy."[4] Beyond this, defining oversight so broadly as to include legislative activities before the administrative process begins renders it almost meaningless by encompassing practically everything that the legislature does. One should nonetheless bear in mind the important relationship between oversight and Congress's authorization and appropriations powers.

Resources and Techniques

Congress relies on a variety of resources and techniques in its efforts to monitor and influence bureaucratic performance. Much has been made of frequent efforts by legislators to aid constituents and other individuals in obtaining favorable treatment from agencies in decisions involving licenses, contracts, exemptions from regulations or taxes, and a wide array of other matters.[5] Such casework is usually carried out by individual legislators and their personal staffs located in Washington and (especially) their home states or districts. Although attempts to describe the extent and effects of casework have come to different conclusions, it is safe to say that it is often a high priority that receives a significant amount of attention from a majority of legislative staff. In 1978, for example, an average of 10 aides for each individual senator were regularly engaged in casework, and an average of 5 staffers were formally designated for that task. The comparable figures for the House were 7 and 3.5.[6] Indeed, most legislators actively solicit casework from their constituents, using a variety of techniques to do so.[7]

Review of a more programmatic nature is conducted largely by congressional committees and subcommittees in their areas of specialization. This is not to say that committees do not respond to complaints as well, either directly or at the behest of congressional colleagues. Moreover, the distinction between casework and policy-oriented oversight tends to blur at the margins in that the former can bring to light problems of a more general nature. This is especially true to the extent that one includes interest groups as beneficiaries of casework. At any rate, responsibility for reviewing agencies' spending activities is vested in relevant appropriations subcommittees from each chamber, while responsibility for overseeing the accuracy and effectiveness of program implementation rests with the relevant authorization committees or subcommittees in the House and Senate. One should not infer too much from this functional distinction, however, for the tasks of auditing and "legislative" review frequently run together. The organizational structure of oversight is further complicated by the fact that different committees or subcommittees may supervise the implementation of different programs by an agency, or may share oversight responsibility for a given activity. In the latter regard, the only limitation on a committee's ability to oversee an area of interest to it is that the activity must bear some reasonable connection to its legislative duties (which themselves may be vaguely defined).

Oversight can focus on how agencies do things as well as on what they do. Considerations of substance and process are frequently difficult to separate, and most standing committees and subcommittees are inevitably concerned with both when they conduct review in their areas of concern. In addition, the House Government Operations and Senate Government Affairs committees have oversight responsibilities throughout the federal bureaucracy pertaining to agency procedures and organization, as well as to other matters relating to the "economy and efficiency" of administration. Among other things, these committees have primary responsibility for assessing and revising the other types of institutional controls on bureaucracy discussed in this book. Thus, they study the effects of procedural requirements and judicial review, and play a central role in the consideration of generally applicable statutes dealing with the administrative process (such as proposed amendments to the APA). The Government Operations committees also represent Congress's interests in reviewing presidential oversight practices such as those instituted by E.O. 12291. Many committees in the House also have their own subcommittees with jurisdiction-wide responsibilities similar to those of Government Operations.

Given the magnitude of the task, committee staff are central to Congress's efforts to review agency performance. Although their priorities vary substantially from committee to committee, a great majority of the roughly 2,600 staffers in the House and Senate devote a substantial portion their energies to conducting oversight.[8] In addition, legislators can call on several in-house organizations for help in conducting oversight. The Congressional Research Service provides assistance in collecting and analyzing data, scholarly literature, and documents that are relevant to the performance of program review (as well as the enactment of new legislation). The Office of Technology Assessment and the Congressional Budget Office also provide expertise and staff assistance in performing various tasks that are part of the oversight process. The most important general-support organization for oversight is the General Accounting Office, which employs about five thousand specialists in fields such as accounting, economics, and public management. Although the agency initiates some studies on its own, it estimates that between 80 and 100 percent of its work is generated directly or indirectly by requests from Congress (depending on the area). In 1980, about 7 percent of its workload was devoted to financial auditing, 29 percent to managerial studies, 50 percent to program evaluation, and 14 percent to "special studies."[9]

Oversight occurs in a number of formal contexts. The most visible forum is the oversight hearing at which administrators and other parties are called before committees or subcommittees to testify about agency practices and program effects. Although it seldom has to rely on them, Congress has subpoena powers to compel testimony and the provision of other kinds of evidence at such proceedings. Varying from year to year, roughly 18 percent to 25 percent of all committee hearing and meetings days are devoted to oversight.[10] Agencies are also frequently required to describe and assess their activities in formal reports. In addition, much oversight naturally occurs as a by-product of other congressional functions such as hearings on new legislation.

At the same time, Congress does not rely exclusively or perhaps even primarily on formal devices in its efforts to review and correct administration. Legislators and their staff obtain information about bureaucratic performance and its ramifications from a variety of sources, including the media, other agencies with overlapping and conflicting responsibilities, and other members of Congress and committee staff. Complaints from constituents or interest groups can be especially important in this regard. In the most comprehensive work on congressional oversight to date, Joel Aberbach identifies seventeen ways in which committees keep track of agency activities, and fourteen distinct techniques for communicating with and influencing administrators.

Much oversight occurs through telephone conversations, private meetings, and other off-the-record contacts. Representatives and their staff often prefer such measures for a number of reasons. "Informal" oversight can obviously be more expedient than reliance on hearings and reports. It can also avoid adverse publicity that might prove damaging to worthwhile programs and to the careers of legislators and administrators associated with those programs. Finally, informal oversight may facilitate efforts by legislators to change the course of administrative policy in directions that are unpopular with constituents. Thus, for example, Ogul notes that some southern congressmen found it prudent to rely on such techniques in prodding the Department of Justice toward more aggressive civil rights enforcement in the 1960s.[11] The use of informal communications is nurtured by the institutional stability of committee-based review. Committee members and their staff frequently spend years interacting with the same agency officials, developing well-defined working relationships in the process.

Of course, the viability of informal oversight is determined in part by the formal tools Congress holds in reserve. If legislators are frequently inclined to rely on informal methods, the adverse publicity associated with formal hearings can also be an especially strong inducement for administrators to cooperate with such efforts. In addition, the actual or threatened use of congressional powers not directly associated with oversight is inextricably tied to the review and control of ongoing administrative activities. Congress can influence bureaucracy through its traditional powers to reorganize and relocate agencies; through senatorial prerogatives to confirm political appointees; through its powers otherwise to influence the numbers and types of personnel within agencies; and through its ability to shape the constitutional character of agency decision making by defining procedural requirements, terms of access by outside participants, and standards of justification and judicial review.

Foremost among Congress's powers with regard to the bureaucracy are its control over budgets and enabling statutes, which are the lifeblood of the administrative process. Again, the "surgical" use of amendatory enabling legislation and appropriations bills to clarify agency mandates is, to many, the most legitimate means by which Congress may seek to correct misinterpretations of congressional intent discovered during oversight. Although members of Congress often prefer to exert influence over the bureaucracy through other techniques, recourse to the legislative process occurs often enough. Beyond this, legislation is important as an implicit or explicit threat that Congress can use to attain desired results in administration through less-formal devices.

Although the power to amend enabling statutes provides the ultimate institutional authority for oversight in most instances, a number of special mechanisms may enhance Congress's capabilities beyond those it enjoys by virtue of its normal legislative prerogatives. The most common of these are temporary authorizations, which require the legislature to reapprove particular activities or bureaus after a certain amount of time has elapsed. Temporary authorizations thus institutionalize periodic oversight, at least of a cursory nature, by forcing Congress to review and act on arguments prepared by administrators and perhaps other interested parties concerning the effects and continued viability of programs. Although their applicability as corrective tools or as threats is limited in most cases by the crude, all-or-nothing character of congressional action (through inaction), temporary authorizations enable the legislature to address sufficiently disturbing problems without recourse to the process of passing a new law and obtaining the president's signature. Evidence suggests that they do serve as important cues in identifying areas of administration that will receive serious oversight attention.[12]

The legislative veto provided a more convenient tool by which Congress could systematically monitor and assert itself in the administrative process. Under the most common variants of this device, proposed actions of a given type were required by an agency's enabling legislation to be submitted to Congress, and could not go into effect until a mandatory waiting period had elapsed. Either one or both houses of the legislature, or committees in a few cases, could disapprove agency decisions during that time. As such, the veto had advantages over both the normal legislative process and temporary authorizations as a means of controlling the bureaucracy. Unlike either, it provided a mechanism for bringing specific actions to Congress's attention before they took effect. Unlike the latter, moreover, it gave Congress the flexibility to address individual decisions (as opposed to entire programs), and unlike the former it circumvented the need to secure presidential approval of legislative initiatives in the administrative process.[13]

Although the most popular forms of the legislative veto were declared unconstitutional in the Supreme Court's *Chadha* (1983) decision,[14] Congress has continued to enact such devices on a more limited basis. The veto's continued use in appropriations bills has been especially notable. In addition, Congress can rely on several analogous but more cumbersome mechanisms that enhance its ability to review and influence specific agency actions. "Report-and-wait" provisions require agencies to submit specific types of proposals for legislative scrutiny, often by designated committees, and allow Congress a fixed period of time in which it can block or amend those actions through the normal legislative process. Another alternative that remains legal in the wake of *Chadha* is the statutory requirement that both houses and the president affirm administrative proposals through the enactment of legislation.

Legislative Oversight in Perspective

Institutional resources work in conjunction with congressional incentives to determine the impact of oversight. If it is to have meaning, moreover, whatever results from these two organizational characteristics must be assessed in terms of some external standard. In this latter regard, the concept of effectiveness has provided the focus for most descriptive analyses of oversight. Despite the multiplicity of tools available to Congress, many scholars have found legislative involvement in the administrative process to be sporadic and ineffectual. This "conventional" assessment of oversight's limited effectiveness outlined below may not correspond in its entirety with any particular work, but it is accurate as a rough synthesis of common assumptions and arguments that once dominated the literature. As such, it provides a point of departure for considering the impact of legislative review.

Although the conventional view retains a good deal of currency, its popularity has suffered under the weight of recent evidence. The reassessment of the effectiveness of oversight centers around two interrelated challenges. A number of observations suggest that Congress considers review of administration to be an important activity worthy of substantial organizational resources. In this regard, key institutional changes evince an increased legislative interest and presence in the administrative process over the past three decades. A reinforcing observation concerns the definition of effectiveness. Thus, perhaps a more fundamental challenge to the conventional view is that, by equating effectiveness with comprehensive or at least very extensive review, it reflects an unrealistic view of the relationship between policy implementation and Congress's institutional goals.

The Conventional View

The conventional assessment of oversight is based in part on the observation that Congress cannot conduct comprehensive review or even a systematic sampling of bureaucratic actions. A key premise is that the legislature simply lacks the wherewithal to monitor the administrative process. Notwithstanding committee staff and other institutional resources, the sheer size of bureaucracy and the diversity of its activities are alleged to render anything beyond haphazard oversight an unrealistic expectation.[15] This problem is compounded by Congress's lack of expertise in complex areas of policy implementation, by bureaucracy's well-known inclination to preserve its autonomy through information control and other means, and by competition from the president, interest groups, and other actors with a stake in the administrative process.[16]

To the extent that Congress is able to monitor agency action, many authorities also note limitations in the tools that it can rely on to influence statutory implementation. Terry Moe observes that legislative and budgetary powers are unwieldy instruments that give congressional committees only limited bargaining power in their relations with the bureaucracy. The utility of these devices is discounted by the fact that they require bicameral majorities and presidential approval, as well as by the same asymmetries of information and expertise that constrain efforts to review bureaucratic performance. Moe further contends that the Senate's confirmation power is a crude means of control at best, and that in practice Congress defers strongly to the president in personnel matters.[17]

Congress's characteristics as an organization are frequently alleged to reinforce the inherent limitations of its constitutional powers to perform oversight. The decentralization of authority among individuals, among committees and subcommittees, and among separate houses, all of which represent different sets of interests, obviously inhibits the legislature's ability to conduct review pursuant to coherent goals. As Dodd and Schott argue, "The highly dispersed nature of oversight responsibility, the lack of strong central oversight committees, and the natural conflict among committees all undermine severely the ability of Congress to conduct serious, rational control of administration."[18] Decentralized and overlapping responsibilities for oversight can also enable agencies to play off one member of Congress or set of legislators against another.

Under the conventional view, the fact that legislators are not motivated to perform systematic oversight both helps to explain and exacerbates the effect of decentralization and limited resources. Ogul, Seymour Scher, and John Bibby discuss a number of these disincentives in their works.[19] The subject matter of day-to-day oversight is often mundane and uninteresting to many legislators. This is particularly true for those assigned to committees responsible for unappealing areas such as the District of Columbia and the Post Office. Moreover, the institutional structure of oversight may discourage critical review given that the same committees that draft legislative policy are responsible for assessing the effectiveness of programs as they are carried out. In a related vein, mutual respect and friendships developed over years of interaction between bureaucrats and committee members and their staff may further inhibit critical review. Members of Congress that belong to the same party as the president may also be reluctant to uncover failures in policy implementation that embarrass the administration.

The most crucial disincentive for vigorous oversight under the conventional assessment is that review of policy implementation is simply not a cost-effective way for representatives and senators to pursue their primary goal of being reelected. Given that most administrative actions are routine matters of low visibility, coupled with the formidable challenge legislators face in attempting to master the substance of agency policy making in most areas, the investment of limited time and staff resources in other activities (such as attaching one's name to prominent legislation) offer much greater dividends in terms of credit claiming and building name recognition. This assessment of oversight's low priority meshes with popular interpretations of congressional behavior that emphasize the influence of careerist incentives and the dominance of individual self-interest over broad policy concerns. As David Mayhew observes in an influential work based on these premises:

> What happens in ... overseeing implementation is ... the result of and interplay between credit-claiming and position-taking impulsions. ... The important point here is that on measures lacking particularized benefits the congressman's intrinsic interest in the impact of legislation vanishes. Hence, it is a misallocation of resources to devote time and energy to ... scrutiny of impact unless ... credit is available for legislative maneuvering.[20]

Contextual Qualifications

Few if any analyses have asserted that legislators are consistently uninterested and uninvolved in policy implementation. Although scholars have traditionally concluded that legislative review of administration is limited and therefore ineffective on the whole, one of the most common themes in the oversight literature is that various contextual factors can be conducive to legislative review. Highly visible issues are a commonly cited exception to Congress's general pattern of neglect. Addressing well-publicized policy failures resulting from bureaucratic malfeasance or incompetence (thalidomide, Times Beach, the Challenger disaster, for example) can provide substantial opportunities for legislators to build name recognition and project themselves to be guardians of the public trust.[21]

In addition, even the most pessimistic assessments of oversight are likely to view intervention in matters that are highly salient to constituents as an important means by which legislators pursue the general reelection strategy of credit claiming (although many do not define such activities as oversight). Morris Fiorina has turned this hypothesis into a cottage industry, arguing that expanded opportunities for casework created by the growth of the administrative state explains the overwhelming electoral advantage incumbents have come to enjoy since the Second World War.[22] Again, studies of casework suggest that it does, in fact, consume a substantial share of congressional resources.[23]

Scholars have examined a variety of other factors affecting oversight as well. Based on his interviews with congressmen and his observations of regulatory oversight between 1938 and 1961, Scher finds that, although "committee review is a spasmodic affair marked by years in which the agencies are virtually ignored," oversight is encouraged by certain political conditions. He suggests, for example, that it can occur as a by-product of widespread congressional interest in policy revision. Scher also finds that oversight is more likely when there is partisan conflict between the administration and congressional leaders. In addition, perceived threats of presidential interference in the affairs of independent regulatory commissions may precipitate reciprocal efforts by Congress to regain control of what it views as its rightful domain.[24]

Aside from responses to transient political opportunities, other studies identify factors that affect Congress's inclination to conduct review in more systematic and predictable ways. Aberbach's hearing data suggest that oversight is taken less seriously in redistributive than other policy areas. This is consistent with Theodore Lowi's thesis that control over redistributive issues is typically the prerogative of the executive and of key leaders in Congress rather than of committees.[25] Relatedly, it may reflect the fact that statutes confer less discretion in redistributive areas. Scholars have also found that structural characteristics within the legislature affect the level and orientation of administrative review. Each committee has a unique mission, task environment, and internal structure and culture that determine the extent to which it performs oversight. As one would predict, for example, a large and capable committee staff and the existence of specialized oversight subunits are both conducive to review.

Several studies have suggested that the degree of committee centralization is an especially important consideration in determining the nature and extent of oversight. While some committees cede much of their responsibility to subcommittees, others are highly centralized, conducting most hearings at the full committee level and giving chairpersons substantial control of the oversight agenda. Analyses by Bibby and Aberbach indicate that committees in which control over hearing agendas and the allocation of staff resources is delegated to subcommittees are more prone to review administration than those in which authority is centralized.[26] One plausible explanation for this is that, because committee chairpersons have more pressing and rewarding concerns, oversight fares better in relation to the more limited range of activities that are available to subcommittees. A related explanation is that the decentralization of authority within a committee makes it a more attractive place for members to further their individual careers. Decentralization may encourage oversight in this regard because it promotes membership stability and the development of expertise. It may also influence the allocation of members' limited time among competing committee assignments.

Aberbach's analysis is especially valuable because of its efforts to explain both the extent and the character of oversight as functions of institutional design. He finds, for example, that special oversight committees or subcommittees are more likely to conduct critical, objective review than are other units, which tend to view their role in the administrative process as one of program advocacy. In addition, Aberbach's interview data indicate that the structure of oversight has much to do with whether review occurs primarily in response to constituent complaints or whether it reflects active efforts by committee members to investigate agency performance. For instance, Congress is more likely to show initiative in examining administrative performance when oversight occurs in the context of reauthorization. The impressions of staffers also suggest that active oversight is much more prevalent in appropriations committees than in standing subject-matter committees.[27]

Reassessing Congressional Incentives and Capabilities

Although many still adhere to the thesis that oversight is ineffectual on the whole, variation in the nature and extent of congressional review obviously undermines the generalization that it is consistently neglected. The fact that the structural arrangements which seem to account for much of this variation are controlled by Congress, presumably in accordance with its own interests, further contradicts the assertion that the legislature is relatively powerless to perform effective oversight. Beyond these qualifications, a number of observations indicate that there has been a marked increase in oversight, both in absolute terms and in relation to other activities that compete for congressional resources. If oversight of the bureaucracy ever bore a weak relationship to Congress's institutional goals, it is clearly an important function today.

Scholars have probably always tended to underestimate the legislature's interest in and influence over policy implementation, especially to the extent that they have equated oversight with the use of formal mechanisms such as hearings and reports. Foreman's analysis of congressional involvement in the administration of social regulatory policy illustrates this well. He observes that informal oversight occurs frequently and in a wide array of contexts. It may take the form of direct communications or of indirect signals that are nonetheless effective in shaping agency decisions. Foreman argues that focusing on "formal structure can be misleading in at least two respects. First, it encourages the nonsensical perception that oversight is something that happens entirely apart from the other two processes [authorization and appropriation]. Second, it probably biases discussion toward an underestimation of cumulative congressional influence."[28] Whether informal communications are to be considered oversight is again a matter of definitional choice. At any rate, they have often been ignored in assessing the extent and impact of legislative involvement in agency affairs.

Aberbach's latest work provides extensive evidence that oversight is taken seriously by Congress. Based largely on interviews with committee staff, it indicates that various types of review consume a large share of legislative attention and resources. In contrast to what the conventional view would predict, it suggests that authorization, appropriation, and oversight committees all engage in a significant amount of active as well as reactive monitoring (although the mix between these two strategies varies significantly).[29] Those who conduct oversight also frequently possess considerable substantive knowledge. Administrators generally know more about their day-to-day operations than anyone else, of course, and legislators and their staff sometimes have a poor understanding of the cause-and-effect relationships that provide the bases for bureaucratic decisions. Yet although it varies substantially from one area to the next, committee-based oversight is hardly devoid of relevant expertise. The specialization and division of labor provided by committees, as reinforced by the seniority system, are means through which Congress has adapted as an organization to demands for more and increasingly complex policy. The result is that the legislators who are primarily responsible for oversight often have years of experience in their respective areas. Indeed, it is not uncommon for individual representatives and senators to be widely respected as policy experts.[30] Legislators almost always compare quite favorably in these respects with the transitory political executives who manage agencies for the president.[31]

A complementary point is that the committee staff who do much of the work in conducting oversight are, like their bureaucratic counterparts, typically careerists. Like agency officials, moreover, many have benefited from extensive professional training in fields relevant to their responsibilities. One can go too far in developing these similarities; in the aggregate, top committee staffers tend to have somewhat less experience and somewhat more general educations that their opposite numbers in the executive branch. [32] The former are nevertheless a talented and experienced group who possess considerable expertise in their substantive policy areas. The general support organizations that aid legislators in conducting oversight add significantly to Congress's technical capabilities. The General Accounting Office and the Congressional Research Service both employ highly competent people, some of whom are nationally recognized authorities in their areas. [33]

Congress, itself, largely determines the types and amounts of institutional resources that are devoted to oversight. In this regard, a number of observations suggest that the legislature has become increasingly intent on reviewing administrative behavior over the past several decades. Although congressional review of administration can occur in a variety of contexts, for example, formally designated oversight hearings as a percentage of all legislative hearings rose from about 2.5 percent to about 15 percent between 1970 and 1976, and the figure has remained fairly stable since then. [34] Similarly, there has been a dramatic increase in the number and days of oversight hearings per session, both in absolute terms and as a percentage of all hearing activity. As Aberbach notes, congressional committees devoted 146 out of a total of 1,789 hearing days to oversight (or 8.2 percent) in 1961. After 22 years of more or less secular growth, the comparable figures for 1983 were 587 out of a total of 2,331 hearing days (or 25.2 percent) devoted to oversight. [35] This trend correlates very closely with what was roughly a trebling in the total number of House and Senate committee staff over the same period. [36] These data obviously suggest growing congressional interest in oversight (at least assuming that the comparative attractiveness and incidence of informal versus informal review have not changed in any fundamental way).

Other institutional developments further belie the claim that Congress has maintained little interest in administrative performance. One is the expanded role of GAO, the most important of the in-house organizations Congress relies on to aid in its oversight activities. Created by the Budget and Accounting Act of 1921, the GAO was originally confined to auditing the legality of agency expenditures and later added accounting to its responsibilities. Since the mid 1960s, however, the agency has become increasingly concerned with program evaluation—a change in orientation that has been facilitated by a tremendous broadening of and improvement in the expertise of agency personnel. This development has been accompanied by

Congress's increased reliance on GAO in performing oversight. Thus, whereas only about 10 percent of its work was generated by congressional requests in the late 1960s, this figure had risen to 35 percent by 1977, and to over 80 percent by 1988.[37]

Another significant manifestation of Congress's increased interest in public administration was its expanded use of the legislative veto. Although this device had existed since the early 1930s, about two-thirds of all vetoes were enacted after 1970. Moreover, the newer provisions tended, to a much greater extent than their predecessors, to facilitate review and control of agency rulemaking and other policy activities as opposed to administrative or presidential decisions applying the law in individual cases. Indeed, all legislative vetoes pertaining to rulemaking were enacted during the 1970s and early 1980s.[38] This suggests that oversight has become more important to Congress, not only as a means of serving individual constituents, but as a way of shaping the direction of administrative policy and of jousting for position with the president. As mentioned earlier, although the most popular forms of the veto were declared unconstitutional in 1983, Congress has continued to enact analogous devices that force systematic review and that enhance its ability to shape bureaucratic policy. For example, there has also been a dramatic increase in the use of temporary authorizations since the 1960s.[39] These trends indicate the legislature's increased desire to exercise effective review over administration (coupled with its frustration over the limitations of traditional mechanisms).

In a direct sense, much of the growth that has occurred in oversight can be attributed to the increased importance of subcommittees in Congress. Whereas the House and Senate, respectively, contained about 85 and 110 subcommittees in the mid 1950s, each chamber had 140 subcommittees by the mid 1970s. This numerical growth was accompanied, in the House especially, by important rule changes that redistributed formal power over the conduct of debate and the disposition of legislation away from committee chairs to the subcommittee level. The effects of these changes were complemented by the reinvigoration of the Democratic Caucus as an instrument for holding committee chairs more accountable to members of their party at the committee level and in Congress as a whole.[40] Given the relationship between committees' decentralization and their proclivity to perform oversight noted earlier, one would expect these developments to have had a substantial impact on the amount of review performed by Congress.

The rise of subcommittee government and growing attention to oversight can be explained partly in terms of the imperative for Congress to accommodate the needs and aspirations of its members. In this regard, both developments have been instrumental to the growth of legislative careerism by allowing more legislators to become important "players" within given policy areas. As Dodd and Schott observe:

> The move to disperse power within committees by instituting subcommittee government derived in large part from the desire by members of Congress to increase the number of positions within Congress that could provide access to subsystem arenas. Members of Congress attempted to increase the number of power positions so that more members could possess reasonably direct access to a subsystem.[41]

If the growth of oversight has been driven by legislators' self-interest coupled with Congress's "organizational maintenance needs," however, it has also reflected important changes in the legislature's political environment. Some authorities have stressed Nixon's efforts to redirect legislative policy through the "administrative presidency" as a factor that precipitated Congress's increased attentiveness to program implementation in the 1970s. While there is undoubtedly some truth to this claim, presidential and congressional interest in and conflict over public administration are also tied to broader systemic developments. It is revealing in this regard that various indexes of oversight activity such as those cited above began to rise before the Nixon presidency and remained high through the Carter years and the 1980s.

The simple dynamic behind expanded oversight is that bureaucracy has come to affect more people in more ways as government's role has increased so dramatically. Yet the relationship between the growth of the administrative state and demands for oversight is more nearly exponential than linear. As discussed in earlier chapters, many of the programs in social regulation and other areas enacted in the 1960s and 1970s created new rights or otherwise legitimated and strengthened old interests. Because of this, coupled with the fiscal concerns that have accompanied changing economic conditions and the growth of federal programs, it has become more likely that implementation decisions in a given area will evoke opposition from other agencies and other congressional constituencies.[42] Like the increased use of statutorily imposed procedural constraints, and like the expansion of presidential efforts to influence public administration, the legislature's efforts to extend its direct influence over agencies can be explained as a function of demands generated by the increased conflict that has come to characterize bureaucratic politics.

The organizational and environmental determinants of increased legislative oversight are thus closely intertwined, and the direction of causality between them is difficult to specify. On the one hand, the decentralization of authority within Congress has probably helped to precipitate fundamental changes within the environment of legislative and administrative policy making. If multiple centers of institutional power provide the "access points" that are conducive to group politics, as pluralists have long argued,[43] then the existence of more policy entrepreneurs with independent bases of authority in Congress has likely contributed to the proliferation of organized interests and associated statutory entitlements so widely observed in the literature. Some theorists have made much of this relationship as evidence of the importance of institutional choice.

On the other hand, the rise of subcommittee government and the growing concern with public administration that has accompanied this structural change can be explained to a considerable extent as organizational efforts to adapt to exogenous social and economic forces. Developments such as continued urbanization, increased levels of income and education, and the evolution of the communications media have thus had independent effects in precipitating new interests in a wide variety of areas. The ability to monitor and influence the administrative process has, in turn, become an important way for Congress to sustain its traditional role of shaping policy as society's demands for government action in these areas have forced it to delegate increasing amounts of discretionary authority to the bureaucracy.

This latter interpretation is consistent with explanations that stress the motives of individual legislators. An increasingly strong linkage between oversight and reelection can thus be explained in terms of Congress's representative function of making policy in accordance with constituent demands. In a similar vein, if decentralization has been a determinant of increased oversight in an immediate sense, it can be viewed from a systemic perspective as an organizational response to the need for more oversight and for more policy specialization generally as Congress's legislative and administrative workload has become larger, more varied, and more complex. In this regard, it is important to bear in mind that the devolution of power to subcommittees largely occurred after the tremendous expansion of social programs during the Great Society and after the enactment of a majority of the social regulatory statutes whose implementation has precipitated so much conflict.

Comprehensiveness, Effectiveness, and Legislative Goals

Notwithstanding its growing interest in administration, whether the legislature is up to the task of effective oversight may be another matter. In evaluating congressional efforts to control bureaucracy, many contend that review is destined to remain reactive and sporadic, and therefore ineffectual under any reasonable augmentation of powers and resources.[44] A complementary point is that, like the institutional presidency discussed in chapter 5, the growth of Congress's organizational capabilities is subject to natural limits. The further expansion of committee personnel and other staff resources required for comprehensive oversight would be so great as to create a congressional bureaucracy as far removed as the executive branch from effective supervision by elected representatives.

A law of diminishing returns may also constrain the effectiveness of decentralization as an oversight strategy. Again, Dodd and Schott observe that, while subcommittee government has led to an increased emphasis on oversight, Congress's capacity for forceful review has become more attenuated as the devolution of authority from committees to subcommittees with overlapping responsibilities has further obfuscated lines of legislative–bureaucratic accountability and has thus undermined the prospects for rational supervision and direction of the bureaucracy. In addition, they feel that the rise of subcommittee government has strengthened the power of agencies in their relations with Congress. One reason for this is that agencies typically have ties to other agencies with similar or related policy concerns, as well as to executive departments, and that these networks of communication and political support often transcend subcommittee jurisdictions. At the same time, subcommittees tend to be more dependent on the bureaucrats they oversee than full committees, whose jurisdictions over a broader range of agencies and programs allow them more freedom in conducting critical review.[45]

Yet it remains to be asked why, if oversight is ineffective, it receives such a substantial portion of Congress's energy and resources. A good part of the answer to this question is that effectiveness is relative to one's choice of goals. Scholars' frequent equation of effective oversight with "continuous watchfulness" implicitly reflects the traditional view of administration as an instrumental process, together with the accompanying prescription that the purpose of legislative review should be to ensure that the bureaucracy serves as an accurate and efficient transmission belt in carrying out substantive statutory intent. Perhaps the most basic challenge to the conventional assessment of oversight from a theoretical standpoint is the argument that legislative review of administration is effective precisely because it is reactive. Two distinct hypotheses are possible in this regard, each of which reflects an alternative conception of delegated authority and its relationship to legislative interests. One assumes that reactive oversight is an effective way of ensuring compliance with the original political (rather than substantive) objectives behind statutes, while the other views it as a means by which Congress shapes policy implementation according to its changing preferences.

Rational choice theorists have played a leading role in reassessing the effectiveness of oversight. The first applications of this perspective to Congress by scholars such as Scher, Mayhew, and Fiorina argued that the electoral incentive dominating legislative behavior was conducive only to sporadic review that had relatively little impact on the general shape of administrative policy. Spurred perhaps by evidence of growing legislative interest in oversight, however, more recent analyses argue that self-interested legislators effectively monitor and control administrative policy for programmatic ends that extend beyond casework and the exploitation of occasional opportunities to generate favorable publicity. Committee members are motivated to do so because of their incentive to ensure that the constituent interests represented by members of winning legislative coalitions are in fact transformed into policy as programs are being implemented. In an early statement and test of this thesis, Barry Weingast and Mark Moran demonstrate a close correspondence between the Federal Trade Commission's policy and the changing composition and policy orientation of the House and Senate Commerce committees.[46]

As part of their argument, Weingast and Moran note that it is cost-effective for legislators to focus limited oversight resources on bureaucratic decisions that evoke opposition from affected groups rather than to attempt comprehensive review or a random sampling of administrative performance. The reason for this is that most agency actions do not adversely affect important constituents and are therefore of little consequence to legislators (who are assumed to be motivated primarily by the need to be reelected). Mathew McCubbins and Thomas Schwartz expand this thesis, likening Congress's preferred oversight strategy to a system of "fire alarms" (as opposed to "police patrols"). McCubbins and Schwartz argue that the reliability of fire alarms is enhanced by legislatively imposed administrative procedures that provide opportunities for constituents to monitor agency decisions and to object to actions that they find offensive. These include notice-and-comment rulemaking procedures, freedom of information requirements, and statutory provisions that create standing for certain types of interests to participate in agency policy making and challenge administration actions in the courts.[47]

As noted in chapter 3, the fire-alarm argument developed by McCubbins and Schwartz is based on an analogy to private-sector transactions known as principal–agent theory. Just as employers (principals) use contractual obligations to ensure that employees (agents) carry out their goals, so it is assumed that legislators use the rewards and sanctions at their disposal to control bureaucratic policy through oversight and other means. Although their original work is vague as to the exact purpose of such control, later articles by McCubbins, Roger Noll, and Weingast view reactive oversight as a technique for ensuring that the interests represented by original winning legislative coalitions are served as programs are implemented. Their argument is based on the assertion that the delegation of discretionary authority to bureaucracy results from Congress's lack of expertise or its inability to anticipate specific issues that will arise in administration. Legislators' fear under this scenario is that bureaucrats will pursue their own agendas to subvert the political goals reflected in the passage of statutes.[48]

The purpose of fire-alarm oversight is thus to correct deviations from the original agreement (usually at the committee or subcommittee level) on the distribution of costs and benefits to constituents. Again, Congress employs administrative procedures to this end as well, not only as strategically placed fire alarms, but as constitutional arrangements within the administrative process that "stack the deck" in favor of the interests represented by winning legislative coalitions. As it has evolved, then, the rational-choice perspective resembles traditional public administration theory in its assumption that oversight and other legislative controls on agencies bear an instrumental relationship to statutory goals. Where it differs is in its (somewhat vague) conception of those goals in political as opposed to substantive terms.

The current version of fire alarms is part of a thought-provoking effort to develop a common framework for understanding direct and indirect legislative controls over the administrative process, yet it suffers from two deficiencies as a general theory of oversight. The first is that, while past experiences may almost always help to focus the application of Congress's scarce investigative resources, a significant amount of legislative review is not precipitated directly by constituent complaints. Aberbach's extensive interviews with legislative staff indicate that committees generally employ a "mixed" approach that reflects their own internally generated initiatives as well as cues from the environment. He finds that special oversight committees and subcommittees are especially inclined to incorporate proactive strategies of review.[49] Foreman's study of Congress's role in the implementation of social regulation similarly finds that committee staff make independent efforts to keep abreast of what agencies are doing.[50]

A more severe problem with the principal–agent model of fire alarms is that it misrepresents the dynamics and policy significance of much of the reactive oversight that does take place. Although legislative oversight can and often does occur in response to the unmet expectations of intended program beneficiaries, the assumption that Congress's relationship with the bureaucracy is instrumental to the interests of original winning coalitions is problematic as a basis for a general empirical theory. One reason for this is simply that the administrative discretion conferred by statutes often reflects more than uncertainty about appropriate means–ends relationships. Indeed, it is a commonplace that delegation is often politically grounded in the sense that it results from Congress's inability to resolve conflicting social interests. To the extent that this obtains, it makes little sense to speak of pre-existing political objectives.

Nor would most observers take exception to the observation that legislative preferences frequently change to the extent that they do exist. Given this, oversight naturally tends to serve not the interests of the original winning coalition but whatever interests dominate Congress at the time administrative issues are brought to its attention. As discussed in chapter 2, it is in this sense that the use of administrative procedures for deck stacking (which is an expression of substantive group interests at the time a statute is enacted) is obviously inconsistent with the realities if not the theory of fire-alarm oversight. Both of these phenomena occur to some extent, but they do not constitute an internally consistent theory of legislative control. Indeed, the earlier analysis of Weingast and Moran, undertaken outside the constraints of principal–agent logic, suggests that oversight reflecting changing committee preferences had substantial effects on the direction taken by the FTC in preventing "unfair or deceptive practices"—a mandate notorious for the political discretion it confers.[51]

As this illustration suggests, however, effective fire-alarm oversight is not contingent on the conditions that Congress's political goals must be clearly defined in the legislative process and that they must remain stable over time. Politically significant groups and individuals tend to be well informed about government actions that might affect them. Further, it is almost axiomatic that, when these interests are dissatisfied with policy outcomes produced by one set of institutional actors, they will redirect their efforts at other parts of the political system. Fire alarms exist, then, regardless of whether they have been instituted as such. And if they are neither infallible nor the exclusive basis for oversight, they do enable legislators to identify and respond to a large share of agency policy decisions that are politically salient. In this sense, reactive oversight can serve Congress's electoral needs as well as any other programmatic concerns. The expansion of Congress's oversight efforts and institutional capabilities described above can be explained from this standpoint as a function of growing conflict within the administrative process and the accompanying demand for legislative intervention.

This latter formulation of reactive oversight may not be a revelation to those who have observed congressional–bureaucratic relations. Indeed, a number of scholars have remarked that the original fire-alarm thesis (in which the protective strategy of winning coalitions is not explicit) is a pretentious restatement of a fact that everyone already knew. Such criticisms miss the point in an important respect, however, for although the legislature's tendency to intervene reactively was well known and often reported, this observation was seldom used to make the case that oversight was effective in terms of Congress's institutional needs. Again, comprehensive review designed to ensure the attainment of substantive statutory objectives has been and continues to be the most prevalent evaluative standard. Ogul notes that legislators themselves often express regrets that their involvement with bureaucracy tends to be haphazard and reactive, and that systematic and comprehensive review is seldom attained, even within isolated programs.[52] As discussed in chapter 8, the issue of effectiveness ultimately cannot be divorced from normative questions regarding the institutional responsibilities and prerogatives of Congress and the bureaucracy.

Conclusion

This chapter has described the institutional resources and techniques used to conduct legislative oversight. It has also discussed the expansion of oversight that has occurred in recent decades. Congress's increased interest in the administrative process is probably attributable to a number of interrelated factors. To some extent, it has been a natural reaction to heightened efforts by recent presidents to control the bureaucracy. It has also resulted from the rise of subcommittee government and from the changes in institutional incentives that have accompanied this development. In a broad sense, however, these explanations for the expansion of congressional oversight are tied to the growth of bureaucracy and to increased conflict in many areas of program implementation. This dynamic is closely related to the issue of effectiveness and how it should be defined. Although vigorous program review is destined to be sporadic, oversight does provide an effective if limited means by which Congress can monitor and influence those areas of administration that are most salient to it.

It remains to be asked what Congress's expanded efforts to control the administrative process have meant in terms of policy. In contrast to the substantial body of literature dealing with the "input" side of legislative oversight, there has been little systematic research assessing the nature and extent of its effects. At a more basic level, the literature devotes little explicit attention to the process values by which Congress's role in the administrative process should be judged. Yet this is not to say that scholars have been bashful in offering conclusions about the policy implications of oversight (often in passing as appendages to empirical analyses). A majority have held that, to the extent it occurs, active involvement by legislators in public administration is a source of irrationality, parochialism, or inequity in program implementation. As such, oversight is sometimes judged to undermine the objectives that inform Congress's enactment of statutes.

Chapter 7 examines the implications of legislative oversight for public policy. In so doing, it necessarily blends a consideration of the values to which bureaucracy should be accountable with a consideration of the institutional characteristics that link Congress to the administrative process. Indictments of Congress's administrative role derive from plausible inferences based on the organizational features and constituency principles that determine legislative behavior. These assessments can also be supported with anecdotal evidence. At the same time, they oversimplify and misrepresent Congress's relationship to the bureaucracy in important respects.

Notes

1. Joseph P. Harris, *Congressional Control of Administration* (Washington, D.C.: Brookings Institution, 1964), p. 9.

2. Lawrence C. Dodd and Richard L. Schott, *Congress and the Administrative State* (New York: John Wiley and Sons, 1979), chap. 5.

3. Morris S. Ogul, *Congress Oversees the Bureaucracy* (Pittsburgh: University of Pittsburgh Press, 1976), p. 11.

4. Christopher H. Foreman, Jr., *Signals from the Hill: Congressional Oversight and the Challenge of Social Regulation* (New Haven: Yale University Press, 1988), p. 13.

5. Morris P. Fiorina, *Congress: Keystone of the Washington Establishment* (New Haven: Yale University Press, 1977).

6. John R. Johannes, *To Serve the People: Congress and Constituency Service* (Lincoln: University of Nebraska Press, 1984), p. 63.

7. Ibid.

8. For a very thorough and insightful discussion of committee staff, their backgrounds, and their orientations toward oversight, see Joel D. Aberbach, *Keeping a Watchful Eye: The Politics of Congressional Oversight* (Washington, D.C.: Brookings Institution, 1990).

9. Frederick Mosher, *A Tale of Two Agencies: A Comparative Analysis of the General Accounting Office and the Office of Management and Budget* (Baton Rouge: Louisiana State University Press, 1984).

10. Aberbach, *Keeping a Watchful Eye.*

11. Ogul, *Congress Oversees the Bureaucracy.*

12. Aberbach, *Keeping a Watchful Eye.*

13. See, for example, Joseph Cooper and Ann Cooper, "The Legislative Veto and the Constitution," *George Washington Law Review* 30 (1962): 467–517.

14. *Immigration and Naturalization Service v. Chadha,* 462 U.S. 919 (1983). Chapter 8 of this book contains a fairly extensive discussion of this and related cases.

15. James L. Sundquist, *The Decline and Resurgence of Congress* (Washington, D.C.: Brookings Institution, 1981). Sundquist observes that even many members of Congress share this view of the limitations of oversight.

16. Ibid.; See also Dodd and Schott, *Congress and the Administrative State;* Ogul, *Congress Oversees the Bureaucracy.*

17. Terry M. Moe, "An Assessment of the Positive Theory of 'Congressional Dominance,' " *Legislative Studies Quarterly* 12 (November 1987): 475–520.

18. Dodd and Schott, *Congress and the Administrative State,* p. 173.

19. Ogul, *Congress Oversees the Bureaucracy;* John F. Bibby, "Committee Characteristics and Congressional Oversight of Administration," *Midwest Journal of Political Science* 10 (February 1966): 78–98; Seymour Scher, "Congressional Committee Members as Independent Agency Overseers," *American Political Science Review* 54 (December 1960): 911–20; Scher, "Conditions for Legislative Control," *Journal of Politics* 25 (August 1963): 526–51.

20. David R. Mayhew, *The Electoral Connection* (New Haven: Yale University Press, 1974), pp. 121–22.

21. For an early development of this argument, see Scher, "Conditions for Legislative Control."

22. Fiorina, *Congress: Keystone of the Washington Establishment.*

23. Johannes, *To Serve the People.*

24. Scher, "Conditions for Legislative Control."

25. Aberbach, *Keeping a Watchful Eye;* Theodore Lowi, "Four Systems of Policy, Politics, and Choice," *Public Administration Review* 32 (July/August 1972): 298–310.

26. Bibby, "Committee Characteristics and Congressional Oversight"; Aberbach, *Keeping a Watchful Eye.*

27. Aberbach, *Keeping a Watchful Eye.*

28. Foreman, *Signals from the Hill,* p. 12.

29. Aberbach, *Keeping a Watchful Eye,* p. 35.

30. For example, Wilbur Mills was widely reputed to be one of the most knowledgeable men in Washington on tax policy when he chaired the House Ways and Means Committee. Sam Nunn currently enjoys similar respect for his knowledge of defense policy.

31. For a fairly recent discussion of political executives' limited experience, see Patricia W. Ingraham, "Building Bridges or Burning Them? The President, the Appointees, and the Bureaucracy," *Public Administration Review* 47 (September/October 1987): 425–35.

32. Aberbach, *Keeping a Watchful Eye.*

33. Mark Nadel, for instance, in the GAO, and Louis Fisher and Morton Rosenburg in the CRS.

34. Congressional Research Service Index (Washington, D.C.: Congressional Research Service, 1993).

35. Aberbach, *Keeping a Watchful Eye.*

36. Ibid., p. 44.

37. Harry S. Havens, "What We Were, Who We Are," *The GAO Journal* 8 (Winter/Spring 1990): 33–42.

38. Joseph Cooper and Patricia A. Hurley, "The Legislative Veto: A Policy Analysis," *Congress and the Presidency* 10 (Spring 1983): p. 5. According to Cooper and Hurley, 14.5 percent of all veto provisions enacted between 1970 and 1976 pertained to rulemaking, and 7.5 percent pertained to administrative plans and proposals. This latter figure also represented a substantial increase over previous decades.

39. Arthur Maass, *Congress and the Common Good* (New York: Basic Books, 1983).

40. Many have discussed the rise of subcommittee government. The changes in question were precipitated by liberal Democrats, sometimes acting in concert with Republicans, who had become frustrated by the successful efforts of entrenched Democratic committee chairs from the South to slow down and block civil rights and welfare legislation. See, for example, Lawrence C. Dodd and Bruce I. Oppenheimer, "The

House in Transition," in *Congress Reconsidered,* ed. Dodd and Oppenheimer (New York: Praeger Publishers, 1977).

41. Dodd and Schott, *Congress and the Administrative State,* p. 173.

42. Hugh Heclo, "Issue Networks and the Executive Establishment," in *The New American Political System,* ed. Anthony King (Washington, D.C.: American Enterprise Institute, 1978). For a qualification of this argument, see Daniel McCool, "Subgovernments as Determinants of Political Viability," *Political Science Quarterly* 105 (Summer 1990): 269–74; McCool, "Subgovernments and the Impact of Policy Fragmentation and Accommodation," *Policy Studies Review* 8 (winter 1989): 264–87.

43. See, for example, David B. Trues, *The Governmental Process* (New York: Knopf, 1951); Norton E. Long, "Power and Administration," *Public Administration Review* 9 (Autumn 1949): 257–64.

44. See, for example, Sundquist, *The Decline and Resurgence of Congress.*

45. Dodd and Schott, *Congress and the Administrative State,* pp. 170–84.

46. Barry R. Weingast and Mark J. Moran, "Bureaucratic Discretion or Congressional Control? Regulatory Policymaking by the Federal Trade Commission," *Journal of Political Economy* 91 (1983): 765–800.

47. Mathew D. McCubbins and Thomas Schwartz, "Congressional Oversight Overlooked: Police Patrols Versus Fire Alarms," *American Journal of Political Science* 28 (February 1984): 165–79.

48. Mathew McCubbins, Roger Noll, and Barry Weingast, "Administrative Procedures as Instruments of Political Control," *Journal of Law, Economics, and Organization* 3 (Fall 1987): 243–77; "Structure and Process, Politics and Policy: Administrative Arrangements and the Political Control of Agencies," *Virginia Law Review* 75 (1989): 431–82.

49. Aberbach, *Keeping a Watchful Eye.*

50. Foreman, *Signals from the Hill.*

51. Weingast and Moran, "Bureaucratic Discretion or Congressional Control?"

52. Ogul, *Congress Oversees the Bureaucracy.*

7

The Politics of Congressional Influence

Congressional oversight has not enjoyed enthusiastic support as a means of controlling bureaucratic discretion because of two assessments of its impact. As discussed in the previous chapter, many scholars have argued that Congress lacks both the resources and the incentive to conduct sound program review. These accounts typically lament Congress's inability or unwillingness to perform oversight more effectively. At the same time, legislative involvement in administration has also been greeted with sharp criticism where it has occurred (and often by the same authorities). Negative assessments of the effects of oversight are not embraced universally, nor do they ultimately constitute a theoretically coherent whole. Like the generally positive or at least hopeful view of the administrative presidency, however, they are sufficiently popular that they provide a logical starting point for institutional policy analysis.

Negative assessments of legislative oversight are grounded in its defining characteristics. The fact that much oversight is reactive arguably provides a mechanism by which special interests can subvert programs designed to promote the public interest. The fact that most oversight is done by committees and subcommittees similarly is alleged to allow unrepresentative elements of the whole to warp agency policy according to their perspectives and the narrow interests of their constituents. In both of these regards, oversight is frequently viewed, not as a potential solution to the problem of bureaucratic fragmentation, but as a force that amplifies pathological tendencies widely thought to beset public administration.

Although these charges contain some merit, they also constitute an oversimplified and inconsistent description of the political dynamics of oversight. To say that much legislative review is reactive is not to say that it is usually dominated by the interests of program opponents. The standards of statutory intent and the public interest that often provide the reference points for criticizing legislative review as a tool of special interests tend to be highly subjective. Beyond this, an obvious fact that characterizations of reactive intervention frequently ignore is that the coincidence of legislative and oversight responsibilities in subject-matter committees ensures that the latter process is often a vehicle for program advocacy.

Perhaps the most important misrepresentation of oversight is the claim that the decentralization of responsibility among committees and subcommittees is a source of policy fragmentation that contributes to "subgovernment politics." Assessments of oversight frequently exaggerate the degree to which committees are unrepresentative of the whole. To the extent that parochialism is a committee characteristic, moreover, assessments of oversight also frequently misrepresent the kinds of unrepresentative policy preferences that motivate legislative review. Beyond these observations, single committees or subcommittees are rarely able to dominate congressional review and influence over agencies in controversial policy areas. Although it frequently contributes to uncertainty and delay in policy implementation, the decentralized structure of oversight often facilitates rather than inhibits the expression of a broad range of relevant interests in administrative policy making. Indeed, the need for Congress to accommodate more diverse interests has been closely associated with both the growth of oversight and the devolution of power to subcommittees that has occurred since the 1960s.

Legislative Oversight and Prescriptive Theory

As noted in chapter 6, the term *legislative oversight* is used in a number of ways. As a prescriptive definition, however, Congress's legitimate role in the administrative process was traditionally conceived of in terms of passive supervision, with legislation viewed as the only appropriate means of addressing administrative deficiencies that oversight might uncover. The confinement of oversight to a monitoring role precluded legislative interference with the performance of executive functions, and thus fit neatly with a formal conception of separation of powers. Aside from its grounding in what seemed to be straightforward constitutional principles, this restricted conception of oversight was judged to be desirable for the practical reason that it precluded "meddling" by politically motivated amateurs in "details of administration" best left to the applied technical and managerial expertise of bureaucratic professionals. In both these respects, the traditional model could be justified on the premise that politics and administration were distinct and institutionally separable activities. As such, it fit reasonably well with the traditional conceptions of administrative law and executive management discussed in earlier chapters. All three were consistent with the popular view of administration as an instrumental process.

Advocates of the traditional model never bothered to explain why, if congressional interference in administration was informed by politics and technical ineptitude, the process of monitoring bureaucracy and enacting corrective legislation would be informed by objectivity and managerial competence. The truth behind this inconsistency is probably that, although expectations for the quality of passive oversight were not very high, few were prepared to deny that Congress had a legitimate right to inquire about the accuracy and efficiency of program implementation as an extension of its legislative prerogative. At the same time, concern over the effects of legislative meddling for other, less-defensible ends was mitigated by the perception that Congress would not become involved in policy implementation very often. Indeed, congressional oversight was a matter of relatively little interest to scholars from either a prescriptive or a descriptive standpoint until the 1960s.

Enthusiasm for legislative involvement in administration has remained low. This has been due in part to the continued belief that Congress lacks both the will and the capacity to supervise bureaucracy effectively. As an extension of the latter assertion, some have argued that, regardless of its intent and notwithstanding any conceivable augmentation of resources, Congress's mistaken assumption that it can subsequently monitor and constrain the exercise of administrative discretion through oversight provides an unfortunate excuse for neglecting its primary constitutional responsibility to control implementation through sound, specific statutes. This is especially apt to be true for contentious issues, where there are strong incentives to defer hard political choices. Ironically in this regard, the net effect of oversight may be to undermine rather than to strengthen the legislature's influence over policy outcomes. Law professor Antonin Scalia felt that this was true, even under the more systematic and forceful oversight made possible by legislative vetoes. Testifying before Congress, he noted that:

> Another deleterious effect ... will be an increase of that very practice of congressional delegation of vague and standardless rulemaking authority which has placed us in our current predicament. That is to say, the delusion that it will be able to control agencies through the legislative veto will render Congress all the more ready to continue to expand the transfer of basic policy decisions to the agencies.[1]

Many of the same people who characterize oversight as an ineffectual means of controlling the bureaucracy also criticize Congress for excessive interference in agency decision making.[2] Thus, a traditional theme that

remains popular is that micromanagement by uninformed legislators undermines effective and efficient policy implementation. As James Sundquist
argues, for example:

> The suggestion that Congress is carrying oversight too far has been heard
> from both ends of Pennsylvania Avenue. As early as 1974, just when the
> Bolling committee was recommending more attention to oversight, Senator
> George Aiken . . . protested that Congress was overreacting to its loss of
> status and its clash with Nixon. "Congress wants to tell the executive how to
> run things, down to small details," he said. "We just can't do it." And execu-
> tive branch officials were complaining about congressional "micromanage-
> ment" of programs as exemplified by an 862-page report of the House
> Agriculture Committee advising the Department of Agriculture how to ad-
> minister the food stamp program, or a 446-page House Appropriations report
> "littered with demands for information on scores of subjects" from the De-
> partment of Defense.[3]

To an increasing extent, however, indictments of congressional intervention in agency affairs have focused on its political motives and policy
effects rather than on its futility or its subversion of administrative values.
The unwholesomeness of legislative influence allegedly derives from the
very features of oversight that contribute to its viability as a way of promoting congressional interests in the administrative process. Thus, the reactive
nature of much congressional review and its reliance on the committee
system arguably serve parochial interests at the expense of broader national
concerns. Given these underlying dynamics, oversight is frequently portrayed as an activity that reinforces rather than confronts the inherent fragmentation of a large and uncoordinated administrative state. In an effort to
disassociate it from Congress's constitutional policy-making responsibilities, oversight is also frequently portrayed as an activity that reflects political influences that differ from those that inform the legislative process.

In these respects, many authorities have expressed concern, not that congressional intervention in agency affairs is driven by politics, per se, but
that it is driven by undesirable political forces. The popularity of such
arguments helps to explain the ironic fact that, of the three branches, Congress has benefited the least from prescriptive theories of institutional control based on the premise that administration is an extension of the
legislative process. Many have endorsed the administrative presidency as a
source of focused political accountability that naturally serves to rationalize
public administration pursuant to broad national interests. Although expectations for due process are more mixed, many have also defended administrative procedures and judicial review as means of promoting balanced
interest representation in what is essentially a political process. In contrast,

the minority who have defended legislative intervention in agency decision making have rarely developed their case in explicitly political terms. Rather, they have tended to portray congressional influence in defensive and vaguely instrumental terms as a means of ensuring that agencies faithfully comply with "legislative intent."[4]

Characterizations of legislative involvement in administration as a venue for special interests and as a source of policy fragmentation are not universal, but they are sufficiently popular and plausible that they provide a logical basis for examining the effects of oversight. The equation of reactive and committee-based oversight with parochialism would not have such widespread currency if it did not reflect important elements of the truth. Yet if it is still at a comparatively early stage of erosion, this assessment of oversight's policy effects has begun to encounter challenges analogous to those that have undermined the conventional view of its limited significance. Several recent studies as well as key developments in the institutional structure of congressional review suggest that criticisms of oversight on policy grounds are based on important oversimplifications and misconceptions about legislative behavior. Beyond this, assessments are also frequently based on questionable assumptions about the normative criteria that should be used to evaluate the effects of legislative influence in the administrative process. A balanced assessment of Congress's involvement in administration suggests a reality that is much more complex than the facile generalizations offered by its critics.

Oversight and Special Interests

Perhaps the most common characterization of legislative oversight is that it provides an additional round of opportunities for groups to alter, delay, or block the administration of programs they do not like. Terry Moe observes in this vein that institutional arrangements facilitating congressional review and influence over bureaucracy, such as temporary authorizations and the legislative veto, can typically be explained as concessions to those who lost at the time statutory programs were enacted. As he argues, "currently advantaged" groups:

> oppose formal provisions that enhance political oversight and involvement. The legislative veto, for example, is bad [for them] because it gives opponents a direct mechanism for reversing agency decisions. Sunset provisions . . . are also dangerous because they give opponents opportunities to overturn the group's legislative achievements.[5]

By the same token, Moe notes that opponents of programs "want structures that allow politicians to get at the agency. . . . They are enthusiastic support-ers of legislative veto and reauthorization provisions."[6]

Continuing in this spirit, critics of Congress's role in the administrative process often add that reactive intervention at the behest of program oppo-nents inhibits the effective implementation of statutes intended to benefit the general public and other poorly represented interests. Not all groups can sustain their influence throughout the policy-making process according to this argument; it is usually only intense and well-organized interests that are able to monitor agency performance and lobby Congress to intervene on their behalf. Thus, while Congress may enact programs to serve diffuse or otherwise weak interests, either as the result of short-term pressures or its own sense of what is equitable, it cannot be expected to sustain its support for such efforts over time. As Robert Gilmour observes regarding the ef-fects of the legislative veto, "the public most likely to take timely notice of an unfavorable regulatory proposal, to understand its implications, and ar-ticulate its objections with enough clarity and force to be intelligible to Congress are those interests that can support on-going lobbyist activities and maintain continuous contacts with legislators and their staffs."[7]

Numerous anecdotes have been cited in support of this thesis. Indeed, considerable publicity has surrounded some of these episodes, such as the efforts of several senators to influence savings-and-loan regulators on be-half of well-heeled clients. By itself, the history of the Federal Trade Com-mission in recent decades provides an imposing list of cases in which Congress has intervened at the urging of various industries to deflect rules or adjudicative actions intended to protect consumers. Doctors, cigarette manufacturers, and insurance companies are among the groups that have been spared by the enactment of special amendments to the FTC's enabling legislation. An action that was especially offensive to many was Congress's veto of a regulation requiring used car dealers to disclose the known defects of vehicles to potential buyers.

Similar illustrations can be drawn from across a broad spectrum of regu-latory and nonregulatory programs.[8] Reacting to an intensive letter-writing campaign by manufacturers of nutritional supplements, Congress recently passed legislation curbing the Food and Drug Administration's efforts to proscribe misleading claims that such products could cure cancer, arthritis, and a variety of other afflictions. In an influential set of case studies assess-ing the legislative veto, Bruff and Gellhorn found pressure by special inter-ests to be a common motivation for congressional review and influence in administrative areas ranging from energy regulation to the distribution of student loans.[9]

At the same time, the political dynamics of legislative oversight are not nearly as uniform as many imply. To say that fire alarms are central to Congress's political stakes in the administrative process is not to deny that much oversight is driven by instrumental criteria. As discussed in chapter 6, Joel Aberbach's work suggests that a good deal of committee-based review is proactive and is concerned with the efficiency and effectiveness of program implementation. The generalization that oversight systematically subverts program goals at the behest of special interests is also inconsistent with the output of congressional staff organizations, such as the scores of GAO reports that are issued each year. Research of this kind is not completely dispassionate in the sense that it often reflects Congress's broad interest in maintaining its control over administration. This institutional bias is especially evident in studies dealing with legislative–executive conflict over the control of administration. Yet the vast majority of such efforts are clearly devoted to managerial concerns, often focusing on what most would consider to be quite mundane details of administration.

A fact that is often not given its due in assessments of oversight is that Congress frequently has a strong incentive to ensure that its statutory aims are carried out accurately and efficiently. One need not embrace the principal–agent model as a general theory to note that legislators are often motivated by electoral self-interest to ensure that programs serve the constituents they were intended to benefit.[10] Fashionable cynicism notwithstanding, moreover, legislators and their staffs are often sincerely committed to the programs they create. In these respects, reactive oversight and oversight designed to see if programs work are not mutually exclusive. Political coalitions are not static, and a changing balance of forces may induce Congress to influence agency performance at the behest of those who stand to lose in the administrative process—especially if they are politically powerful. Yet legislative review and influence over administration is just as often energized by complaints arising from program beneficiaries.[11]

Both proactive and reactive oversight can thus serve to protect the integrity of program implementation against subversive influences from outside the legislature. If charges of agency clientelism and capture have been exaggerated, they also contain some truth. An extensive body of scholarship over the past fifty years suggests that bureaucrats can become attuned to narrow group interests. Many have also attested to the tendency of agency officials to become wedded to existing policies and to resist initiatives that would require organizational change. In a related vein, administrative decision making can be dominated by technical orientations that preclude the consideration of important decisional criteria. Based on studies of several executive-branch agencies, Thomas McGarity observes that "techno-bureaucratic rationality is inclined to narrow options early in the decisionmaking process and to be unreceptive to new options that come to light later on. The very definition of the problem may eliminate options."[12]

In these regards, one can easily cite instances in which legislative review has confronted bureaucratic or executive actions based on what would normally be classified as special or otherwise narrow concerns. One such case was when Congress forced the Department of Housing and Urban Development to abandon a rule defining eligibility criteria for housing assistance payments for new construction and other purposes. It did so after mayors and other local officials testified during oversight hearings that, while the policy would benefit some builders, it would place a substantial relocation burden on tenants—many of whom were poor or senior citizens.[13] In a recent work, Cathy Johnson finds that the legislature frequently uses its oversight power to counter the influence of entrenched interests and other sources of parochialism within the administrative process. As she concludes from an extensive longitudinal study of Congress's relations with four agencies:

> ... the legislators on the committees responded to interest-group demands, yet the congressional committees were not merely a point of access for vested interests. Several conflicts [between Congress and the bureaucracy] developed as legislators reacted to the complaints of interest groups adversely affected by a bureau's decision or inaction, but new interest groups were able to challenge the dominant interests. Environmental arguments were raised effectively in the 1960s before the full-fledged environmental movement began, and in the 1970s Interior Committee members responded to the need for greater environmental protection.[14]

As discussed in chapter 5, moreover, the president's attempts to influence administration are naturally motivated by executive interests rather than by a concern with legislative intent. Here, too, Congress has often exercised its oversight prerogatives in order to promote the faithful implementation of its programs. For example, congressional support was instrumental in successful efforts by career bureaucrats and environmentalists to resist the Reagan administration's attempts to stifle the enforcement of environmental regulations.[15] Congress also reacted against efforts to curtail health, safety, and environmental rulemaking at the behest of business groups under the provisions of E.O. 12291 and E.O. 12498. Precipitated in part by information gathered in oversight hearings by the Senate Government Operations Committee, the threat to eliminate funding for the Office of Information and Regulatory Affairs secured a concession that future communications between OMB and agencies would be made a part of the public record.

Again, this is not to say that legislative oversight is always motivated by broad national goals or by a desire to ensure the effective implementation of statutory intent. As with efforts to assess the president's role in public administration, however, these evaluative criteria often present more fundamental ambiguities in and of themselves. An obvious point that characterizations of oversight frequently ignore is that statutes may further special or parochial interests. Beyond the examples of subsidies, public works, loans, and other distributive policies, some would argue that so-called social programs to protect the environment, consumer rights, health and safety, and other concerns often promote the personal interests and patronizing impulses of elites as opposed to the broad public welfare they purport to represent. This interpretation is often supported by the assertion (again, by elites on behalf of society) that such policies impose economic costs that go well beyond those who profit directly from regulated enterprises.

The fact that this latter claim may have some merit raises a further issue regarding the conceptual underpinnings of many assessments of oversight. No matter how much we might like to cloak our policy preferences in terms of general or public interests, the distinction between these and special interests is often highly subjective. Who is to say, for example, that legislative pressure on the Office of Education to broaden its eligibility criteria for student loans to include segments of the middle class served special or general interests?[16] Or who is to say that Congress's inducement of the FTC to abandon its Children's Advertising Rule served special or general interests? To one observer, this latter action may represent a concession to industry pressure at the expense of broad consumer interests; to another it may represent a decision to protect Americans from an agency that would assume the role of a "national nanny" by usurping dietary decisions best left to parents.[17] Indeed, Ernest Gellhorn, who is among the strongest critics of congressional intervention in agency affairs as a tool of special interests, cites approvingly the legislature's curtailment of this and other FTC initiatives as justly deserved "wages of zealotry."[18]

A related and equally important conceptual limitation of many descriptions of oversight's effects is that, however one chooses to describe the interests that might precipitate congressional intervention, contentions that it either undermines or supports legislative intent are the product of wishful thinking as often as not. Legislative intent is frequently invoked to support competing claims on scarce resources in the administrative process or otherwise to legitimate assessments of agency actions. Much like claims to divine favor, however, assertions as to its meaning are often articles of faith drawn from vague or conflicting principles. As noted in chapter 6, it is true in some cases that Congress has a reasonably clear notion of who should benefit from legislation, but may delegate substantive discretion to an agency because it lacks appropriate technical knowledge or because it wishes to allow for administrative flexibility in coping with policy needs that change over time or from one location to the next. But it is probably just as often the case that delegated authority results from Congress's inability to resolve conflicting interests.

The Implications of Decentralized Review

In addition to the biases attributed to special interests, an equally prevalent characterization of the effects of oversight focuses on its institutional structure. Because review is usually conducted by committees and subcommittees, many claim that influence over administration tends to be informed by policy concerns that are different from those that motivate the full House and Senate. Oversight is frequently portrayed as an element of subgovernment politics in this regard. As discussed in earlier chapters, this is a widely criticized phenomenon in which alliances of committees or subcommittees, agencies, and clientele groups allegedly control individual policy areas in their own interests—typically at the expense of overarching national concerns or at least at the expense of coherent policy. According to many accounts, the legislature's contribution to this systemic fragmentation through oversight (and legislation) has been reinforced by the further devolution of institutional authority from committees to subcommittees that occurred during the 1960s and 1970s.[19]

The hypothesis that the structure of oversight is a source of parochialism and fragmentation is based in part on the assertion that committees and subcommittees are unrepresentative of the whole. Representation is a complex concept that can be defined according to any number of subjective criteria. It is true by definition, however, that committees are unrepresentative in the sense that their individual responsibilities for substantive policy comprise only a fraction of Congress's total workload. Subcommittees obviously have responsibilities that are still more narrowly defined. The parochialism associated with the legislature's functional differentiation is arguably reinforced by the fact that committee and subcommittee membership is determined in large measure by the personal preferences of legislators themselves. According to the classical conception of subgovernment politics, representatives and senators seek committee assignments that enable them to serve their constituents and other interests that can contribute to their reelection. The following indictment of the legislative veto as an institution that amplifies the effects of "interest group liberalism" clearly reflects this general assessment of the motives that inform oversight:

> The veto . . . exacerbates the problem of divisive interest group pressure on modern government. . . . This kind of politics erodes the center, rules by fiefdoms, and evades the national will. . . . The veto fragments rather than unifies power in Congress. It points toward making every member of Congress, and the interests for whom he speaks, a de facto co-administrator of the agency programs within his committee's assigned area of oversight.[20]

Of course, committees and subcommittees play central roles in almost everything that Congress does. Thus, the assertion that congressional review and influence distort policy in the direction of unrepresentative interests is often based on the further claim that committees are able to accomplish policy ends through oversight that they are unable to accomplish through the legislative process. Although few studies rigorously develop the premises of this argument, an assumption that seems implicit in much of the literature is that, unlike the drafting of legislation, where the final product must be approved by congressional majorities, the oversight process permits committees to (re)shape policy through informal communications with administrators that fall outside the purview of the full Congress and the president. It follows that, to the extent committees are unrepresentative, oversight distorts policy toward their goals and away from the preferences of the whole. Discussing the parochial bias of committee-based oversight in environmental protection and a variety of other areas, for example, Jeremy Rabkin notes that

> getting such deals through the entire Congress and past the president, especially in general legislation, is difficult. That explains why Congress had postponed the reconsideration of Clean Air Act Amendments (supposed to be enacted in 1982) for almost a decade. Enter micromanagement.[21]

In an enthusiastic version of this thesis, some argue that committee members secure legislation that is ostensibly designed to serve broad, national goals, knowing that they can subsequently use their influence over administrators to divert policy toward narrow interests as it is carried out.[22] Given that statutory intent is often difficult to discern, an alternative possibility is that oversight permits committees to pursue objectives that may be consistent with vague legislation, but that congressional majorities would not endorse.

The equation of committee-based oversight with narrow policy goals is grounded in plausible assumptions about the dynamics of congressional behavior that approach the status of conventional wisdom. If it contains some truth, however, it must also be tempered in important respects. Characterizations of oversight frequently misrepresent the parochial influences brought to bear through review by committees or subcommittees. They also frequently ignore the fact that individual committees or subcommittees are seldom able to dominate the oversight process in important policy areas. In the latter regard, the decentralization of power within Congress has facilitated rather than inhibited the accommodation of conflicting interests as the environment of policy implementation has become more contentious in recent decades.

Committee Motives and Program Goals

Assessments of oversight often exaggerate the narrowness and the homogeneity of committees' policy orientations. In fact, many committees have responsibilities for reviewing diverse and conflicting programs. A single committee in the Senate oversees environmental protection and public works, for example, presumably because policy decisions in these two areas are functionally and politically interdependent. In the most thorough descriptive study on the subject, Steven Smith and Christopher Deering consider only eight of twenty-one House committees and four of sixteen Senate committees to be low in "jurisdictional fragmentation."[23]

In a related vein, much evidence suggests that the "overrepresentation hypothesis" linking committee and subcommittee membership to the interests of subgoverment clientele is in need of substantial qualification.[24] As a rough assessment, so-called constituency committees tend to be overrepresentative of states or districts that stand to benefit from the implementation of the substantive policies they oversee. Thus, for instance, the Agriculture committees in the House and Senate have disproportionate numbers of legislators from southern and midwestern states, and the committees on Energy and Natural Resources, and Interior and Insular Affairs are heavily overrepresentative of the West.

For the majority of committees, however, the literature suggests that legislators are attracted, not primarily to secure electoral benefits through constituent service, but to cultivate power within Congress or to make a policy contribution in an area that they feel to be worthwhile or stimulating.[25] The latter types of committees may well differ from their parent chambers in terms of their members' priorities. They also sometimes have close ties to external groups, such as environmentalists or education organizations, that may promote their members' electoral goals. They do not, however, tend to be overrepresentative of the kinds of economically based interests normally associated with cozy triangles.

Johnson's study attests to the fact that committee oversight is used, not just to transmit constituent pressures and promote members' electoral goals, but to further legislators' policy interests as well:

Legislators realize that a subcommittee or committee can be a forum to
explore an intriguing issue, an opportunity to cover new ground on a difficult
problem, or the chance to hold forth on an ideological position. These legislative entrepreneurs are able to place an issue on an agenda because they
often hold committee leadership positions.[26]

Johnson finds that such motives are even important in describing the relationship between the Interior Committees and the Bureau of Reclamation—
a policy area traditionally assumed to be dominated by the politics of pork
barreling.

To the extent that committees and subcommittees do represent narrow
interests, moreover, it remains to be asked why and in what respects they
should be motivated to change the course of administration. There would
seem to be little need for this under the classic characterization of pork-barrel
politics, where policy benefits are concentrated and costs are diffused, and
where committee members and bureaucrats share the largess that comes
from pleasing clientele groups. Yet again, it is here that the composition of
committees and subcommittees is most likely to be biased in terms of
economic interests. Under this scenario, committee-based review might be
expected to contribute to the distortion of policy only in that it lends encouragement for what bureaucrats are inclined to do on their own.

One might also ask why committees that are unrepresentative in terms of
their members' policy interests (rather than constituency ties) should be inclined to change the direction of programs as they are being carried out. If
senators are attracted to the Labor Committee because of their commitment to
health policy, for example, one would not expect them to distort the implementation of health-related programs. As mentioned above, the 1980s witnessed just the opposite, as congressional policy advocates used their influence
in the administrative process to counter efforts by the Reagan administration to
curtail various kinds of social regulation and other programs. To the extent that
policy bias might have resulted from oversight in such instances, it involved
the emphasis of what most would consider to be primary program objectives at
the expense of competing goals, such as an industry's economic health. This
logic is consistent with Aberbach's finding that, in the minds of top committee
staff, program advocacy is the defining focus for much of the oversight conducted by subject-matter committees and subcommittees.[27]

The Institutional Structure of Oversight:
Parochialism Versus Pluralism

An even more important limitation of arguments equating the institutional
structure of oversight with parochialism is that, regardless of their inten-

tions, individual committees and subcommittees seldom enjoy complete control over their areas of concern. Whatever leverage they have in their dealings with agencies is usually dependent on formal sanctions that must be exercised by Congress as a whole. Agencies that might resist attempts at informal influence by unrepresentative elements of Congress are bolstered in their resolve by the fact that corrective action normally requires new legislation. With a few exceptions, even institutional shortcuts for shaping agency policy through oversight, such as the legislative veto and its kin, usually demand the approval of one or both houses. Nor are committees unmindful of the sentiments of their parent chambers. These are given weight by a variety of formal and informal mechanisms that Congress can (and occasionally does) use to check committees or subcommittees that abuse their oversight (or legislative) prerogatives by straying too far from the preferences of its majority or its leadership. Such measures range from rejection of committees' proposals, to replacement of their members, to ridicule or loss of prestige.

To observe that there are limits on committee autonomy is not to say that oversight normally expresses goals formulated by the full chambers of Congress. Congress as a whole has neither the time nor the inclination to seek consensus or majority approval on all but a few issues of administrative policy. Although review of agency programs occasionally reflects the initiative and authority of congressional leaders, generally in the form of scrutiny by ad hoc select committees, standing committees and subcommittees are usually the key players in the oversight process.[28] At the same time, individual committees and subcommittees are prevented from having their way at the expense of other legislators and the constituents they represent on significant, controversial issues. The ability of committees to monitor and influence administrative behavior unilaterally is thus generally contingent on a lack of interest from other elements of Congress. This condition sometimes exists, to be sure, but not in policy areas that are salient to the legislature as a whole or to other committees or subcommittees. Indeed, it has become less common in direct proportion to the expansion of oversight itself.

A number of observations about the structure and dynamics of oversight, both within and among legislative committees, are relevant here. Subcommittees have more homogeneous and parochial concerns than full committees, of course, and much has been made of the autonomy they enjoy in performing both legislative and oversight functions. Yet although it varies substantially (subcommittees tend to be much less independent in the Senate than in the House, and their autonomy varies considerably within the latter chamber as well), the independence of subcommittees from full committees and their chairpersons is never absolute.

Conversely, to the considerable extent that oversight authority is decentralized in Congress, it is a structural feature that often results in conflict as opposed to logrolling. This is attributable in part to overlapping jurisdictions and interests among committee subunits organized along substantive lines. In addition, the majority of House committees include "oversight and investigation" subcommittees with jurisdiction-wide responsibilities for program review. Although the existence of these special units does not preclude review by other subcommittees in most cases, it does prevent the latter from monopolizing oversight in their areas of specialization. Intracommittee differences may be settled through negotiation among the principals or by appeal to the leadership at the full-committee level.[29] Alternatively, the competing perspectives of different subcommittees may be transmitted to agencies for them to resolve.[30]

Competition and conflict concerning the direction of administrative programs frequently spills over committee (and chamber) boundaries as well. As discussed earlier, standing subject-matter committees in the House and Senate share oversight responsibilities for the agencies under their jurisdictions with the Government Operations/Affairs committees and with Appropriations subcommittees. Although this arrangement theoretically reflects a division of labor among legislative, procedural, and fiscal concerns, review by all three types of committees is frequently driven by substantive policy issues. This overlap naturally increases the likelihood that oversight will be conducted by a sample of legislators with individual perspectives and constituency ties that more closely reflect the distribution of such characteristics within Congress as a whole. The orientations brought to bear by different types of committees may also vary in more systematic and predictable ways. Thus, government operations committees and appropriations subcommittees tend to be more critical of agencies and less concerned with program advocacy than authorization committees.[31]

Finally, review by multiple authorization committees is also an important source of redundancy and conflict in oversight. In general, the only limitation on the ability of a committee or subcommittee to oversee an agency is that it demonstrate some linkage between the program in question and its legislative responsibilities. This is usually not difficult. For example, twenty-nine committees and fifty-five subcommittees in the House and Senate review the implementation of various defense programs.[32] As another illustration, Richard Lazarus observes that at least eleven standing committees in the House and nine in the Senate (and up to one hundred of their subcommittees) have taken an active interest in the affairs of EPA. As he notes:

because EPA's jurisdiction has affected so many interest groups, the demand for the agency's oversight has grown exponentially among the committees and subcommittees in Congress, as has the number of oversight hearings regarding the agency's work. Most committees can find a nexus between their assigned jurisdiction and an aspect of the EPA's work. . . . Those committees utilize the full panoply of oversight tools.[33]

Although EPA and Defense are extreme cases, administrative program review by multiple legislative committees is the norm in conflictual policy areas.[34] In this regard, the argument that oversight is generally motivated by concerns that are more parochial than those that inform legislation seems especially suspect. At the committee level, the oversight process is clearly more amenable to the expression of competing interests than the legislative process. Whereas committees encounter few constraints in investigating agency programs, bill referrals must generally be secured through the House and Senate parliamentarians, who base their decisions on considerations of formal committee jurisdiction and precedent. Indeed, a recent study by Bryan Jones, Frank Baumgartner, and Jeffrey Talbert argues that the review of agency programs is a primary means by which committees insert themselves into new areas, breaking up stable subgovernment relationships that center around the legislative process. Oversight hearings may thus be used to create precedent for the purpose of redefining committee jurisdictions (and redirecting the assignment of future legislation).[35]

Decentralized and Overlapping Review in Systemic Perspective

Agency review by multiple committees and subcommittees has become increasingly prevalent during the second half of this century. For example, Dodd and Schott observe that the average number of committees overseeing individual "departmental areas" in the executive branch increased dramatically in both the House and Senate between 1947 and 1970.[36] More recent data collected on oversight in four policy areas between 1945 and 1985 strongly suggest that this trend has persisted. Thus, the numbers of oversight bodies active in smoking, nuclear power, pesticides, and drug abuse all increased and remained high during the 1970s and the first half of the 1980s.[37] A sample of oversight of specific agencies reveals the same trend. The number of different House and Senate subcommittees holding hearings on the Forest Service, the Office/Department of Education, the Federal Trade Commission, and the Agricultural Marketing Service increased from a total of 35 in 1962, to 56 in 1977, to 61 in 1992.[38]

The growth of overlapping and often conflicting program review by different elements of Congress has naturally accompanied the decentralization of legislative power and the expansion of oversight that occurred during the 1960s and 1970s. This package of developments can be largely appreciated as a closely interrelated set of institutional responses to fundamental changes in Congress's political environment. Thus, while the rise of subcommittee government may be consistent with the career needs of rankand-file legislators to reign within their own fiefdoms, as many have argued, it also reflects the need for the legislature to accommodate a broader and more interdependent array of interests. As subgovernments, if one wishes to call them that, have become more numerous, their boundaries have either become more permeable or more inclined to overlap with one another.

Developments in the formal structure of oversight are consistent with this interpretation of how its representative character has evolved. Although the use of legislative vetoes grew dramatically during the 1970s, for example, a sharply diminished proportion of the new mechanisms gave individual committees or sets of committees in the House and Senate direct legal authority over administrative outcomes. Thus, whereas 11.8 percent of all legislative vetoes enacted during the 1940s gave individual committees the authority to disapprove agency actions, only 2.5 percent of the mechanisms created between 1970 and 1977 were so structured. Similarly, the percentage of "affirmative" vetoes that required dual, joint, or multicommittee approval for agency proposals to become effective (as opposed to approval by one or both Houses) dropped from high levels of 23.5 percent and 21.2 percent in the 1940s and 1950s to 6.8 percent in the 1970–1977 period.[39] These observations are difficult to reconcile with the argument that the primary institutional dynamic behind oversight is to accommodate particularistic policy concerns through logrolling.

Structural developments within committees reinforce this interpretation of the relationship between oversight and Congress's institutional needs. The fact that most committee jurisdictions have become moderately or highly fragmented is at least partly a function of the imperative to reconcile competing demands in both the oversight and legislative processes as policy-making environments have become more complex. The argument equating the expansion of legislative review with the politics of mutual noninterference is further belied by the increased popularity of oversight subcommittees whose jurisdictions duplicate those of other subcommittees organized according to policy area (and, again, that tend to apply a more critical perspective in performing oversight). The percentage of House committees employing such bodies increased from 18.8 percent (three out of sixteen substantively defined standing committees) in the first session of the

88th Congress (1963)[40] to 58.8 percent (ten out of seventeen) in the first session of the 103d Congress (1993).[41] One can easily cite instances in which oversight and investigation subcommittees have been used by enterprising committee members to intrude upon their colleagues' domains.[42]

Again, therefore, to recognize that oversight is decentralized and that the participants in the process often apply narrow policy orientations is not to say that it is always fragmented and parochial in a political sense. The review of agency programs by multiple committees and subcommittees with differing perspectives and constituencies is not without its costs. Administrative efficiency and effectiveness can suffer as agencies are pulled in different directions.[43] Lazarus observes that the EPA has had to endure a constant crossfire between legislative proponents and opponents of aggressive regulation, each with their own bases of committee or subcommittee power. Agency morale and initiative have declined as a result. In the latter regard, Lazarus argues that the political uncertainty arising from multiple lines of accountability has left administrators reluctant to try innovative approaches to regulatory problems.[44] Similarly, Foreman notes that, in social regulation, oversight is not guided by any consensus as to what programs should achieve:

> What Congress lacks . . . is a stable and shared understanding of what, and how much, regulators ought to do. Given the nature of the tasks assigned to them, regulators will often stand accused of either doing too much or doing too little—frequently on the same issue and in the same breath. Disagreement among attentive interests within Congress . . . is inevitable.[45]

In any case, these are very different problems than the ones traditionally attributed to oversight. Again, the fact that individual legislators or committees represent parochial interests of varying kinds does not mean that Congress is parochial. Indeed, the conventional critique of oversight as an element of subgovernment politics (and as an often-neglected function) is contradicted by growing sympathy in some quarters for a more rational division of committee responsibilities (such as that established by the Legislative Reorganization Act of 1946) that would curtail overlapping review.[46] The problem posed by such a reform is that, while it may contribute to the coherence and efficiency of program implementation in a narrow sense, it is implicitly based on the assumption that clear statutory goals exist and that individual committees can be trusted to ensure the attainment of such objectives. It also seems to ignore the fact that, insofar as they are established in the legislative process, program goals often conflict with one another.

Congressional involvement may, in fact, expedite politically sound decision making where administration is legislative in nature. There is little reason to believe that mutual partisan adjustment within Congress will yield coherent policy across administrative issues. This is even more true with regard to the legislature than it is with regard to the pluralistic balancing of interests in executive oversight discussed in chapter 5. In any case, Congress is more adept at fashioning compromises than the bureaucracy, which is often dominated by technical and legalistic rather than political orientations, and the conflicting perspectives that legislators bring to bear often facilitate decisions that accommodate the various legitimate interests at stake in administration. Not surprisingly, the limited evidence that is available on this subject indicates that intercommittee communication and negotiation naturally accompany overlapping review of agency programs.[47] Congress's superiority to the bureaucracy in accommodating interests is reinforced by the contrary effects of administrative due process. As discussed in chapter 3, formal adversary proceedings and decision making on the record often severely inhibit the ability of agencies to engage in the kind of political give and take that is appropriate for decision making pursuant to open-ended mandates.

Conclusion

Perhaps the most accurate generalization about legislative oversight is that it defies neat characterization along any of the dimensions commonly used to evaluate its systemic role. Effectiveness is relative to one's expectations, of course, but oversight is clearly not the inconsequential activity it is sometimes claimed to be. Although it is not and cannot be a comprehensive or systematic management tool, it allows legislators substantial opportunities to review and influence policy implementation in those areas that are especially relevant in terms of their interests and the interests of important constituents. At the same time, oversight is far from being the instrument of "legislative dominance" portrayed in some revisionist accounts by rational choice theorists. If it is an important means of pursuing legislative goals on salient issues, it is also constrained by a lack of resources and by the fact that Congress must share administrative power with the other constitutional branches.

A reasonable description of the strategies that shape Congress's oversight agenda must be similarly mixed. Reactive oversight is undoubtedly an important technique that allows the legislature to allocate limited time, staff resources, and political capital to those areas of administration that are most important to it. Nevertheless, strong evidence suggests that Congress also conducts a good deal of proactive review. A further point is that these two types of oversight are not as discrete as they might initially seem to be. As mentioned, legislators and their staffs naturally devote much of the finite resources available for proactive review to areas where they expect to find problems. The identification of such areas is, in turn, partly a reaction to past controversies and other experiences. Conversely, reactive oversight is often conditioned by pre-existing standard operating procedures and informal networks of communication that predispose legislators to monitor some parts of their political environments more closely than others.

Most important, perhaps, the politics and the policy effects of oversight are not consistent with simple descriptions offered by many scholars. This is not to deny that legislative review is frequently motivated by parochial forces, as its critics contend. Congress is responsive to changing political conditions, and sometimes it intervenes in the administrative process at the behest of intense interests that stand to lose as the result of accurate, aggressive program implementation. The committee system can also be a source of parochialism. Congress must decentralize and specialize in order to cope with numerous and complex policy demands. If differentiation of responsibilities produces "suboptimization" in most organizations, this effect is amplified in Congress by the fact that legislators are accountable more to their constituents than to the leadership of the House and Senate.

Yet these characterizations easily can be overdone. Legislative review and influence over administration frequently come to the aid of program beneficiaries. Moreover, if the incentives and institutional arrangements that define Congress's relationship to the bureaucracy sometimes allow individuals or subunits to influence administrative policy pursuant to their own narrow perspectives, oversight also frequently entails a very different process of program review by legislators representing varied interests. In fact, the character of much oversight can be appreciated in terms of a fundamental but little-noted inconsistency that mars many assessments of its effects. To the extent committees or subcommittees do engage in the kind of program advocacy predicted by the standard conception of iron triangles, the effect is to counteract critical oversight by program opponents. Each of these forces exists to some extent and each may often be described as a reflection of narrow interests, but in combination they do not suggest that Congress as an institution applies a narrow orientation in monitoring and influencing the implementation of its programs. In much the same way, it is curious that scholars who clearly recognize the conflict that often accompanies involvement by multiple committees and subcommittees nevertheless characterize oversight as having "parochial" effects. Thus, for example, James Sundquist goes on at length about the diverse and conflicting orientations brought to bear on administrators through oversight (and the inefficiency this causes), but also observes that "whether parochialism is a dominant or secondary characteristic of Congress, it is one of its inbred and ineradicable traits."[48]

All of this is essentially to say that the political dynamics of legislative review usually reflect the political environment surrounding public administration. While oversight may be dominated by the narrow and homogeneous interests of subgovernment actors in areas of low salience, it facilitates rather than inhibits the expression of diverse policy concerns where they exist. A point that bears reemphasis here is that committees and subcommittees have more freedom in conducting oversight than in securing bill referrals. It is a fact of life that legislative involvement in administration is often a function of group influence, and that some legitimate interests fare better than others under the system. In a broad sense, however, the expansion of Congress's role in the administrative process since the 1960s has both resulted from and nourished a more inclusive dialog in many policy areas. The decentralization of power that has provided the institutional authority and the resources for this development is associated more closely with pluralism than with feudalism.

The down side of pluralism probably deserves more attention than it has received in this discussion. The accommodation of interests is time-consuming and wasteful of administrative resources. Moreover, there is little guarantee that it will produce coherent policy from one decision to the next. Yet the counter to these arguments is arguably the central premise of our system of constitutional democracy: that efficiency should remain subordinate to representative goals. As discussed in the following chapter, to criticize congressional oversight because of its representative nature is to raise fundamental issues about the desirability of legislative power. Indictments of oversight that focus on the conflict and the messiness it produces in the administrative process implicitly represent a return to the traditional prescription that controverted issues be resolved in the legislative process. If one assumes that Congress must delegate political discretion to the bureaucracy, then to attack oversight is to attack its prerogative as the central policy-making institution in American government.

Notes

1. Testimony of Antonin Scalia, *Regulatory Reform and Congressional Review of Agency Rules: Hearings before a Subcommittee of the House Rules Committee,* 96th Cong., 1st sess. (1979), p. 541.

2. See, for example, Lawrence C. Dodd and Richard L. Schott, *Congress and the Administrative State* (New York: John Wiley and Sons, 1979); James L. Sundquist, *The Decline and Resurgence of Congress* (Washington, D.C.: Brookings Institution, 1981).

3. Sundquist, *The Decline and Resurgence of Congress,* p. 333.

4. This is true even of sophisticated and thorough scholars, such as Louis Fisher. See, for example, Louis Fisher, *The Politics of Shared Power* (Washington, D.C.: Congressional Quarterly Press, 1981).

5. Terry M. Moe, "The Politics of Structural Choice: Toward a Theory of Public Bureaucracy," in *Organization Theory: From Chester Barnard to the Present and Beyond,* ed. Oliver E. Williamson (New York: Oxford University Press, 1990), p. 137.

6. Ibid., p. 138.

7. Robert S. Gilmour, "The Legislative Veto: Shifting the Balance of Administrative Control," *Journal of Policy Analysis and Management* 2 (1982): p. 18.

8. Rabkin, "Micromanaging Administrative Agencies," *The Public Interest* (Summer 1990): 116–30.

9. Harold Bruff and Ernest Gellhorn, "Congressional Control of Administrative Regulation: A Study of Legislative Vetoes," *Harvard Law Review* 90 (May 1977): 1369–1440.

10. See Mathew McCubbins, Roger Noll, and Barry Weingast, "Administrative Procedures as Instruments of Political Control," *Journal of Law, Economics, and Organization* 3 (fall 1987).

11. See, for example, Cathy M. Johnson, *The Dynamics of Conflict Between Bureaucrats and Legislators* (Armonk, N.Y.: M.E. Sharpe, 1992).

12. Thomas O. McGarity, *Reinventing Rationality: The Role of Regulatory Analysis in the Federal Bureaucracy* (Cambridge: Cambridge University Press, 1991).

13. *Disapproving and Invalidating HUD Regulations Concerning Section B: Hearings Before the Subcommittee on Housing and Community Development of the House Committee on Banking, Finance, and Urban Affairs,* 96th Cong., 1st sess. (1979).

14. Johnson, *The Dynamics of Conflict,* p. 152.

15. Christopher H. Foreman, Jr., *Signals from the Hill: Congressional Oversight and the Challenge of Social Regulation* (New Haven: Yale University Press, 1988).

16. Bruff and Gellhorn make this argument in "Congressional Control of Administrative Regulation."

17. The proposed regulation would have limited advertising for foods with a high sugar content during children's programs.

18. Ernest Gellhorn, "The FTC Under Siege," *Regulation Magazine* (January/February 1980): 33–40.

19. Dodd and Schott, *Congress and the Administrative State.*

20. Testimony of Robert G. Dixon, *Regulatory Reform and Congressional Review of Agency Rules: Hearings Before a Subcommittee of the House Rules Committee,* 96th Cong., 1st sess. (1979), p. 549. See also Dixon, "The Congressional Veto and Separation of Powers: The Executive on a Leash?" *North Carolina Law Review* 56 (1978): 423–94.

21. Rabkin, "Micromanaging the Administrative Agencies," p. 123.

22. William P. Schaefer and James Thurber, "The Legislative Veto and the Policy Subsystems" (paper presented at the annual meeting of the Southern Political Science Association, Atlanta, November 1980).

23. Steven S. Smith and Christopher J. Deering, *Committees in Congress,* 2d ed. (Washington, D.C.: Congressional Quarterly Press, 1990).

24. For what is still perhaps the most comprehensive discussion of this literature, see Keith Hamm, "Patterns of Influence Among Committees, Agencies, and Interest Groups," *Legislative Studies Quarterly* 8 (August 1983): 379–426.

25. Smith and Deering, *Committees in Congress.* For the classic development of this thesis, see Richard Fenno, *Congressmen in Committees* (Boston: Little, Brown, 1973).

26. Johnson, *The Dynamics of Conflict,* p. 150.

27. Aberbach, *Keeping a Watchful Eye.*

28. Morris S. Ogul and Bert A. Rockman, "Overseeing Oversight: New Departures and Old Problems," *Legislative Studies Quarterly* 15 (February 1990): 5–24.

29. Smith and Deering, *Committees in Congress,* p. 161.

30. For a thorough corroboration of this, see Sundquist, *The Decline and Resurgence of Congress,* pp. 332–40.

31. Joel D. Aberbach, *Keeping a Watchful Eye: The Politics of Congressional Oversight* (Washington, D.C.: Brookings Institution, 1990); Dodd and Schott, *Congress and the Administrative State.*

33. Richard J. Lazarus, "The Neglected Question of Congressional Oversight of EPA: *Quis Custodiet Ipsos Custodes* (Who Shall Watch the Watchers Themselves)?" *Law and Contemporary Problems* 54 (1991): p. 211.

34. Sundquist, *The Decline and Resurgence of Congress,* pp. 332–40.

35. Bryan Jones, Frank Baumgartner, and Jeffrey Talbert, "The Destruction of Issue Monopolies in Congress," *American Political Science Review* 87 (September 1993): 657–71.

36. Dodd and Schott, *Congress and the Administrative State,* figure 5–2, p. 178. In the case of the House, it rose from about 2.2 to 3, and in the case of the Senate, it rose from about 2.7 to 4.5.

37. Jeffrey Talbert, Frank Baumgartner, and Bryan Jones, "The Legislative Importance of Non-Legislative Hearings" (paper presented at the 1994 annual meeting of the Midwest Political Science Association, Chicago, April 14–16, 1994).

38. Data collected from the Congressional Research Service index.

39. Joseph Cooper and Patricia A. Hurley, "The Legislative Veto: A Policy Analysis," *Congress and the Presidency* 10 (Spring 1983): p. 9.

40. *Congressional Quarterly Almanac* 1963. The Appropriations, Governmental Operations, House Administration, and Rules committees were not included in the total count.

41. *Congressional Yellow Book, Spring 1993* (New York: Monitor Publishing) XIX, no. 1. The Appropriations, Budget, Government Operations, House Administration, Rules, and Standards of Official Conduct committees were excluded from the total count.

42. John Dingell has done this on the House Energy and Commerce Committee, for example. See Smith and Deering, *Committees in Congress,* p. 135.

43. Sundquist, *The Decline and Resurgence of Congress,* pp. 332–40.

44. Lazarus, "The Neglected Question."

45. Foreman, *Signals from the Hill,* p. 7.

46. The Joint Committee on the Organization of Congress is currently working on ways to eliminate jurisdictional overlaps, although most feel that the extent of any such reform will be limited.

47. Talbert, Baumgartner, and Jones, "The Legislative Importance of Non-Legislative Hearings."

48. Sundquist, *The Decline and Resurgence of Congress,* pp. 332–40, quotation p. 451. For similar inconsistencies, see Dodd and Schott, *Congress and the Administrative State.*

8

Constitutional Issues

The preceding chapters have provided an overview of administrative due process, executive management, and legislative oversight. They have described the powers and resources that provide the bases for these three types of control over administration. They have also sought to examine the effectiveness and the effects of each in light of the expectations we hold for it. As with institutional policy analysis generally, normative and empirical issues are closely intertwined in this regard. Normative theory is based in part on empirical premises, but it also inevitably informs the questions we ask regarding institutional effects.

This concluding chapter focuses in a more direct and comprehensive way on the normative issues surrounding administration and its place in our constitutional system. As such, it provides a basis for reviewing important points about theory and practice made earlier. In addition, it entails a broader consideration of how different kinds of control relate to one another, and of the implications posed by the growth of bureaucracy for the roles of the three constitutional branches of government. A point that underlies much of the following discussion is that administration is hardly monolithic, and that different constraints and process values are appropriate for different kinds of agency action. To say this, however, is not to contend that the issues surrounding the control of bureaucracy can be neatly resolved by dividing policy implementation into executive, legislative, and judicial components. In large measure, the solutions to issues of accountability in public administration involve striking an acceptable balance among competing controls.

Many theorists have been slow to recognize this fact. In confronting institutional tension within the administrative process, judges and legal scholars have relied on two contradictory models, each of which is designed to parcel out authority discretely. The courts have assumed that administration consists of functionally distinct activities that correspond with the three powers of government in dealing with the proper role of due process. In contrast, judges have usually assumed that all administration is executive in dealing with the conflict between presidential and congressional influence over the bureaucracy. Neither of these approaches yields realistic solutions. Although the emphasis placed on different kinds of constraints should arguably vary according to the type of agency action in question, a sharing of influence is both inevitable and desirable in most areas of administration. This is an especially sound constitutional prescription with regard to presidential and congressional controls over agency policy making.

The Constitutional Context

All of the issues treated in this book are directly or indirectly related to prescriptive theory. An important addition to what has been said so far is that due process and executive and legislative oversight cannot be considered in isolation from one another, for each tends to vitiate the effectiveness of the other two. This observation underscores the fact that institutional constraints on public administration must ultimately be evaluated on the basis of constitutional principles. At the same time, however, the Constitution provides little specific guidance on the matter of bureaucratic accountability. The ambiguous relationship between public administration and the prerogatives of the president, Congress, and the courts has become the most important general source of tension in American government today.

As discussed in previous chapters, issues of administrative control were once less complex and could be addressed by applying a widely embraced doctrine that viewed administration as an instrumental process. The fact that agencies were given the authority to adjudicate obviously made it difficult to reconcile all administration with a neat separation of powers, but the anxiety this caused was mitigated by the assumption that procedural constraints and judicial review would ensure accurate and consistent decisions in cases where substantial individual interests were at stake. With the exception of adjudication (especially regulatory adjudication), adherence to the politics/administration dichotomy meant that the residual of what bureaucracy did could be neatly designated as an executive function. This, in turn, yielded straightforward (if somewhat naive) prescriptions for presidential and congressional oversight. The purpose of the former was to promote economy and efficiency through active control of the bureaucracy, both in the implementation of individual programs and in the coordination of the federal government as a whole. The purpose of the latter was passively to evaluate administrative performance according to the standard of legislative intent.

As also discussed, however, the traditional model has broken down as its empirical premise has become increasingly untenable. Doctrinal conflict and inconsistency have reigned in the wake of its demise. The realization that agencies make policy choices has led some to assert that public administration should be informed by political values. One manifestation of this premise is the prescription that bureaucratic policy makers themselves should be drawn from a representative cross-section of society in order to ensure that their personal predilections accurately reflect the values and interests of those affected by their decisions.[1] Given the inherent limitations of "representative bureaucracy,"[2] a more practical recommendation is that agencies should be encouraged or required to respond to relevant interests. This is manifested in procedural requirements imposed by Congress and the courts designed to facilitate participation in agency decision making. The view of administration as a political process also underlies arguments that the proper goal of presidential and congressional oversight is to transmit constituency preferences.

Yet these positions have by no means supplanted traditional prescriptions of objectivity and technical competence. Many still advocate administrative due process and policy analysis as means of promoting instrumental rationality. In addition, many still portray executive and legislative oversight as means of ensuring that statutory goals are carried out effectively and efficiently. Confusion concerning the proper nature of administration and the values that should guide it is evident, not only among academic theorists, but in conflicting statutory constraints on agency decision making and in muddled efforts by the courts to reconcile administration with the three core functions of government.

This ambivalence is partly attributable to the need to legitimate bureaucracy within the framework of separation of powers. We cannot live without delegated authority given the imperative for government to confront society's problems effectively, but we cannot live comfortably with it either—at least in an abstract, intellectual sense.[3] Policy making by non-elected officials is not only difficult to reconcile with the tenets of representative democracy; it also has unsettling implications for the balance of power among the executive, legislative, and judicial branches. The latter fact explains many disingenuous attempts to justify executive and legislative oversight in instrumental terms rather than as means of creating policy.

In part, however, our failure to develop a coherent normative doctrine of control over the bureaucracy reflects rather than ignores the nature of what agencies do. A colleague's picturesque characterization of the politics/administration dichotomy as the "undead" illustrates a common (though certainly not universal) feeling among sophisticates that neutral competence has persisted well beyond its appropriateness as an ideal for public administration. It is true that, if administration was never purely an instrumental process, the political content of policy implementation has expanded dramatically with the continued delegation of authority since the New Deal. This trend has been amplified over the past two-and-a-half decades by the increased use of rulemaking. Relatedly, the normative dimensions of bureaucratic discretion have become more visible and more problematic as agencies' political environments have become more contentious. Yet these observations do not imply that the instrumental dimensions of administration that once rendered the traditional model an appealing general theory have vanished. To say that the criteria of objective and efficient administration are not absolutely controlling is not to say that they are no longer relevant.

Tension between political and technical values necessarily pervades normative analysis of institutional controls over the bureaucracy. Although the task of reconciling these conflicting visions is insuperable to some extent, prescriptive issues can be addressed more intelligently by considering different types of agency decisions. Without any pretense to an exhaustive typology or to a rigorous treatment of the subject, a recognition of two basic dimensions of administrative action is useful for understanding and evaluating institutional controls.[4] One can be labeled "applicability." As discussed in chapter 2, some decisions apply policy in individual cases, whereas others create general standards. A second has to do with the underlying criterion for administrative action—whether it is based on technical, instrumental determinations pursuant to statutory intent, or whether it rests on political judgments.

The four types of decisions defined in the cells of table 8.1 are not all necessarily desirable, nor do they exist independently of institutional choices. Indeed, these two facts were central to the examination of internal constraints in chapter 2. A basic goal of formal due process has been to ensure that application decisions are instrumental rather than political in nature, for example, just as devices such as hybrid rulemaking procedures and cost–benefit analysis have been used to ensure that decisions of general applicability are arrived at objectively. To the extent that administration must be political, moreover, the use of rulemaking has been advocated in part as a means of ensuring that such discretion is removed from application decisions.

In any case, administration is far from being monolithic in a functional sense. The fact that different agency actions have different effects and rest on different types of premises naturally suggests that decision making should reflect different process values. For example, cells 1–3 in table 8.1

Table 8.1

Dimensions of Administrative Action

	Basis for agency decision	
	Instrumental criteria	Political criteria
Applicability of agency decision		
Particular	Due process (1)	Patronage/incrementalism (4)
General	Policy analysis (2)	Interest representation (3)

correspond closely with the familiar "trichotomy" of bureaucratic actions and associated decision-making paradigms that provides the basis for Christopher Edley's thoughtful analysis of the courts' role in public administration. In cell 1, "adjudicatory fairness" demands that the qualities of neutrality, reason, and consistency should guide administration. Cell 2, which Edley labels the paradigm of "science or expertise," calls for "rationality, objectivity, deductive reasoning, and specialized knowledge." Finally, the "politics" paradigm of cell 3 implies that processes of "interest accommodation or balancing" should guide decision making.[5] These observations obviously have important prescriptive implications for institutional control of the bureaucracy. Thus, as Edley also argues, the paradigms of adjudicatory fairness, science, and politics respectively correspond with popular, idealized conceptions of the judicial, executive, and legislative functions.

Yet issues of institutional control are not nearly as straightforward and easy to resolve as these simple analogies suggest. One reason for this is that real-world agency actions seldom fit neatly into functional categories. The dimensions in table 8.1 represent aspects or ideal types of administration rather than discrete characteristics that define actual decisions. There is often a fuzzy line between applying and making policy. Application decisions often have broad policy implications, just as abstract policy statements may affect only a small number of individuals. In addition, most administrative decisions must inevitably be based on some combination of objective and subjective considerations. This is especially true of agency policy making.

Even to the extent that it is possible to place agency decisions into discrete categories, many would balk at relying on such distinctions to prescribe hegemonic control by any branch of government in its respective sphere. As Edley also notes, for example, the courts and the executive/bureaucracy only imperfectly promote the values with which they are ideally linked. A fact that Edley curiously ignores in this latter regard is that the association of the president and other officials at the top levels of the executive with the value of scientific expertise is especially tenuous. Conversely, to the extent that they do provide the bases for decision making, each of the three models of Edley's trichotomy have potential liabilities that accompany their strengths. If adjudicatory due process can promote neutrality and fairness, it can also be a source of rigidity. If science can promote objectivity and rigor, it can also be a source of parochialism. If politics can promote the accommodation of relevant interests, it can also result in patronage, excessive partisanship, and tyrannical majoritarianism. It is because of the possibility that the three branches will fail to promote their associated values as well as because of the undesirable things that can occur when they do that we have a system of shared as well as separated powers.

These brief observations provide a context for considering two general and logically sequential issues. The first concerns the respective roles of objectivity and politics in administration. This question is, in turn, closely related to but not conterminous with an evaluation of administrative procedures and judicial review. Although such constraints have frequently been justified in terms of interest representation, the controlling assumption of due process—that agency decisions are demonstrably correct or incorrect—precludes the consideration and accommodation of interests, as such. Given that the effectiveness of due process is contingent on the absence of extraneous influences, its desirability as a means of promoting empirically rigorous and accurate decision making also determines the degree to which Congress and the president should be excluded from the administrative process.

Insofar as administration is political rather than instrumental, a second and even more fundamental question concerns the kinds of political representation that should come to bear in policy implementation. This, in turn, is largely a matter of defining the respective roles that the two political branches of government should play in controlling the bureaucracy. Attempts by the president and Congress to influence what agencies do have been a natural extension of their competing efforts to determine the allocation of scarce resources. The definition of executive and legislative roles within the administrative process thus has profound implications, not only for the kinds of institutional motives and constituency influences that inform policy, but for the fundamental balance of policy-making power in American government.

The judiciary is largely responsible for resolving these issues. To the extent that the courts have addressed the first, they have relied on a functional analysis that focuses on the specific character of agency action as a basis for determining the limits of due process in constraining administration. Adjudicatory decisions having substantial effects on individual interests have been singled out for more demanding procedures and more exacting judicial scrutiny, while policy actions have been accorded more deference. This is not to deny the strong presence of administrative procedures and judicial review in the latter area. As discussed in chapter 2, due process imposed by Congress and the courts has become more popular as a means of holding agencies accountable for their policy decisions. Although it has been ignored in many instances and applied inconsistently in others, however, the distinction between adjudication and policy making has remained the common basis for attempts by judges and scholars to define the proper balance between due process and the often-conflicting values of bureaucratic expertise and presidential and congressional influence.

Separation-of-powers analysis based on functional distinctions among agency actions is much less useful in determining the kind of politically based control that should hold sway over administration. The explanation for this is obvious, for the logical extension of such reasoning to issues involving presidential and congressional influence is to proscribe the former in areas where administrative decision making resembles legislation. Few would endorse this solution, especially given the popularity of the idea that a strong administrative presidency is necessary as a means of rationalizing bureaucracy and holding it accountable to the public interest. In confronting this dilemma, the courts have usually relied on a premise that is sharply at odds with the reasoning they have applied in resolving conflict between politics and the goals of due process. Thus, they have most often employed a formal (rather than functional) separation-of-powers analysis that simply defines all administration as being executive. Aside from its facile assumptions about the nature of administration and its inconsistency with the functional logic used to define the limits of due process, this approach has the untenable effect of precluding direct legislative influence over bureaucracy.

Due Process and the Role of Objectivity in Administration

Although each of the three types of control discussed in this book has been justified as a means of ensuring the faithful execution of statutory intent, administrative due process is the only one whose central goal is to promote objectivity. As such, its desirability, as well as the desirability of competing influences from Congress or the president that might undermine its effects, is logically contingent on the degree to which administration can and should be an instrumental process. It is further contingent on the ability of procedural constraints and judicial review to promote accurate, rational decision making where that goal is theoretically attainable. In these regards, many have argued that due process is most appropriate as a constraint on the adjudication of individual cases and least appropriate as a guide for the kinds of political and technical judgments involved in agency policy making. Within the bounds of this general prescription, however, there remain a variety of specific issues regarding the role of administrative procedures and the courts that defy neat resolution.

Due Process, Adjudication, and Individual Interests

The role of procedural constraints and judicial review under the traditional model of administrative law was to ensure that policy would be applied accurately and consistently in individual cases. At least in regulatory areas, formal adversary proceedings and the requirement that decisions be based on evidence in a record would serve these ends by forcing agencies to defend the factual and legal premises behind their actions in a rigorous way. Administrative due process was thus based on the assumption that application decisions could be justified in instrumental terms. Given this, it was designed to guard against incompetence as well as to preclude arbitrariness, capriciousness, and bias in relations between bureaucracy and the individual. The traditional model's premise that adjudication should be dispassionate and accurate remains compelling. Its appeal explains the extension of procedural constraints and more demanding judicial review to many areas of nonregulatory administration as the expansion of public authority has led to a fundamental reconceptualization of the kinds of individual interests that should be protected from unjust agency action.

At the same time, it is important not to exaggerate the degree to which due process really does ensure accuracy and fairness in adjudication. Competing needs for administrative effectiveness and efficiency have prevented its extension to all types of application decisions, and have resulted in relatively lax constraints in many areas of adjudication where interests protected by the Fifth and Fourteenth amendments have been found to exist. To the extent that such constraints do apply, moreover, administrative due process is far from perfect as a means of ensuring the accurate application of policy to individuals. It hardly precludes the interjection of bias in agency decision making. In the case of the Social Security Administration, for example, wide variation exists in the decision-making patterns of the seven hundred administrative law judges charged with hearing individual appeals. Thus, the average rate of reversal of benefit denials is about 50 percent, but 10 percent of the ALJs reverse 75 percent of the decisions appealed to them and 10 percent of the judges reverse only 25 percent.[6] The effects of due process are further circumscribed by the fact that some individuals lack the resources needed to assert their interests through agency hearings and judicial review. Its natural limits are partly defined by the fact that, the more demanding the constraints, the less accessible they are to many types of interests.

The administrative costs and limited effectiveness of due process have led some to advocate alternative controls that are more effective in promoting fairness and accuracy in adjudication. As Emmette Redford notes, for example, "democratic morality" in "micropolitics" can also be furthered through internal standards that define objective criteria for making individual decisions, as well as through the recruitment of competent and neutral personnel.[7] Another suggestion has been the use of ombudsmen who would listen to complaints and apply their own resources in investigating allegations of incorrect decisions. Another has been the institution of internal quality-control systems that would enable agency managers to identify and correct problems in policy application.[8] The Social Security Administration has applied this last approach in an effort to ensure more decisional consistency and more uniform productivity among its ALJs. With the encouragement of Congress, it has adopted statistical analysis and peer review among its judges to identify problem areas, together with techniques such as counseling, training sessions, and output targets designed to regulate the performance of its adjudicatory personnel.[9]

The use of ombudsmen is poorly developed in the United States, however, and other alternatives to due process are limited by their failure to recognize participation by affected parties as an intrinsic source of legitimacy that is deeply embedded in American political culture. The potential of internal controls for producing objective, substantively correct decisions is further limited by the fact that they rely primarily on the willingness of agencies to police themselves. Indeed, standard operating procedures and quality-control mechanisms arguably provide opportunities for political appointees and other agency managers to undermine the neutrality of the adjudicatory process, either by systematically interjecting their own policy biases or by acting as conduits for affected interests. Thus, if it is far from being a perfect means of ensuring individual justice, and if it should therefore be supplemented in some contexts, one can make a strong case that due process should serve as the primary control over agency adjudication. This argument is especially persuasive with regard to administrative regulation, where the individual stakes in decision making tend to be very significant

and where the parties involved are generally capable of effectively representing themselves.

In this same vein, it is appropriate that influences over agency decision
making by the two political branches be tightly constrained in areas of administrative adjudication that are governed by formal procedures and that
involve important and narrowly defined interests. Although it is not entirely
clear, the law regulating ex parte communications is generally consistent
with this prescription. In seeking to limit its own potential for abuse, as well
as to protect the integrity of administrative procedures and judicial review,
Congress has circumscribed its role in APA-controlled adjudication to that of
securing "status reports" concerning ongoing proceedings.[10] In theory, at
least, corrective action in such matters is confined to the subsequent passage
of legislation. To this end, the text of the APA further prohibits "communications relevant to the merits of the proceeding" (as opposed to procedural
inquiries and other communications),[11] and its legislative history cautions
that, "in doubtful cases, the agency official should treat the communication
as ex parte so as to protect the integrity of the decision making process."[12]
Judicial precedent has reinforced the principle that legislative influence over
agency adjudication is unwarranted. Perhaps the leading case in this area is
Pillsbury Co. v. FTC (1966), in which the Fifth Circuit reversed the
commission's disapproval of two acquisitions on the grounds that its decision had been tainted by pressures from members of the Senate.[13]

The courts have held that similar principles should constrain the relationship between adjudicatory decision makers and other executive officials
such as the president, members of the Executive Office, and interested staff
and political appointees from within and outside their own agencies. In
*Professional Air Traffic Controllers Organization (PATCO) v. Federal
Labor Relations Authority (FLRA)* (1982),[14] for example, the D.C. Circuit
upheld a decision by the Federal Labor Relations Authority that was pre-
ceded by ex parte contacts from the secretary of labor, but it based its
decision on the fact that the communications did not involve questions or
preferences regarding the substance of the case, and that there was otherwise little to suggest that the agency's decision had been affected in a
material way by the communications. Instead, the secretary had only expressed a "managerial" or "procedural" concern that the case be resolved as
expeditiously as possible. As such, his queries could be justified pursuant to
a legitimate "executive" interest in administrative efficiency and effectiveness rather than an interest in the substance of individual decisions. Even
here, however, the court indicated that it had severe reservations about the
secretary's actions.

Ex parte contacts in adjudication are, by definition, only possible in the context of on-the-record proceedings. In this regard, the legal and ethical principles governing interference by politicians and other officials in less-formal adjudicatory actions are much more ambiguous. Efforts by representatives to help their constituents are widely viewed as a legitimate protection of individual interests in a myriad of areas where procedural constraints and judicial review are lax. Yet casework is also readily subject to abuse. The responsibility for channeling such efforts within acceptable bounds rests largely with Congress itself. Aside from criminal sanctions associated with egregious actions such as bribe taking, the House and Senate have sought to regulate the behavior of their members through rather vague codes of ethics enforced by peer review.[15]

Due Process and Administrative Policy Making

As discussed in chapter 2, rulemaking and application decisions having broad policy effects have also been exposed to more rigorous procedural constraints and judicial review in recent decades. The most important element of this trend has been the creation of standards for agency rulemaking that go well beyond the notice-and-comment format spelled out in the Administrative Procedure Act. These requirements can be understood from a normative perspective as an effort to legitimate fundamental changes in the character of administration. Although the rulemaking revolution of the late 1960s and 1970s was viewed as a positive development by many, increased reliance on such a powerful, quasi-legislative tool also rendered agencies' policy-making discretion much more visible and more difficult to reconcile with the tenets of representative democracy. Procedures requiring agencies to conduct formal hearings and to justify their actions on a record subject to rigorous judicial scrutiny thus became popular as a means of ensuring that bureaucrats would rely on sound evidence and reasoning, and that they would not stray beyond the substantive goals of their mandates.

Some scholars have also argued that institutional constraints on bureaucratic policy making have been informed by the assumption that administration pursuant to broad mandates should be a matter of accommodating relevant interests. This provides a compelling explanation for the expansion of standing by the courts and for Congress's inclusion of various participatory rights in enabling statutes. The extension of formal due process to rulemaking can also be viewed as an effort to ensure that agencies give adequate consideration to public comment. Yet while efforts by the courts and Congress to expand the breadth and effectiveness of participation in bureaucratic decision making may well reflect their awareness of its political nature, the input facilitated by such devices is ultimately constrained by procedural requirements and judicial review whose purpose is to ensure that actions accurately and effectively promote legislative intent. The appeal of the latter goal explains the relatively infrequent use of techniques, such as negotiated rulemaking, that go beyond participation within an instrumental framework and explicitly seek to accommodate competing interests as a basis for policy.[16] It also explains the fact that, where they are used, such political exercises only result in proposals that must be subjected to the same standards of reasoned justification as other rules.

The use of formal due process as a constraint on the exercise of quasi-legislative discretion must be assessed in terms of its appropriateness for the tasks that agencies are called upon to perform. Many feel that administrative procedures and judicial review are ill suited for dealing with kinds of empirical issues that typically provide the bases for broad policy decisions. Judges are alleged to lack the training and experience required to participate effectively in such areas. This may be true, not only with regard to their limited substantive expertise, but with regard to important "process knowledge" as well. As one authority argues, judges

> are not, as they might be apt to regard themselves, specialists in the decisionmaking processes necessary to managing a large governmental division. As expert as they might be in the formal adversary process of our nation's courts, many judges are unfamiliar with the manner in which important decisions are made by most other kinds of institutions in the United States. Many judges are abysmally ignorant of the techniques involved in bureaucratic decisionmaking, scientific decisionmaking, management science, quality control, and statistics.[17]

Aside from the limitations of judges themselves, the adversary process, with its highly structured participatory format and its rigid insistence that assertions are either right or wrong, can inhibit the critical exchange of ideas among experts. Such dialogue is often essential to an intelligent examination of the kinds of hypotheses about probable rather than known cause-and-effect relationships that frequently inform rules and other actions having broad policy effects.[18]

Administrative due process is often limited in even a more basic way by the incompatibility between its underlying logic and the political issues that must often be resolved in making policy decisions. Instrumental rationality is a relevant goal for public administration only insofar as Congress has defined clear objectives. Whether it is possible or desirable for statutes to provide precise guidance that removes administration from politics perhaps are still unsettled questions. Certainly, however, few would disagree with the assertion that substantial obstacles confront this prospect and that enabling statutes, as they exist, often require agencies to balance competing interests. The tension between the assumptions and decisional constraints of due process, on the one hand, and the political demands of administration on the other is acute in many areas of rulemaking, as well as in areas of adjudication that involves diverse and conflicting interests. As discussed in chapter 3, while formal procedures and exacting standards of review imposed by Congress and the courts have produced more rigorous attempts to justify policy actions in such areas, they have also precluded the accommodation of interests and values, as such. Agencies have struggled to formulate and defend tight means–ends justifications for actions whose premises are (and must be) essentially political.

Of course, political considerations inevitably underlie many administrative policy decisions that are made. In this regard, an inverse limitation of due process is that, by placing a premium on technical and legal arguments, it artificially recasts debate into technical languages that undermine accountability and that are more accessible to some groups than to others. Democratic principles also suffer under the prospect of policy-based oversight by unelected and unaccountable judicial elites. As Martin Shapiro comments:

> Not all of us are equally charmed by the discovery that a set of Ivy League lawyers are the ideal medium for introducing ethical discourse into public affairs and creating and enforcing our public values. Nor are all of us equally charmed that courts, as opposed to legislatures, or executives, or political parties, or voters are to be the seat of principles of right and wrong that are to replace group struggle as the criteria for public policy.[19]

Yet to note these limitations is not to imply that prescriptive issues regarding the role of administrative procedures and the courts are clear-cut and easy to resolve. Many would be uncomfortable relying on the vagaries of executive and legislative oversight as the sole means of assuring that bureaucracy is accountable in making policy decisions. Given this, it is difficult to abandon objectivity as the only legitimate criterion for administration—notwithstanding the fact that the instrumental goals that due process seeks to promote may be unrealistic in some contexts. Agency officials, like judges, have limited credibility as arbiters of social equity. As a practical matter, moreover, decisions pursuant to even the broadest mandates inevitably rest, not only on value judgments, but on empirical determinations that should arguably be made as rigorously as possible. In these same respects, one cannot easily dismiss the potential for executive and legislative oversight to undermine the neutrality that administrative procedures and judicial review are designed to promote.

The arguments that can be made both for and against due process in agency policy making underlie the vagueness and inconsistency of the courts on the subject. As discussed in chapter 2, the Supreme Court's *Vermont Yankee* decision in 1978 reproved lower courts for requiring rulemaking procedures that went beyond the APA's simple notice-and-comment format.[20] Justice Rehnquist's opinion in the case clearly expressed the need for judicial deference and for freedom from rigid procedures in areas where agencies are required to weigh competing interests and to render judgments on complicated technical issues. *Chevron* (1984) and other decisions have subsequently emphasized that judges should not interject their preferences within the political latitude afforded by imprecise legislative mandates.[21] As also discussed, however, the hard-look doctrine remains very much alive. Recent court decisions still generally assume that agencies will base their decisions on a record and often stress the need for agencies rigorously to justify and defend their actions to judges' satisfaction.

The same ambivalence that underlies efforts to fashion appropriate administrative procedures is also evident in efforts by the courts to define the limits of executive and legislative influence over agency policy making. This is illustrated by the tension between two leading decisions from the 1980s, each of which dealt in part with the balance that should be struck between the president's administrative prerogatives and the integrity of due process in rulemaking. In *Chevron* (1984), the Supreme Court approved of influences by the Reagan administration to have the EPA allow states to apply the "bubble concept" in defining a "stationary source" pursuant to the Clean Air Act Amendments of 1977. As a basis for its action, it reasoned that policy judgments under vague mandates were better informed by input from a politically accountable official than by on-the-record proceedings and judicial review. In the previous year, however, the Court reversed a decision by the National Highway Traffic Safety Administration to rescind a passive restraint rule that was similarly motivated by the president's anti-regulatory agenda. Although NHTSA's action also took place under a broad mandate that required it to balance competing social objectives, the Court held that its decision was not supported by the rulemaking record.[22]

In these regards, a fundamental challenge facing efforts to structure bureaucratic discretion is to define the proper role for the kind of objectivity provided by due process. To the extent that courts have sought to confront this issue, they have done so primarily through a distinction between quasi-legislative and quasi-judicial decisions. In *Vermont Yankee,* for example, the Court intimated that formal procedures might be appropriate in areas of what was technically rulemaking, but where the issues and outcomes nonetheless resembled those involved in adjudication. Relying on precedents established early in the century, it noted that "additional procedures may be required in order to afford aggrieved individuals due process" when an "agency is making a 'quasi-judicial' determination by which a very small number of persons are exceptionally affected, in each case upon individual grounds."[23] As noted earlier, this same criterion has been used to determine the appropriateness of ex parte communications in rulemaking.

The courts' functional approach to defining the role of due process is limited, however. As discussed in chapter 2, the distinction between quasi-legislative and quasi-judicial actions is fuzzy in many practical contexts. Just as general policy statements may have intense effects on a narrow range of interests, individual decisions implementing statutory programs may have broad effects. In addition, many adjudicatory actions whose immediate effects are confined to one or a few parties may nevertheless create broad policy through precedent. This is illustrated by the *Pillsbury* case mentioned above. Thus, an initial point of contention between Congress and the FTC was whether the agency should use the "per se rule" or the "rule of reason" as a general criterion for evaluating acquisitions under the Clayton Act. If the commission's change in course had been based on an abandonment of the latter standard in favor of the former, as some legislators had urged it to do, the broad policy content of its adjudicatory decision to disapprove proposed acquisitions might arguably have justified politically based intervention. Beyond such conceptual difficulties, the most fundamental problem with the rulemaking/adjudication distinction is that the strict limitation of due process to quasi-judicial actions would, to many, be an unacceptable restriction of procedural and judicial constraints on agency policy making. Again, neither lower courts nor the Supreme Court itself have been willing to return to anything approaching the lax standards of justification and judicial review contemplated by the framers of the APA.

Given an unwillingness to abandon administrative procedures and judicial review as assurances of accountability in agency policy making, an alternative approach is to limit their applicability to appropriate elements of policy decisions. Some authorities feel that formal due process is useful for examining complex or technical issues of fact, especially when they involve conflicting data or expert opinions. The task, then, is to segregate these empirical components of policy making from the political balancing of competing interests that must also inform many decisions. To this end, some statutory provisions for hybrid rulemaking stipulate that constraints such as cross-examination, rebuttal, and decision making on the record should be confined to controverted factual issues. Some judges and legal scholars have also argued that the courts should adhere to this distinction as a basis for self-restraint.

Yet as noted above, others have questioned whether adversary procedures and judicial review are effective means for dealing with the kinds of empirical issues that typically lie at the heart of most policy decisions. Even to the extent that due process is useful for getting at the truth on questions of legislative fact, moreover, agency officials and judges have found it difficult confidently to separate these premises from other subjective or political considerations in the context of actual decisions. This has been true in the case of the FTC, for example, which is instructed by its enabling legislation to confine adversary procedures to "issues of material fact that are necessary to resolve." Unable to isolate these elements of its decisions and highly sensitive to the threat of reversal on appeal, agency hearing examiners have typically been reluctant to exclude any disputed questions from formal scrutiny under the hybrid rulemaking procedures imposed by Congress.[24]

The tension between the goal of instrumental rationality and the reality of administrative policy making is not only central to the evaluation of due process; it also helps to explain the popularity attained by cost–benefit analysis and similar techniques. Economic efficiency has been inserted as a basis for the rigorous scientific assessment of agency proposals in the absence of clear legislative goals. Yet the attempt to objectify political choices by translating them into market values also presents important problems. The goal of economic efficiency as a basis for objectivity is itself grounded in assumptions about social equity that are inherently political. Further, the bias of economic efficiency in favor of the existing distribution of resources in society is a goal that probably would not have been endorsed by the legislative coalitions responsible for enacting many programs to which it has been applied. As discussed in chapter 2, this is especially evident in areas of social regulation, where there is little doubt of the redistributive intent behind many statutes.

In brief, the only neat solutions to the problem of defining the role of administrative procedures and the courts in agency policy making are to resurrect the nondelegation doctrine or to apply a functional analysis that proscribes such constraints in areas where agencies make broad legislative judgments. Short of these extremes, which most find to be unrealistic, there are no magic keys for defining the appropriate nature of due process in policy making. This is perhaps not surprising, for most important constitutional issues in American government involve finding a workable balance between competing principles and institutional prerogatives. In any case, a starting point for more intelligent discourse in this area is to develop a more refined understanding of the "task environment" of public administration and how it conditions the effects of administrative due process.

Although there is no simple formula for defining its role, due process should be treated with caution as a solution to the problem of bureaucratic discretion. Judges and legislators have certainly extended it too far as a constraint on agency decisions that involve broad political issues. The converse of this point is that preserving the integrity of administrative procedures and judicial review is not nearly as compelling a reason to limit input by the president and Congress in administrative policy making as it is in adjudication. If the premise that administration is an extension of the legislative process requires a modification of the traditional compartmentalization of powers, there can be little doubt that politically based control by the elected branches of government is more compatible with the spirit of the Constitution than politically based control by the courts. At the same time, this raises further issues regarding the proper balance between executive and legislative power within the administrative process. Here, too, there are no easy solutions.

Executive and Legislative Prerogatives

Perhaps the most important set of constitutional questions presented by the rise of the bureaucratic state has to do with the respective roles of the president and Congress in administrative policy making. The central point of contention in this area involves who should exercise direct influence or control over agency decisions. As discussed in chapter 5, many have argued that the executive should play a prominent role in administration and that the legislature should confine itself to passive monitoring. Recent court decisions have, for the most part, sought to institutionalize these prescriptions by striking down Congress's efforts to extend its own power over administration and to limit executive prerogatives. As also discussed, however, critics of legislative oversight and advocates of a powerful administrative presidency base their arguments on oversimplifications and misconceptions about institutional motives and capabilities as they relate to public administration. As developed in this section, they also tend to rely on simplistic normative and legal arguments that give insufficient weight to the relationship between the administrative process and the legislature's constitutional responsibilities.

Institutionalizing the Model of Executive Dominance

Analysis of institutional behavior has frequently led to the conclusion that presidential control of the bureaucracy is salutary, while legislative influence exacerbates fundamental pathologies in American government. Thus, congressional oversight is widely alleged to lack appropriate expertise and to occur in response to special interests. Because of its structure, moreover, it is alleged to reinforce the fragmentation inherent in the committee system and subgovernment politics. Executive management of administration is frequently portrayed in the opposite terms, and indeed is often prescribed as an antidote to the problems associated with congressional power in the administrative and legislative processes. There is a good deal of disagreement concerning the president's institutional capabilities, and many have lamented the executive's apparent lack of interest in economy and efficiency. Nevertheless, the character of executive influence over administration—insofar as it occurs—is less frequently questioned. The presidency is viewed by most as a centralizing and rationalizing political force that, by its essential nature, promotes broad national interests. This assumption about the effects of executive management has provided the basis for numerous successful and unsuccessful attempts throughout this century to augment the president's institutional capabilities.

As is frequently the case with constitutional interpretation, the evolution of legal doctrine in the area of legislative and executive oversight has reflected dominant trends in thinking about sound institutional policy. The president and Congress have naturally sought to extend their influence over administration in recent years given the continued shift of discretionary authority to the bureaucracy and given the increased political saliency of agency decision making in many policy areas. Yet while the expansion of executive capabilities has been successful for the most part, legislative initiatives have often been nullified. As Harold Bruff notes, "Recent decisions [by the Supreme Court] have generally promoted a unified executive branch under presidential direction, as opposed to a more fragmented executive that makes many decisions free of presidential participation."[25] This trend has combined a strong endorsement of executive influence as a means of promoting rationality and accountability with efforts to limit direct congressional participation in administration as a force that necessarily undermines the president's managerial prerogatives.

The most dramatic recent precedent furthering presidential hegemony within the administrative process was the Supreme Court's *Chadha* decision of 1983, which declared most forms of the legislative veto unconstitutional.[26] Chief Justice Burger's sweeping majority opinion in the case was based on two quite different arguments. One was that, because the exercise of vetoes had legislative effect (presumably in the sense that they had the same practical implications as amending an enabling statute), forms that failed to provide for the president's signature and the approval of both houses of Congress were unconstitutional. In addition, Burger stated that the veto was an unwarranted infringement by the legislature on the president's executive power to control public administration.

This latter position has provided the basis for a number of other reinforcing decisions concerning the potential for congressional influence over the bureaucracy through personnel actions. In *Buckley v. Valeo* (1976), for example, the Court forbade Congress to appoint members of the Federal Election Commission.[27] *Bowsher v. Synar* (1986) ruled that the legislature could not delegate authority for implementing portions of the Gramm-Rudman Act to the comptroller general, since he was removable only by a joint resolution of Congress.[28] Both decisions were based on the premise that, because the selection and retention of personnel was an instrument of presidential control, Congress was interfering with an executive prerogative. Indeed, the Court has emphasized repeatedly in recent years the importance of presidential appointment and removal powers as "means of supervising and controlling" executive officials charged with policy implementation.[29]

If the courts have not been consistent on the subject, they have also endorsed direct presidential influence over agency policy making in a number of recent decisions dealing with ex parte communications. In *Chevron*, for example, a unanimous Supreme Court stated that, when Congress delegates policy decisions to an agency, that agency can "properly rely on the incumbent administration's view of wise policy to inform its judgments." It justified its position by arguing that, "While agencies are not accountable to the people, the Chief Executive is, and it is entirely appropriate for this political branch of government to make such policy choices. . . ."[30] The same view was expressed by the D.C. Court of Appeals in *Sierra Club v. Costle* (1981), which some cite as the leading authority on the propriety of presidential influence in rulemaking.[31] This opinion stressed the desirability and the constitutionality of a unified executive, observing that "executive power under our Constitution . . . rests exclusively with the President." Building on that premise, it reasoned that presidential communications with agencies must only be made a part of the rulemaking record when specifically required by Congress. As it stated:

> The court recognizes the basic need of the President and his White House staff to monitor the consistency of executive agency regulations with Administration policy. . . . Regulations such as those involved here demand a careful weighing of cost, environmental, and energy considerations. They also have broad implications for national economic policy. Our form of government simply could not function effectively or rationally if key executive policymakers were isolated from each other and from the Chief Executive. Single mission agencies do not always have the answers to complex regulatory problems. An over-worked administrator exposed on a 24-hour basis to a

dedicated but zealous staff needs to know the arguments and ideas of policy-makers in other agencies as well as in the White House.

Again, the courts have distinguished between legislative and adjudicative issues as a theoretical basis for weighing the integrity of administrative due process against the need for political accountability. As a consequence, they have generally accepted congressional contacts with rulemaking officials as well. Given that legislative monitoring and direct legislative influence go hand in hand, however, this application of functional analysis to ex parte communications has naturally run athwart of the strict separation-of-powers scheme that underlies the courts' preference for presidential over congressional control within the administrative process.

As a practical matter, judges have shown little of the same enthusiasm for legislative communications with agency officials that they have shown for presidential input. In a 1971 case that is still frequently cited, in fact, the D.C. Circuit invalidated a decision by the secretary of transportation to build a bridge across the Potomac River because it was tainted by pressures from Congress.[32] Although *Sierra Club* also approved of communications that had taken place between EPA and legislators who sought to discourage the regulations in question, it echoed common reservations about the policy effects of congressional oversight. Thus, it added that such influences were only permissible "so long as individual congressmen do not frustrate the intent of Congress as a whole as expressed in statute."[33]

Encouraged by the Court's endorsement of unified executive control, some proponents of a strong administrative presidency have advocated the reconsideration of an issue seemingly disposed of during the New Deal—the constitutionality of independent regulatory agencies. Their arguments sometimes portray *Humphrey's Executor* (1935) as an historical anomaly brought about by unprecedented conflict between an activist president and a conservative Court.[34] They further contend that *Humphrey's* characterization of independent commissions as quasi-judicial entities that are properly insulated from political influences has become less convincing since the late 1960s given the emphasis now placed on rulemaking as a means of carrying out regulatory mandates. In making this argument, they have often conceived of presidential control in political terms, basing their appeals for centralized management on the premise that administrative regulation cannot be a neutral, expert process.

Hope that the Court might abolish independent agencies has been frustrated by two recent decisions affirming the status of such bodies. *Morrison v. Olson* (1988)[35] upheld the law providing for the appointment of special prosecutors, while *Mistretta v. United States* (1989)[36] permitted Congress to create an independent agency for the purpose of establishing sentencing guidelines to bind federal judges. The fact that there was only one dissent in each of these decisions has been an especial source of alarm for some advocates of executive power. Yet if these cases perhaps represent a dead end on one possible avenue of advancement, it is unclear whether they reflect a general softening of recent trends. On balance the courts have still shown a strong preference for unified executive control over administration at the expense of direct congressional influence.

The Struggle to Justify Executive Dominance

Again, it is likely if not provable that judges' recent efforts to limit congressional influence over administration in favor of executive power are ultimately attributable to the popularity of the belief that Congress's decentralized structure and its delegation of authority have undesirable policy effects. If they have been driven by considerations of good policy, however, such decisions must also be legitimized on the basis of constitutional theory. Two considerations are relevant here. As discussed later, the abstract goals that institutional arrangements are designed to achieve must be reconciled with constitutional objectives. In a closely related but more immediate mechanical sense, institutional devices themselves must be reconciled with the Constitution's prescriptions regarding the roles of the three branches of government. Whereas the neat fit between the traditional model of public administration and separation of powers provided an elegant response to this latter need, the task of reconciling presidential dominance with constitutional principles has proven much more difficult under the realization that agencies make important policy choices.

As described above, judges have most often applied a "formalistic" conception of separation of powers in defending the president's administrative prerogatives against congressional infringement. As Bruff notes, the courts have "adopted a formal definition of the boundary between legislation and execution, and forbade Congress to control the latter through nonstatutory means."[37] This position essentially defines away any functional distinctions among bureaucratic actions; once delegated, all administrative authority becomes "executive" by fiat. For example, Chadha states that "although some agency action—rulemaking, for example—may resemble lawmaking, . . . the President's power to see that the laws are faithfully executed refutes the idea that he is to be a lawmaker." As a conceptual distinction intended to provide a rational basis for its position, Chief Justice Burger's majority opinion adds that "the Executive's administration of the laws" is not legislative because "his administrative activity cannot reach beyond the limits of the statute that created it."[38]

Although it produces prescriptions that are attractive to many, the formalistic model used to justify presidential hegemony within the administrative process suffers from important limitations. The heart of the problem is that the concepts of executive, legislative, and judicial power become meaningless in the absence of functional distinctions among them. Given that agency rulemaking often involves balancing conflicting social interests subject to few substantive constraints, for example, the argument that all power automatically becomes executive once delegated becomes an appeal to blind faith in which government functions are defined, not according to their essential nature, but according to who performs them. This certainly violates any common-sense understanding of separation of powers. The inherent difficulty of such an approach is reflected in the *Chadha* majority's characterization of presidential control of administration as an executive function and congressional control of the same activities as having legislative effects (notwithstanding the fact that Congress, too, could not legally "reach beyond the limits" of statutory law in performing oversight). It is also reflected in the incompatibility of a formalistic approach with the reasoning used to limit the role of due process and to permit ex parte contacts. Thus, *Chevron, Sierra Club,* and other decisions have taken pains to characterize agency rulemaking as a political, legislative function.

Some scholars have smugly dismissed these objections in their belief that, if the courts' reasoning has been faulty, it has nonetheless produced good policy. Their willingness to stoop to this is understandable given the difficulty of formulating a more convincing theory that produces the results they desire. As discussed in the preceding section, an alternative model that judges have applied in defining their own administrative role is to determine whether agency actions are legislative, executive, or judicial, and then to parcel out oversight responsibilities among the three constitutional branches accordingly. Justice White argued in his *Chadha* dissent that the Court might have used this strategy to arrive at the same conclusion in the case without invalidating the legislative veto entirely. Given that the administrative decision in question involved an individual's prospective deportation and that it was based on a formal hearing, direct congressional intervention could be rejected as an intrusion into the judicial realm. This approach would have avoided the logical and presumably unacceptable extension of *Chadha*'s reasoning to the conclusion that the courts should abstain from reviewing agency adjudication in order not to interfere with an executive prerogative.

Yet such a functional separation-of-powers analysis, which conceives of constitutional controls over bureaucracy in terms of discrete responsibilities, is just as Procrustian in its results as a formalistic approach. As discussed above, few would accept the absolute confinement of judicial review to administrative adjudication implied by a strict application of this perspective. If used in *Chadha,* moreover, the result of a functional approach would have been not only to sanction the congressional veto as a control on quasi-legislative activities such as rulemaking but to preclude executive influence in those areas as well. Even the most ardent defenders of legislative prerogatives would be reluctant to endorse a restriction of the president's role in the administrative process to activities such as internal management and agenda setting.

In these regards, the only alternative to analysis based on either a functional or a formalistic division of responsibilities is to proceed on the assumption that constitutional powers are intermixed, both within the administrative process and within American government generally. This is a premise that should hardly seem novel to anyone who has benefited from a civics course. Institutions such as the president's ability to veto bills and judicial review of statutes' constitutionality require Congress to share its legislative authority, just as the Senate's prerogative to confirm appointees requires the president to share his executive power. Although law scholars have been surprisingly slow to develop theories based on the principle of shared as opposed to separated powers, "checks and balances" has gained some currency in recent years as a paradigm for analyzing the constitutional dimensions of congressional and presidential control of administration. The leading advocate of this approach is Peter Strauss, who has used it in an attempt to provide a more convincing legal justification for presidential dominance over agency policy making.[39]

Strauss does not abandon functional distinctions within the administrative process. Instead, the task of constitutional analysis under his model is to define the roles performed by Congress, the president, and the courts, as well as to assess particular administrative actions as they relate to the performance of those "core functions." As he observes:

> Each . . . agency is to some extent "independent" of each of the named branches and to some extent in relationship with each. The continued achievement of the intended balance and interaction among the three named actors at the top of government, with each continuing to have effective responsibility for its unique core function, depends on the existence of relationships between each of these actors and each agency within which that function can find voice.[40]

If this analytical framework is appealing, however, Strauss applies it in a convoluted and speculative way. Thus, he prescribes a strong role for the president in precisely those areas of administration that are legislative in nature. At the heart of his analysis is a definition of the president's core function that corresponds closely with the model of politically based executive leadership discussed in chapter 5. As is frequently the case in efforts to extract specific meaning from the Constitution's broad language, Strauss bases this interpretation on an historical analysis of the Framers' intent. Drawing on the debates of the Constitutional Convention, he maintains that the Founding Fathers sought to establish a strong chief executive who could respond to exigencies at the time statutes were passed and who could provide centralized, coordinative control over government's actions. He does not specify whether the executive function was meant to entail direct control over agencies' policy-making discretion. At the least, however, Strauss feels that the president's authority to "require opinions in writing" permits the kind of direct and systematic Executive Office scrutiny of proposed agency rules instituted under recent administrations.

The most striking dimension of Strauss's analysis is the extension of his reasoning to prescribe limited congressional influence over agency policy making. This conclusion is based on the further historical argument that the executive's role within the administrative process was intended not only as something that would promote accountability and coordination, per se, but also as a check against congressional power. He feels that the Framers were motivated in this latter regard by their perception that the president's influence would serve as a balance against Congress's tendency toward tyrannical majoritarianism. This argument seems curious given that institutional power and constituency interests have always been more fragmented in the legislature than in the presidency. Indeed, this generally accepted comparison provides a justification for centralized executive coordination in Strauss's analysis. In any case, it is for the purpose of preserving the president's administrative role as a political counterweight to Congress that Strauss argues against direct legislative control over agency rulemaking. Since rulemaking authority is typically delegated to agency heads (and not the president), he feels that such a practice creates the potential for congressional dominance in the realm of policy making, defeating the constitutional intent that the president's administrative prerogatives serve as check on Congress's legislative authority in this functional area.

The Case for Congressional Influence

In brief, scholars have struggled to formulate a sound legal justification for unilateral executive control as a rationalizing force in public administration. Despite its appeal, the prescriptive model of presidential dominance over agency policy making suffers from two general limitations. One is that it is based on exaggerated empirical assessments of both executive and legislative behavior. More important, it reflects a simplistic interpretation of constitutional goals. Although Strauss's formulation of the issue as a matter of defining the correct balance between executive and legislative policy-making authority is the only analytical approach that makes sense, his application of this model fundamentally misrepresents the implications of the rise of bureaucracy for the balance of institutional power in American government.

Again, it is difficult to separate legal justifications for executive dominance over agency policy making from the underlying belief that presidential control produces desirable results. An evaluation of this prescription must therefore be based in part on an examination of the empirical premises about institutional capabilities and motives discussed in earlier chapters. A point that has received little attention is that the resources Congress devotes to oversight are probably superior both in quality and quantity to those of the president. Political executives are notoriously transient, and careerists in the Executive Office are relatively small in number and often lack a detailed knowledge of specific programs. While Congress also compares unfavorably with the bureaucracy in terms of its size and substantive knowledge, the committee system provides it with a substantial measure of institutional stability and policy specialization. On the whole, committee members and their staffs undoubtedly have more experience in dealing with the administrative issues under their purviews than presidential appointees.

One should also take care not to misrepresent either the degree to which, the manner in which, or the ends for which the administrative presidency serves to coordinate bureaucratic performance. Little evidence suggests that presidents or their surrogates have sought to screen and rationalize agency actions in any systematic way. Insofar as executive coordination does occur, moreover, it often involves a different dynamic than that envisioned by advocates of executive leadership. The president's administrative priorities are often determined reactively and incrementally as his or her team of departmental and Executive Office appointees deal with policy issues that arise during implementation. Relatedly, the diversity in ideology and constituency ties that characterize presidential administrations to one degree or another often dictate that "executive influence" is characterized by a pluralistic accommodation of interests as opposed to centralized planning and hierarchical control. Finally, much presidential oversight gives voice to the same kinds of particular interests that are frequently alleged to motivate congressional intervention.

By the same token, legislative oversight is neither as uncoordinated nor as parochial as its critics contend. It is cynical to assume that legislators' narrow self-interest always supersedes their sense of justice or of the public good. If many anecdotes can be cited in which oversight has served wealthy and well-organized groups, many others can be cited in which Congress has sought to promote general or disenfranchised interests in the administrative process. Moreover, the committees that conduct oversight are ultimately agents of the whole that must respond to widespread sentiment in their parent bodies on salient issues, and that can be and are disciplined in a variety of formal and informal ways. Nor is Congress's failure to emphasize systematic and explicitly coordinative oversight a legitimate basis for invidious comparisons. As with presidential intervention, some of the legislature's oversight promotes single interests, but some of it facilitates the accommodation of conflicting views. Even to the extent that committees have parochial orientations, the fact that different committees or subcommittees with different constituencies and substantive priorities frequently share oversight responsibility for particular programs tends to promote a kind of political coordination.

This is not to say that the effects of executive and legislative influence are the same, or that the former does not frequently promote a more uniform set of policy preferences than the latter. Although executive and legislative intervention in the affairs of bureaucracy are both more pluralistic (and respectively less centralized and less fragmented) in their dynamics than is commonly recognized, the presidency is obviously a more hierarchical institution that is likely to produce more consistent oversight decisions. Yet beyond such managerial concerns, a more basic principle that advocates of executive hegemony have often failed to consider is that questions of efficiency are necessarily subordinate to constitutional, democratic goals in areas of administration that involve significant policy choices. The fact that arguments for centralized executive control are based on empirical oversimplifications regarding the political consequences of presidential and congressional oversight is obviously relevant here. Even more problematic, however, are the normative/constitutional premises that underlie these arguments. Whatever its determinants and whatever direction it takes, a more important issue is raised by the fact that executive hegemony in the administrative process tends to further *one* set of institutional policy preferences.

Again, the president's need to organize a national electoral coalition does not ensure that executive oversight actions will further majoritarian interests across all issues. Even if they did, however, few would endorse a populist model of unquestioned and complete responsiveness to a simple national majority as a general prescription for government action. Similarly, few would argue that one conception of the national interest or of what is otherwise just or proper should guide policy making. Two defining tenets of American democracy are that all constituency principles are imperfect and that all public officials are potentially subject to poor judgment, corruption, and other human failings. These premises are the foundations of our constitutional system, which requires that policy decisions be based on accommodation among different majorities aggregated in different ways through varying electoral principles and representative institutions. The need to preserve this accommodation supersedes the need for sound management, for efficiency is only desirable insofar as it contributes to desirable ends. Making the trains run on time is intended to be subordinate to other values in American government. Viewed in this light, considerations of good institutional policy and of constitutional mechanics merge, for the means through which government seeks to prevent tyranny of one interest or viewpoint over others is its Madisonian system of checks and balances.

Even to the extent that presidential control rationalizes political decision making pursuant to simple majoritarian interests, therefore, the question that remains to be asked is why such a criterion should dominate policy making only in the administrative process. As discussed above, attempts to reconcile this prescription with the notion of separated powers are flawed. The functional version of that model, which differentiates among administrative actions, suggests that Congress and not the president should play the dominant role in guiding activities that are inherently legislative. In light of this, the Supreme Court has relied instead on a formalistic equation of all administration with the executive function. As essentially a resurrection of the politics/administration dichotomy, this approach misrepresents both the nature of agency policy making and the motives of the president for overseeing the bureaucracy. The Court itself has often underscored the deficiency of this model's necessary assumptions. In contrast to the reasoning that it has employed in limiting legislative controls, recent opinions involving ex parte communications have stressed the value of presidential oversight as a means of ensuring political accountability in administrative decisions that require a balancing of competing values.

Again, therefore, the alternative to these approaches is to assume that administrative powers are properly shared among the three branches. Given this, presidential hegemony in the arena of administrative policy making can only be justified through an equation that establishes its necessity as a balance against legislative policy influences exercised elsewhere. Formulated in such a way, the task of assigning oversight prerogatives suggests an important linkage between the empirical examination of institutional power and constitutional theory that is obviously ignored by prescriptions based on a formalistic separation of powers. Strauss's assertion that presidential control over agency policy making was intended to serve as a counterweight to Congress's ability to shape policy through the legislative process seeks to incorporate this relationship. Even assuming that it correctly represents the Framers' intent at the time, however, this analysis ignores tidal changes in American government that have occurred since 1789. A more realistic application of his checks-and-balances principle to modern conditions suggests that executive dominance over agency policy making contributes to an imbalance in the relationship between the political branches.

Two frequently observed trends in the evolution of American government make it logically difficult to exclude Congress from some form of legitimate participation in the implementation of its own statutes. One is the tremendous expansion of delegated authority. Whereas Congress could write detailed legislation during the nineteenth century, confining the discretion of a small bureaucracy, the twentieth century has seen a continual cession of power to the executive. Although administrative decisions are still made pursuant to more general legislative directives, the bureaucracy has come to have more and more discretionary authority in balancing competing values. Given this, a positive role for Congress in helping to shape important administrative decisions can be viewed as an appropriate institutional adaptation for sustaining its constitutional function of establishing domestic policy.

Many have attacked this reasoning, to be sure. As noted, a frequent argument is that Congress simply lacks the resources to perform oversight effectively. A related point is that oversight actually undermines the legislature's ability to shape policy. If Congress is not able to entertain the illusion that it can control policy outcomes as programs are being implemented, then it will arguably legislate in more detail rather than abdicate its authority to the executive. This latter assertion is an appendage to the popular, related beliefs that congressional oversight is pathological in its motives and that delegated authority is the root of most evil in American government.

Again, however, oversight does not have to be comprehensive for it to aid Congress in maintaining its policy-making prerogatives. The most important conflicts in the American political system tend to rise to higher levels of institutional authority for resolution. And although the issue of whether Congress can write laws in significantly greater detail is not soon to be resolved, most scholars agree that it is not feasible for the legislature as presently constituted to enact more specific mandates across the board. The reasons for this are frequently recited. One is that Congress has to spread finite resources over many more areas of policy making than it once did. Another is that it simply lacks the expertise or the foresight concerning changing conditions to articulate precise goals. Finally, delegation is also attributable to Congress's inability to forge majorities in controversial areas, as critics claim. Yet those who feel that this last motive can be overcome by an act of will to behave more responsibly ignore the realities of legislative politics. Given Congress's essential role of representing diverse constituencies, consensus building is destined to be a difficult process that naturally consumes scarce organizational resources. This would remain true even pursuant to the imposition of term limits, the curtailment of campaign spending, or any other conceivable reform designed to improve legislative performance.

Because of such constraints, forcing Congress to choose between specific legislation and no legislation at all would necessarily limit government's ability to respond to society's demands for policy. In turn, if one accepts the premise that the delegation of authority is a legitimate response to the demands of modern government, then it would seem to follow that direct congressional influence over agency policy making is not a perversion of its constitutional role, but a way of sustaining the performance of its legislative function. This interpretation is consistent with the courts' almost unqualified acceptance of delegation as a practical necessity. Efforts to extend the president's administrative authority reinforce the linkage between oversight and Congress's policy-determining role given that executive and legislative influence over administration necessarily occur at each others' expense. As discussed in chapter 5, chief executives tend to prefer the legislative process as a medium for achieving their goals, and the expenditure of presidential resources in administration is often most intense in precisely those areas where they disagree with Congress over the direction policy should take.

Strauss's use of checks and balances to prescribe presidential hegemony in areas of administrative policy making is therefore ahistorical in that it ignores the shift that has occurred during the twentieth century from statutory specification to bureaucratic discretion as a basis for policy making. Of course, constitutional doctrine can either be derived from a reading of the Framers' literal intent at the time or from a more flexible (and even more subjective) interpretation of what the core principles that underlay their prescriptions dictate in the context of modern conditions. Yet the former approach seems especially simplistic when applied to issues posed by the rise of the administrative state. Assuming for the sake of argument that unchallenged presidential control over the bureaucracy was intended as a political counterweight to Congress's legislative prerogatives, the relative importance of such control has grown immeasurably as a direct function of the increased proportion of all systemic policy-making authority located in the administrative process.

In addition to the implications of expanded delegation, a second and complementary way in which Strauss's checks-and-balances argument for executive centralization is ahistorical is that it ignores the corresponding growth of presidential power in legislative policy making. As late as the 1890s, the Senate routinely rejected executive bills out of hand as an unwarranted infringement on congressional prerogatives. Throughout the twentieth century, however, the presidency has acquired an arsenal of powers in budgeting, planning, legislative clearance, program review, and other areas, together with the staff resources needed to utilize them effectively. Congress has generally consented to and in fact has facilitated this fundamental change in constitutional structure, just as the courts have sustained it as a necessary adaptation to the continued growth of national problems and the accompanying need for positive government. As Stephen Wayne observes, "Today, executive initiative and involvement is taken for granted. It has become an expectation, made necessary by demands for activism in a system characterized by its political and constitutional constraints."[41]

The evolution of the legislative presidency has been supported by the same basic arguments used to justify executive control of administrative policy making. Demands for action at the national level, coupled with the erosion of party discipline and centralized leadership in Congress, have rendered presidential government increasingly appealing. This prescription has certainly been qualified and attacked. With the exception of several temporary remissions after perceived abuses of executive authority, however, it has remained a prevailing theme since the New Deal.

By its own logic, which hinges on the functional properties of administration, the checks-and-balances equation used to define executive and legislative roles in controlling the bureaucracy must include this expansion of the president's legislative powers. Policy making in the legislative and administrative processes are not only functionally equivalent in the sense that they both involve choosing among competing social objectives; they are also interrelated. To allow the executive a role in the legislative process is to allow it to influence its own marching orders in the administrative process. To allow the executive centralized control over the administrative process is to allow it substantial control over the direction and success of congressional programs. Moreover, power is transferable between the legislative and administrative processes, both within and across policy areas. Thus, presidential control over administration can be used to influence legislation through bargaining and logrolling. These empirical observations, which few would challenge, have important implications for constitutional analysis that have largely been ignored by legal scholars. If Congress has been forced to abdicate a sizable portion of its core function to the president within the legislative process, blocking its efforts to compete with the executive in the administrative process only exacerbates its loss of systemic policy-making power.

Of course, one should take care not to exaggerate the impact of efforts to exclude Congress from a direct role in administration. Legislators become involved in program implementation on a daily basis, and are able to exert considerable informal influence on the bureaucracy by virtue of their legislative powers. Congress's expanded efforts along these lines are a clear indication of the increasingly strong linkage between public administration and its systemic prerogatives. Yet recent limitations placed on formal congressional control over agency decisions have had substantial effects. The invalidation of the legislative veto has been significant in this regard, denying Congress a flexible and effective means of intervention in administrative policy areas that it finds to be especially important. Beyond its present manifestations, a further extension of the doctrine of executive dominance to areas such as ex parte communications could further undermine Congress's ability to fulfill its policy-making responsibilities.

Conclusion

To an even greater extent than the conflict between due process and the demands of politics, therefore, an inevitable tension exists between executive and legislative oversight of administrative policy making that defies neat resolution. The adjudicative–legislative distinction normally applied in the first instance is a sound criterion for limiting administrative procedures and judicial review, but few would endorse its use as an absolute basis for defining institutional responsibilities. This is illustrated by the inconsistency of the courts themselves in prescribing rulemaking procedures and in confining ex parte contacts. In marked contrast to the functional approach applied to due process issues, moreover, the logic of the formal separation-of-powers analysis favored by the Supreme Court in dealing with legislative–executive conflict denies the political character of much delegated authority. The Court's frequent justification of presidential hegemony in terms of centralized political leadership contradicts the empirical assumptions behind this formalistic model.

Prescriptive issues of institutional control were relatively straightforward (or at least relatively untroubling) under the traditional view of public administration as an instrumental process. Administrative law envisioned procedural constraints and judicial review as means of ensuring objectivity and consistency in the application of policy to individuals. The rigor that should be required in adjudicatory due process depended on the importance of the private interest at stake as balanced against the state's interest in efficient administration. The traditional model similarly conceived of presidential oversight as a means of ensuring through sound organizational management that bureaucracy operated as an efficient transmission belt. Given the neat correspondence between the politics/administration dichotomy and separation of powers and given its decentralized structure, Congress was consigned to the passive monitoring of agency decisions.

Constitutional issues surrounding public administration have become much more difficult pursuant to the realization that agencies frequently make political choices. Although reasonable people can disagree over the institutional constraints that should apply in different adjudicatory contexts, the traditional model's goal of objectivity is still appropriate for structuring the relationship between individuals and the administrative state. In contrast, its prescriptions are much more tenuous when applied to broad policy decisions that require agencies to balance competing social values. It is here that the struggle to define the proper roles of due process and executive and legislative oversight has been the most difficult. It is also here that a consideration of the doctrinal foundations and the effects of institutional controls is especially important. The most popular normative responses to the breakdown of the traditional model suffer from important empirical limitations.

The extension of procedural constraints and judicial review to agency policy making has often been portrayed as an abandonment of the traditional model. Given the realization that agency decision making is political, balanced interest representation has arguably supplanted accuracy and consistency as the goal of administration. Participation in the context of administrative due process is restricted by a variety of factors, however, including its costliness and its confinement of input to the consideration of single, well-developed alternatives. The most fundamental deficiency of the interest-representation model is that participation is ultimately constrained by the central assumption of the adversary process that decisions are demonstrably correct or incorrect. Indeed, the inherent difficulty of reconciling administrative law with the realities of bureaucratic politics is underscored by the fact that the extension of due process to agency policy making has frequently been justified on instrumental grounds as well. Whether or not devices such as formal hearings and decision making on the record are effective means of getting at the truth on the empirical issues that inform actions such as rulemaking, they necessarily inhibit the resolution of conflicting interests.

If the theory and practice of administrative law reflect ambivalence and inconsistency regarding the proper character of agency policy making, appeals for strong executive control over the bureaucracy are based, either implicitly or explicitly, on a plausible argument that integrates political accountability with the traditional values of economy and efficiency. Presidential leadership thus logically should serve as a rationalizing force pursuant to hierarchically ordered goals endorsed by a national constituency. In reality, though, the political incentives that drive the administrative presidency produce results that differ from this model in important respects. Presidents are not particularly interested in the coordination or internal management of programs. Rather, Executive Office intervention in agency affairs tends to occur selectively in response to issues that are controversial or that are otherwise of special interest to the president. Nor does the set of organizations and the network of communications and authority relationships that define presidential oversight always reflect coherent goals or respond to broad national majorities.

Just as scholars have often exaggerated the policy benefits of presidential administration, they have also frequently misrepresented Congress's relationship to the bureaucracy. The criticisms of legislative oversight that have detracted from its popularity are not without some truth. Yet to say that power is fragmented in Congress is not to equate all or even most legislative oversight with the subversion of program goals or with the politics of mutual noninterference. In fact, the increased differentiation and decentralization of Congress in recent decades has produced quite the opposite results. To be sure, the pluralistic character of oversight is often inefficient from a traditional managerial perspective. It is, however, an accurate reflection of complexity and conflict in the environment of program implementation. Indeed, the oversight process has emerged as an important mechanism by which Congress accommodates relevant interests as the policy issues in a given area become more contentious.

None of this is to deny the president's legitimate prerogatives in public administration. To endorse this would be to prescribe a constitutional role reversal that would be unsettling to say the least. Moreover, presidential influence over bureaucracy is defensible in terms of widely shared policy values. If scholars have frequently misrepresented and exaggerated the dynamics of executive oversight, the administrative presidency nevertheless provides a needed measure of "focused political accountability" and of policy coherence in a general sense. It may also render the process of mutual partisan adjustment more democratic by accommodating interests not adequately represented through other institutional means. The point, instead, is that Congress must also be accorded a legitimate, direct role in the administrative process. Presidential dominance may well be preferable in terms of efficiency or even perhaps in terms of direct political responsiveness to national majorities. Yet to focus exclusively on these desirable qualities is to ignore their subordinate relationship to other principles under the Constitution. Although the argument has become less fashionable, it is still difficult to ignore the fact that American government was designed to be pluralistic and messy.

Notes

1. For an early and enthusiastic endorsement of this thesis, see Donald J. Kingsley, *Representative Bureaucracy* (Yellow Springs, Ohio: Antioch Press, 1944).

2. For a critical discussion and empirical examination of representative bureaucracy, see, for example, Kenneth J. Meier and Lloyd G. Nigro, "Representative Bureaucracy and Policy Preferences," *Public Administration Review* 36 (July/August 1976): 458–69.

3. As mentioned in chapter 1, whether bureaucracy really suffers from a "crisis of legitimacy" in the public mind is not at all clear and probably depends on the area of administration in question. For a very accepting view of the constitutionality of bureaucratic policy making, see the so-called Blacksburg Manifesto. Gary L. Wamsley et al., "The Public Administration and the Governance Process: Refocusing the American Dialogue," in *A Centennial History of the American Administrative State,* ed. Ralph Clark Chandler (New York: Free Press, 1987).

4. For a thoughtful and much more elaborate discussion of various dimensions and degrees of administrative discretion, see Martin Shapiro, "Administrative Discretion: The Next Stage," *Yale Law Journal* 92 (July 1983): 1487–1522.

5. Christopher F. Edley, Jr., *Administrative Law: Rethinking Judicial Control of Bureaucracy* (New Haven: Yale University Press, 1990), pp. 13, 14.

6. The agency's ALJs hear about 280,000 cases per year. Richard J. Pierce, Jr., "Bias in Agency Decisionmaking: Lessons from Chevron and Mistretta," *University of Chicago Law Review* 57 (1990): 481–519; pp. 501–15.

7. Emmette Redford, *Democracy in the Administrative State* (New York: Oxford University Press, 1969), chap. IV.

8. Jerry Mashaw, "The Management Side of Due Process: Some Theoretical and Litigation Notes on the Assurance of Accuracy, Fairness, and Timeliness in the Adjudication of Social Welfare Claims," *Cornell Law Review* 59 (1974): 772–824.

9. Pierce, "Bias in Agency Decisionmaking."

10. *Administrative Procedure Act,* U.S. Code, vol. 5, sec. 551(14) (1976).

11. *Administrative Procedure Act,* sec. 557 (d).

12. Arthur Earl Bonfield and Michael Asimow, *State and Federal Administrative Law* (St. Paul, Minn.: West Publishing, 1989), p. 165.

13. 354 F. 2d 952 (5th Cir. 1966).

14. 685 F. 2d (D.C. Cir. 1982).

15. For example, legislators are enjoined to avoid any appearance of using their influence for personal gain and not to take actions that would strike a reasonable, nonpartisan, and fully informed individual as being improper.

16. Cornelius Kerwin observes that most departments and major agencies have experimented with negotiated rulemaking, but the technique is not used extensively. Indeed, it is generally thought to be inappropriate in politically complex areas where many interests have a stake in policy making. Cornelius Kerwin, *Rulemaking: How Agencies Write Law and Make Policy* (Washington, D.C.: Congressional Quarterly Press, 1994).

17. Pierce, "Bias in Agency Decisionmaking," p. 516.

18. Kenneth Culp Davis, *Administrative Law and Government* (St. Paul, Minn.: West Publishing, 1975).

19. Martin Shapiro, *Who Guards the Guardians? Judicial Control of Administration* (Athens: University of Georgia Press, 1988), p. 24.

20. *Vermont Yankee Nuclear Power Corp. v. Natural Resource Defense Council, Inc. (NRDC), 435 U.S. 519 (1978).*

21. *Chevron, U.S.A., Inc. v. Natural Resources Defense Council, Inc.* 467 U.S. 837 (1984). A plantwide definition of the term imposed less of a burden on industry, and was thus consistent with Reagan's basic posture on regulation. Also see *Sierra Club v. Costle,* 657 F. 2d 298 (D.C. Cir. 1981) for a vigorous defense of ex parte influences by political officials over agency rulemaking.

22. *Motor Vehicle Manufacturers Association v. State Farm Mutual Automobile Association,* 463 U.S. 29 (1983). Jerry Mashaw and David Harfst have sought to reconcile these two decisions by arguing that, in the latter case but not the former, administrators failed to satisfy even minimal standards of rationality in arriving at their decision. See Jerry Mashaw and David Harfst, *The Struggle for Auto Safety* (Cambridge, Mass.: Harvard University Press, 1990).

23. Quoting from *Bi-Metallic Investment Co. v. State Board of Equalization,* 239 U.S. 441, 446 (1915). The other leading case in this area was *Londoner v. Denver,* 210 U.S. 373 (1908).

24. Barry B. Boyer, *Trade Regulation Rulemaking Procedures of the Federal Trade Commission: A Report to the Administrative Conference of the United States by the Special Project for the Study of Rulemaking Procedures under the Magnuson-Moss Warranties Federal Trade Commission Improvement Act* (Washington, D.C.: Administrative Conference of the United States, 1979).

25. Harold H. Bruff, "On the Constitutional Status of Administrative Agencies," *American University Law Review* 36 (Winter 1987): 491–518; quotation p. 496.

26. *Immigration and Naturalization Service v. Chadha,* 462 U.S. 919 (1983).

27. 424 U.S. 1 (1976).

28. 106 Sup. Ct. 3181 (1986).

29. *Morrison v. Olson,* 108 Sup. Ct. 2597 (1988) at 2622.

30. *Chevron, U.S.A., Inc. v. Natural Resources Defense Council, Inc.,* 865–66.

31. 657 F. 2d 298 (D.C. Cir. 1981).

32. *D.C. Federation of Civic Associations v. Volpe,* 459 F. 2d 1231 (D.C. Cir. 1971).

33. The regulation in question had important implications in terms of the economic competition between states that produced high- and low-sulfur coal. Senate Majority Leader Robert Byrd, among others, was active in seeking to discourage regulations on power plants that relied on the high-sulfur coal mined in West Virginia and other eastern states.

34. See, for example, Bruff, "On the Constitutional Status of Administrative Agencies." For a dissenting view, see John A. Rohr, "Public Administration, Executive Power, and Constitutional Confusion," *Public Administration Review* 49 (March/April 1989): 108–14.

35. 108 Sup. Ct. 2597.

36. 109 Sup. Ct. 647.

37. Bruff, "On the Constitutional Status of Administrative Agencies," p. 501.

38. 103 Sup. Ct. at 2784, 2785, n. 16.

39. Peter L. Strauss, "The Place of Agencies in Government: Separation of Powers and the Fourth Branch," *Columbia Law Review* 84 (April 1984): 573–669.

40. Strauss, "The Place of Agencies in Government," p. 579.

41. Stephen J. Wayne, *The Legislative Presidency* (New York: Harper and Row, 1978), p. ix.

Index

About the Author

William F. West received his bachelor's degree from the United States Military Academy and his doctorate from Rice University. He has taught Political Science at Texas A&M University since 1981. Most of his research has focused on the role of public administration in American government. He is married with two children and two stepchildren.